BEHAVIORAL MANAGEMENT ACCOUNTING

BEHAVIORAL MANAGEMENT ACCOUNTING

Ahmed Riahi-Belkaoui

QUORUM BOOKS
Westport, Connecticut • London

Library of Congress Cataloging-in-Publication Data

Riahi-Belkaoui, Ahmed, 1943–
    Behavioral management accounting / Ahmed Riahi-Belkaoui.
        p.   cm.
    Includes bibliographical references and index.
    ISBN 1–56720–443–0 (alk.paper)
    1. Managerial accounting.   2. Accounting—Psychological aspects.   I. Title.
    HF5657.4.R5253   2002
    658.15'11—dc21   2001019865

British Library Cataloguing in Publication Data is available.

Library of Congress Catalog Card Number: 2001019865
ISBN: 1–56720–443–0

First published in 2002

Quorum Books, 88 Post Road West, Westport, CT 06881
An imprint of Greenwood Publishing Group, Inc.
www.quorumbooks.com

Printed in the United States of America

The paper used in this book complies with the
Permanent Paper Standard issued by the National
Information Standards Organization (Z39.48–1984).

10 9 8 7 6 5 4 3 2 1

To Dimitra

Contents

Exhibits

Preface

Management accounting deals with the provision of accounting and nonaccounting information to internal users for the purpose of facilitating their decision making. While technical in nature, management accounting still functions in a behavioral environment shaped by the behaviors of management accountants as producers of information and managers as internal users, as they react to the information produced or received, the context created, the attitudes and perceptions generated, and the outcomes desired. Accordingly, this book introduces the concept of "behavioral management accounting" as the study of the behaviors and behavioral contexts created by the production of management accounting information to be used by internal decision makers. Knowledge and appreciation of these behaviors and behavioral contexts contribute to the success and efficiency of management accounting in serving the goals of the firm. These behaviors and behavioral contexts are covered in ten chapters as follows:

1. Chapter 1 examines the multidimensional scope of management accounting and provides a frame of reference for the issues raised by behavioral management accounting. It shows that to meet the diverse needs of today's managers, management accounting has evolved into a multidimensional area of inquiry resting on accounting, organizational, behavioral, and decisional foundations.

2. Chapter 2 examines the nature of the control process, the different basic control systems, and the framework for management control systems as the necessary mechanisms for ensuring an orderly conduct of operations and accountability of actions toward survival and growth of the firm.

3. Chapter 3 covers the linguistic relativism in management accounting by showing

how the Sapir-Whorf hypothesis of linguistic relativity, the sociolinguistic thesis, and the bilingual thesis affect the conduct of management accounting.

4. Chapter 4 examines the cultural relativism in management accounting by postulating that culture, through its components, elements, and dimensions, dictates the organizational structures adopted, the microorganizational behavior, the management accounting environment, and the cognitive functioning of individuals faced with a management accounting phenomenon.

5. Chapter 5 examines the cognitive relativism in management accounting by showing that both judgment and decision are the products of a set of social cognitive operations that include the observation of information on the accounting phenomenon and the foundation of a schema to represent the accounting phenomenon that is stored in memory and later retrieved when needed to allow the formation of a judgment and a decision.

6. Chapter 6 examines the contingency approaches to the design of accounting systems, assuming that the design of various components of accounting systems depends on specific contingencies that can create a perfect match.

7. Chapter 7 covers the functional and data fixation in management accounting, suggesting that under certain circumstances a decision maker might be unable to adjust his/her decision process to a change in the accounting process that supplied him or her with input data.

8. Chapter 8 covers goal setting and participative budgeting by presenting the research results of the effects of goal setting in general, and participative budgeting in particular on task and/or attitude outcomes.

9. Chapter 9 covers the behavioral issues in control by examining the threats to the validity of control judgments.

10. Chapter 10 covers planning, budgeting, and information distortion through an explanation of the nature and ramifications of both organizational and budgetary slack.

The book should be of value to those interested in the impact and the role of behavioral sciences in management accounting, including practicing accountants, business executives, accounting teachers and researchers, and students.

Many people helped in the development of this book. I received considerable assistance from the University of Illinois at Chicago students, especially Shahrzad Ghatan, Ewa Tomaszewska, and Vivian Au. I also thank Eric Valentine, David Palmer, and the entire production team at Greenwood Publishing Group for their continuous and intelligent support.

1

The Multidimensional Scope of Management Accounting

THE ACCOUNTING DIMENSION

Management accounting deals with the provision of information that allows an efficient management of the different parts of the value chain, namely (1) research and development, (2) design of products, services, or processes, (3) production, (4) marketing, (5) distribution, and (6) customer service. It is vital for directing managers to four areas: (a) customer focus, (b) key success factors (cost, quality, time, and innovation), (c) continuous improvement, and (d) value-chain and supply-chain analysis.[1]

Management accounting, which is a more elaborate version of cost accounting, needs to take a multidimensional focus in order to better serve the various and complex needs facing the management accountant. As a result, management accounting rests not only in accounting but also on organizational, behavioral, decisional, strategic, and other foundations and dimensions. An understanding of these dimensions is vital to a better understanding of the management accountant's new role.

This chapter examines the multidimensional scope of management accounting and establishes a frame of reference for the rest of the text.

Management accounting involves consideration of the ways in which accounting information may be accumulated, synthesized, analyzed, and presented in relation to specific problems, decisions, and day-to-day tasks of business management. An appreciation of management accounting requires a good understanding of the different facets of accounting organizations.

Toward a Theory of Management Accounting

Management accounting is generally understood as a process or as referring to the use of techniques. It has been defined as "the application of appropriate techniques and concepts in processing the historical and projected economic data of an entity to assist management in establishing a plan for reasonable economic objectives, and in the making of rational decisions with a view towards achieving these objectives."[2] Similarly, the emergent conceptual framework of management accounting started by the National Association of Accountants (NAA) defines it as

the process of identification, measurement, accumulation, analysis, preparation, interpretation and communication of financial information used by management to plan, evaluate, and control within an organization and to assure the appropriate use of and accountability for its resources. Management accounting also comprises the preparation of financial reports for non-management groups such as shareholders, creditors, regulatory agencies, and tax authorities.[3]

Those techniques are further explicated as follows:

Identification—the recognition and evaluation of business transactions and other economic events for appropriate accounting action.

Measurement—the quantification, including estimates, of business transactions or other economic events that have occurred or may occur.

Accumulation—the disciplined and consistent approach to recording and classifying appropriate business transactions and other economic events.

Analysis—the determination of the reasons for, and the relationships of, the reported activity with other economic events and circumstances.

Preparation and interpretation—the meaningful coordination of accounting and/or planning data to satisfy a need for information, presented in a logical format, and, if appropriate, including the conclusions drawn from those data.

Communication—the reporting of pertinent information to management and others for internal and external uses.

Plan—to gain an understanding of expected business transactions and other economic events and their impact on the organization.

Evaluate—to judge the implications of various past and/or future events.

Control—to ensure the integrity of financial information concerning an organization's activities or its resources.

Assure accountability—to implement the system of reporting that is the closely aligned to organizational responsibilities and that contributes to the effective measurement of management performance.[4]

A generally accepted definition of a theory, as it could apply to management accounting, is that a theory represents the coherent set of hypothetical, conceptual, and pragmatic principles for a field of inquiry. Accordingly, management accounting theory may be defined as a frame of reference in the form of a set of postulates and/or principles from different disciplines by which management accounting techniques are evaluated. The task of justifying the existence of a management accounting theory lies in the definition of appropriate postulates and principles. Given the differences in the objectives between management accounting and financial accounting, the postulates of financial accounting, with some exceptions, do not hold true for management accounting. In fact, the 1961 AAA Management Accounting Committee, charged with determining the relevance of financial accounting concepts to management accounting, concluded that

1. the concepts underlying internal reporting differ in several important respects from those of external public reporting;
2. these differences are due to differences in the objectives of both areas; and
3. it is justified to develop a separate body of concepts applicable to internal reporting.[5]

There is a need, then, for the accounting profession to develop a conceptual framework in management accounting to guide the development and use of techniques. Similar to financial accounting, such a framework would include the following elements:

1. The *objectives* of management accounting as the first and important step for the development of the elements of the conceptual framework for management accounting.
2. *Qualitative characteristics* to be met as essential attributes of management accounting information.
3. *Management accounting concepts* as the foundation for the body of knowledge contained within the conceptual framework.
4. *Management accounting techniques* and procedures that constitute the internal accounting systems.

Although these elements and the total integrated framework have not yet been formalized through a deductive reasoning process, they do exist in the literature as separate attempts to resolve these issues.

A Search for Objectives of Management Accounting

The objectives of management accounting are the first and essential step to the formulation of a management accounting theory. Then, the management accounting concepts will be true because they will be based on accepted objectives. In spite of the importance of management accounting objectives, there has never been a formal attempt by the profession to accomplish such a task. One noticeable exception, which may serve as de facto objectives of management accounting, was provided by the 1972 AAA Committee on Courses in Managerial Accounting. Four objectives were presented:

A. Management accounting should be related to the planning functions of the managers. This involves:
   1. Goal identification.
   2. Planning for optimal resource flows and their measurement.
B. Management accounting should be related to organizational problem areas. This includes:
   1. Relating the structure of the firm to its goals.
   2. Installing and maintaining an effective communication and reporting system.
   3. Measuring existing resource uses, discovering exceptional performance, and identifying causal factors of such exceptions.
C. Management accounting should be related to the management control function. This includes:
   1. Determining economic characteristics of appropriate performance areas that are significant in terms of overall goals.
   2. Aiding motivation of desirable individual performances through a realistic communication of performance information in relation to goals.
   3. Highlighting performance measures indicating goal incongruity within identifiable performance and responsibility areas.
D. Management accounting should be related to operating systems management, by function, product, project, or other segmentation of operations. This involves:
   1. Measurement of relevant cost input and/or revenue or statistical measures of outputs.
   2. Communication of appropriate data, of essentially economic character, to critical personnel on a timely basis.[6]

The NAA's emerging conceptual framework defines the objectives of management accounting as well as management accountants in terms of providing information and participating in the management process. More specifically the true objectives are defined as providing information and participating in the management process.

Providing Information

Management accountants select and provide, to all levels of management, information needed for:

a. planning, evaluating, and controlling operations;
b. safeguarding the organization's assets; and
c. communicating with interested parties outside the organization, such as shareholders and regulatory bodies.

Participating in the Management Process

Management accountants at appropriate levels are involved actively in the process of managing the entity. This process includes making strategic, tactical, and operating decisions and helping to coordinate the efforts of the entire organization. The management accountant participates, as part of management, in assuring that the organization operates as a unified whole in its long-run, intermediate, and short-run best interest.[7]

While these objectives reflect some of the priorities facing management accounting, they do not necessarily represent all the facets of the environment of management accounting. A formal study for the objectives of accounting is a definite must for the profession.

A Search for Qualitative Characteristics of Management Accounting Information

Management accounting information should have certain desirable properties so that benefits are achievable. The 1969 AAA Committee on Managerial Decision Models explored the application to internal reporting of the standards of relevance, verifiability, freedom from bias, and quantifiability.[8] These standards for accounting information were suggested in the AAA Statement of Basic Accounting Theory.[9] This effort was pursued by the 1974 AAA Committee on Concepts and Standards—Internal Planning and Control.[10] The Committee offered the following closely related properties as representatives of the benefits of information or information systems:

1. Relevance/mutuality of objectives
2. Accuracy/precision/reliability
3. Consistency/comparability/uniformity
4. Verifiability/objectivity/neutrality/traceability
5. Aggregation
6. Flexibility/adaptability
7. Timeliness
8. Understandability/acceptability/motivation/fairness[11]

The findings of the Committee are discussed next.

1. *Relevance/mutuality of objectives.* Relevant information is that which bears upon or is useful to "the action it is designed to facilitate or the result it is desired to produce."[12] For example, given different alternatives, the relevant costs and revenues are those expected costs and revenues that will be different for at least one of the alternatives. Historical costs may be only the basis for estimating expected future costs.
   Relevance depends on the structure of the objective function. In other words, rel-

evant information is the information on any variables in the user's objective function and must be very close to the definition implicit in the objective function. Relevance is a qualitative rather than a quantitative characteristic in the sense that information is either relevant or not.

Finally, relevance depends on the particular user receiving the information and on his or her particular decision. Some variables may be relevant to one user and not to others, and to one type of decision and not to others.

Mutuality of objectives refers to the consistency and congruency of the goals of the information users with those established by top management for the whole organization. The information provided by the internal reporting system may contribute to internal goal congruency if the signals of success or failure have the same meaning for both the total organization and its different segments. The mutuality of objectives applies also to the management accountants or the "internal information processors." Their goals should be consistent with the organizational goals.

2. *Accuracy/precision/reliability*. These properties are statistically interrelated in the sense that the notion of accuracy is statistically expressed by the concepts of precision and reliability. The specification of precision requires the specification of reliability, and vice versa.[13] R. M. Cyert and H. J. Davidson define these concepts as follows: "reliability is commonly used to describe the chances that a confidence interval will contain the true value being estimated . . . precision is often used in describing the interval about a sample estimate."[14] While it is generally impossible to reach 100 percent accuracy, it is advisable to specify upper and lower bounds within which accuracy may be an effective property of management accounting information.

3. *Consistency/comparability/uniformity*. Consistency refers to the continued use of the same rules and procedures by the same firm over time, leading to comparability of its own statements with one another from one year to another. Uniformity refers to the use of similar rules by different firms. Consistency, uniformity, and the ensuing comparability are considered desirable criteria for financial accounting. Their relevance to management accounting differs between long-term and short-term decisions. A long-range planning decision relies on diverse, unstructured information and nonrepetitive situations, and it may be unduly hampered by an internal accounting system stressing consistency/comparability/uniformity. However, the areas of short-run planning and performance control rely more on carefully structured information and repetitive situations, and lend themselves to an internal accounting system stressing consistency/comparability/uniformity.

4. *Verifiability/objectivity/neutrality/traceability*. Verifiability and objectivity refer to measurements that can be duplicated by independent measurers using the same measurement methods. They are usually operationally measured by the dispersion of the data in terms of the variance of the data. If the measurement rules are well specified, the verifiability of the measurement may be accomplished through a reconstruction of the initial measurement process and on the basis of evidential documents referred to as the audit trail. Traceability refers to the availability of such an audit trail. Finally, neutrality refers to the impartiality of the data in terms of its impact on different groups. A personal interest of the measurer in the data will not likely lead to neutral measurements. The degree of verifiability/objectivity/traceability of the data generated for management accounting is not as pronounced as when applied to financial accounting. However, neutrality of the information is a desirable objective, especially

when the data are used for information evaluation or as a basis for disturbing resources or settling claims.

5. *Aggregation*. This refers to the process of reducing the volume of data. A loss of identifiability or information is generally attributed to the process of aggregation, which may be compensated by cost savings in accounting for the information. An optimal level of aggregation is difficult to specify for either financial or management accounting. For financial accounting, the preparation of standard financial statements according to well-defined rules has led to a tendency to aggregate the information at an early stage of information processing. For management accounting, the lack of homogeneity in the reports, the flexibility in the choice of rules for preparing these reports, and the objective to meet a variety of information needs argue in favor of a management accounting system with less aggregated data, but that takes into account the user's limitations in handling voluminous data.

6. *Flexibility/adaptability*. Flexibility refers to the degree to which data may be the basis for several types of information and reports. It depends on both the classification used for the database into definite categories and the level of aggregation used in each of the categories. For example, purchase data may be classified under the following categories: (1) by individual product or service, (2) by individual purchaser, (3) by supplier, and so on. These data may be aggregated under the following categories: (1) by transaction, (2) by day, (3) by month, and so on.

Adaptability refers to the extent to which information derived from the database may be tailored to, or harmonized with, the decision processes of the firm. The adaptability of an accounting system requires not only the presence of flexibility, but also an explicit process of harmonizing it with the decision process. The Committee suggested the following procedures for harmonizing: "Such harmonizing is often accomplished iteratively through an understanding of the planning and control process, representing the latter in terms of information parameters and specifying the aggregation rules to be used in going from data base to information and analyzing the impact of such information on the planning processes."[15]

Again, given the lack of homogeneity in the management accounting reports, the large number of these reports, and the desire to meet various decision needs, management accounting requires higher levels of flexibility and adaptability than financial accounting.

7. *Timeliness*. Timeliness refers to the age of the information. It has two components: interval and delay. Interval is the period of time elapsing between the preparation of two successive reports. Delay is the period of time necessary to process the data, prepare the reports, and distribute them. Timeliness is also related to the concept of real time. Wayne Boutell provides the following definition: "It [real time] refers to the time in which information is received by the particular decision maker. If the information is received in sufficient time for a decision to be made without a penalty for delay, the information is said to be received in real time."[16] Although timeliness is a uniquely desirable property of management accounting information, it is affected by cost considerations and may conflict with other criteria, such as accuracy.

8. *Understandability/acceptability/motivation/fairness*. This refers to the extent to which the user is able to use the information. Understandability refers to the ability of the user to ascertain the message transmitted. Acceptability is the recognition by the user

that the problem specification and measurement criteria have been met. Fairness refers to the neutrality of the information as defined earlier. Finally, motivation refers to the attempt to secure goal congruences between the user and the organization. In brief, management accounting information should be understandable, acceptable, fair to the user, and a motivation to the user to perform in the desired manner.

A Search for Management Concepts

Management accounting concepts based on both the objectives and qualitative characteristics of management accounting would constitute the basic foundation for a management accounting conceptual framework. Although the development and formalization of a management accounting conceptual framework remain to be accomplished, the literature contains references to certain identifiable management accounting concepts. For example, the 1972 AAA Committee on Courses in Managerial Accounting identified measurement, communication, information, system, planning, feedback, control, and cost behavior as some of the management accounting concepts "which represent a necessary, if not minimum, foundation for the body of knowledge contained within the structure."[17] Accordingly, each of these concepts will be explained next.

1. Applied to accounting, *measurement* has been defined as "an assignment of numerals to an entity's past, present, or future economic phenomena, on the basis of past or present observation and according to rules."[18] This concept is very essential to management accounting.

2. As defined by Claude Shannon and Warren Weaver, *communication* encompasses "the procedures by means of which one mechanism affects another mechanism."[19]

3. *Information* represents significant data upon which action is based. It refers to those data that reduce the uncertainty on the part of the user. Thus, data produced by management accounting should be evaluated in terms of their informational content. Although not exhaustive, management accounting information includes the following categories:

    a. financial information resulting from the flow of financial resources within the organization,

    b. production information resulting from the physical flow of resources within the organization,

    c. personnel information resulting from the flow of people within the organization, and

    d. marketing information resulting from the interaction with the market for the organization's products.

4. *System* refers to an entity consisting of two or more interacting components or subsystems intended to achieve a goal. Management accounting is generally a subsystem of the accounting information system, which is itself a subsystem of the total management information system within the organization. The interaction of the management accounting system with all the other systems within the organization, and

especially the integration of all these systems, is essential for an efficient functioning of the organization. A management accounting system may be defined as *the set of human and capital resources within an organization that is responsible for the production and dissemination of information deemed relevant for internal decision making.*

5. *Planning* refers to the management function of setting objectives, establishing policies, and choosing means of accomplishment. Planning may be practiced at different levels in the organization, from strategic to operational, and may have behavioral implications.

6. *Feedback* refers to the output of a process that returns to become an input to the process in order to initiate control. It is basically a revision of the planning process to accommodate new environmental events.

7. *Control* refers to monitoring and evaluation of performance to determine the degree of conformance of actions to plans. Ideally, planning precedes control, which is followed by a feedback corrective action or a feedforward preventive action.

8. *Cost behavior*: cost results from the use of an asset for the generation of revenues. The identification, classification, and estimation of costs are essential to any evaluation of courses of action.

Although not exhaustive, this list represents concepts that are representative of those foundation components essential to a grasp of the management accounting process. This is very much in line with the NAA's definition of the responsibilities of a management accountant:

1. *Planning*. Quantifying and interpreting the effects on the organization of planned transactions and other economic events. The planning responsibility, which includes strategic, tactical, and operating aspects, requires that the accountant provide quantitative historical and prospective information to facilitate planning. It includes participation in developing the planning system, setting obtainable goals, and choosing appropriate means of monitoring the progress toward the goals.

2. *Evaluating*. Judging implications of historical and expected events and helping to choose the optimum course of action. Evaluating includes translating data into trends and relationships. Management accountants must communicate effectively and promptly the conclusions derived from the analyses.

3. *Controlling*. Assuring the integrity of financial information concerning an organization's activities and resources; monitoring and measuring performance and inducing any corrective actions required to return the activity to its intended course. Management accountants provide information to executives operating in functional areas who can make use of it to achieve desirable performance.

4. *Assuring accountability of resources*. Implementing a system of reporting that is aligned with organizational responsibilities. This reporting system will contribute to the effective use of resources and measurement of management performance. The transmission of management's goals and objectives throughout the organization in the form of assigned responsibilities is a basis for identifying accountability. Management accountants must provide an accounting and reporting system that will accumulate

and report appropriate revenues, expenses, assets, liabilities, and related quantitative information to managers. Managers then will have better control over these elements.

5. *External reporting.* Preparing financial reports bases on generally accepted accounting principles, or other appropriate bases, for nonmanagement groups such as shareholders, creditors, regulatory agencies, and tax authorities. Management accountants should participate in the process of developing the accounting principles that underlie external reporting.[20]

Management Accounting Techniques

Management accounting techniques should be derived and supported by the management accounting conceptual framework. Given the absence of such a framework, there is no consensus on a list of management accounting techniques. Most management accounting textbooks include standard cost accounting techniques and only a few attempts at introducing behavioral and/or quantitative considerations in separate chapters. What is needed is a structure that will allow an integration of accounting, organizational, behavioral, quantitative, and other techniques of relevance to internal decision making. The AAA Report of the Committee on Courses in Managerial Accounting proposes such a structure:

Introductory Material

 Systems theory and accounting

 Communications, measurement, and information concepts

 Criteria development

 Feedback and control mechanisms

 Information systems

 Accounting for management planning and control

 Cost concepts and techniques

Cost Determination for Assets

 Job order and process costing

 Standard costing system

 Direct versus absorption costing

 By-product and joint product costing

 Cost allocation practices

 Accounting for human resources

Planning

 Strategic planning

 Continuous planning

 Investment decisions

 Comprehensive budgets

Cost-volume-profit analysis

Problems of alternative choice

Management Control

Responsibility accounting

Cost centers

Financial performance centers

Investment performance centers

Centralized versus decentralized structures

Concern for goal congruence

Transfer pricing

Evaluation methods

Performance reporting

Operational Control

Internal control

Project control

Inventory control[21]

DECISIONAL DIMENSIONS

Anthony Framework

Although a typology of managerial activities, the Anthony framework may also be conceived as a hierarchy of decision systems, each requiring different planning and control systems. The decision systems are categorized as strategic planning, management control systems. The decision systems are categorized as strategic planning, management control, and operational control.[22]

Strategic planning as defined by R. N. Anthony is "the process of deciding on objectives of the organization, on changes in these objectives, on the re-sources used to attain these objectives, and on the policies that are to govern the acquisition, use, and disposition of resources."[23] The main concern of the strategic planner is the relationship between the organization and its environ-ment. This concern is expressed in the formulation of a long-range plan that defines the intended future orientation of the firm. Strategic planning is the responsibility of senior managers and analysts who will approach problems on an ad hoc basis as the need for a solution arises.

Management control is "the process by which managers assure that resources are obtained and used effectively and efficiently in the accomplishment of the organization's objectives."[24] The concern is with the conduct of managerial ac-tivities within the framework established by strategic planning. These activities require sometimes subjective interpretations and involve personal interactions. Management control involves both top management and the middle managers, who will approach problems following a definite pattern and timetable to insure efficient and effective results.

Operational control is "the process of assuring that specific tasks are carried out effectively and efficiently."[25] The concern is with individual tasks or transactions. The performance of these tasks or transactions is accomplished according to rules and procedures derived from management control. These rules and procedures are often expressed in terms of a mathematical model.

Although, as recognized by Anthony, the boundaries between the three categories are often not clear, they are useful for the analysis of the different activities and their information requirements. The decision categories form a continuum and require different information.

Anthony's framework has the advantage of simplicity, and it facilitates communications between individuals in the organization by categorizing different types of decisions and their information requirements. For management accounting, it implies a tailoring of the data produced to the context and category of the particular decision. It also calls for different approaches to planning and control in each of the strategic planning, management control, and operational control areas.

Simon Framework

Similar to Anthony's framework, H. A. Simon's framework presents a taxonomy of decisions.[26] However, while Anthony's framework focuses on the purpose of decision-making activity (strategic planning, management control, and operational control), Simon's framework focuses on the question of problem solving by individuals regardless of their position within an organization. Simon maintains that all problem solving can be broken down into three distinct phases: intelligence, design, and choice. Intelligence consists of surveying the environment for situations that demand decisions. It implies an identification of the problem(s), the collection of information, and the establishment of goals and evaluative criteria. Design involves delineating and analyzing various courses of action for the problems identified in the intelligence phase. It implies an enumeration of a combination of feasible alternatives and their evaluation on the basis of the criteria established in the intelligence phase. Choice involves selecting the best alternative. Although not mentioned by Simon, decision making involves a fourth phase, implementation, designed to insure the proper execution of choice.

Simon's framework also makes the distinction between programmed and non-programmed decisions:

Decisions are programmed to the extent that they are repetitive and routine, to the extent that a definite procedure has been worked out for handling them so that they don't have to be treated de novo each time they occur. Decisions are nonprogrammed to the extent that they are novel, unstructured, and consequential. There is no cut-and-dried method of handling the problem because it hasn't arisen before, or because its precise nature and structure are elusive or complex, or because it is so important that it deserves a custom-tailored treatment. . . . By nonprogrammed I mean a response where the system has no specific procedure to deal with situations like the one at hand, but must fall back on whatever general capacity it has for intelligent, adaptive, problem-oriented action.[27]

Because they are repetitive and routine, programmed decisions require little time in the design phase. On the other hand, nonprogrammed decisions require much more time in the design phase. In general, the terms *structured* and *unstructured* are used for *programmed* and *nonprogrammed* to imply less dependence on the computer and to show more dependence on the basic character of the problem-solving activity in question. The two classifications advanced by Simon may be viewed as polar types for a continuum of decision-making activity. For example, "semistructured" decisions may be those for which one or two of the intelligence, design, and choice phases are unstructured.

That decisions may fall on a continuum going from structured to unstructured has implications for management accounting. Structured decisions are solvable by analytic techniques, while unstructured decisions generally are not. The analytic techniques required for the structured decisions may be either based on clerical routine and habit or formalized techniques from operations research and electronic data processing. The decision techniques required for unstructured decisions may be either based on human intuition and judgment or heuristic techniques. While the role of management accounting for structured decisions appears without doubt to be one of providing and assisting in the use of fixed outlines, it is not very obvious in the case of unstructured decisions. Users may rely more on their decision style, intuition, or heuristics for the unstructured decisions or tasks.

Gorry–Scott Morton Framework

As mentioned earlier, Anthony's framework is based on the purpose of the decision-making activity, while Simon's framework is based on the methods or techniques of problem solving. The Gorry–Scott Morton framework provides a combination of both frameworks in the form of a matrix that classifies decisions on both a structured-to-unstructured dimension and an operational-to-strategic dimension.[28]

The implications for management accounting from both the Anthony and Simon frameworks apply to the Gorry–Scott Morton framework. The synthesis, however, presents additional implications. First, different information requirements and different methods of data collection and maintenance are required not only for the three decision categories borrowed from Anthony, but also for the types of decisions borrowed from Simon. This implies that the design of a management accounting support system is flexible enough to cope with the various complex demands. For example, in the structured case, the goal of management accounting may be to facilitate the flow of information, while in the unstructured case, it may be to improve the organization and presentation of information inputs.[29] Second, different organizational structures, different managerial skills and talents, and different numbers of managers may be required for each decision category. The decision process, the implementation process, and the level of analytic sophistication will differ among the three decision categories and call for different organization structures:

On strategic problems, a task force reporting to the user and virtually independent of the computer group may make sense. The important issues are problem definition and problem structure; the implementation and computer issues are relatively simple by comparison. In management control, the single user, although still dominant in his application, has problems of interfacing with other users. An organizational design that encourages cross-functional (marketing, production, distribution, etc.) cooperation is probably desirable. In operational control, the organizational design should include the user as a major influence, but he will have to be balanced with operational systems experts, and the whole group can quite possibly stay within functional boundaries.[30]

Finally, the model requirements may be different between the three areas, given the differences in the information requirements, the frequency of decisions in each area, and their relative magnitude. The operational control system calls for frequent decisions, and the models for these decisions need to be "efficient in running time, have ready access to current data, and be structured so as to be easily changed."[31] The models in strategic planning, and to a lesser extent management control, are infrequent, individual, and dependent on the managers involved.

While not referring to management accounting per se, but to a more general information systems concept labeled "Decision Support Systems," P.G. Keen and Scott Morton identified several implications of the framework to the design and implementation of a decision support system:

1. The skills and attitudes of the people involved in building a DSS (decision support system) for semistructured decisions need to differ from those building similar systems for structured decisions.

2. Ill-structured problems require a different technology to support decisions than structured problems.

3. While a well-structured operational control problem may require the use of optimization algorithms, most other problems will rely on different models.

4. The design of a DSS should be accomplished through a continuous evolutionary process to accommodate future needs, learning, and growth.[32]

Because management accounting is a decision support system, the above implications apply also to it. It requires people with different skills and attitudes, different technologies, different models, and different processes to accommodate both structured and unstructured decisions on the one hand and strategic planning, management control, and operational control on the other hand.

Forrester Framework

As developed by Professor Jay Forrester, the essence of industrial dynamics is that social systems such as business organizations can be understood through nonlinear feedback systems concepts.[33] Any system is characterized by its closed-loop (information feedback) structure. Forrester describes the state of the organization by information on the levels of variables in the organization, such as inventory, manpower, open orders, money, sales, and so on. The activity in the organization takes the form of instantaneous flows of the physical values of these variables or rates between the levels in each network. In addition to these physical values, each level produces information representing those values with the result of an information network superimposed on the physical network and controlling it.

Forrester expands this notion as follows:

The industrial system . . . is a very complex multi-loop and interconnected system. . . . Decisions are made at multiple points throughout the system. Each resulting action generates information that can be used at several but not all decision points. This structure of cascaded and interconnected information-feedback loops, when taken together, describes the industrial system. Within a company, the decision points extend from the shipping room and the stock clerk to the board of directors.

The interlocking network of information channels emerges at various points to control physical processes such as the hiring of employees, the building of factories, and the production of goods. Every action point in the system is backed up by a local decision point whose information sources reach into other parts of the organization and the surrounding environment.[34]

Forrester viewed management in terms of the sequence information-decision-action, with the decision-making process as a response to the gap between the objectives of the organization and its actual progress toward the accomplishment of these objectives.

Thus, industrial dynamics views organizations from a control perspective. It is intended mostly as a method of designing organizational policies. Nevertheless, industrial dynamics is a useful framework for information systems, management accounting in particular, in several ways:

1. It places information as an explicit and integral part of organizational decision making.
2. The information's function is to represent the physical values of the levels of various activities and entities in the organization.
3. It emphasizes the identification of decision points, objectives, and information requirements.

Dearden Framework

John Dearden observes that the concept of a single information system is "too large and all-encompassing to be a meaningful and useful classification."[35] He suggests instead to break down the systems and data-processing activities both horizontally and vertically. Horizontally, systems activities can be classified by the type of work performed; vertically, systems activities can be classified by the kind of information handled.

The horizontal classification includes three stages: systems specification, data processing implementation, and programming. These tasks are assumed to be different and should be treated differently. Systems specification should be decentralized to operating management or users because they have the best knowledge and capabilities required to determine what information should be provided by the system. Data-processing implementation can and should be centralized because it improves the economics of integration of the data-processing requirements, and should also be controlled by staff specialists because knowledge of equipment and data requirement is the primary requirement. Programming as a process of converting flowcharts to working programs lends itself best to centralization. Dearden gives the following three reasons:

1. Programming is more economically accomplished on a centralized basis.
2. Writing business programs requires a special knowledge of equipment and programming languages, and there is practically no difference in the skills required to program the different systems.
3. Management must delegate the task of programming to someone, and it makes little difference whether it is a staff unit or a department reporting directly to the manager.[36]

The vertical classification is based on the presence of three major information systems in a typical company, and a varying and indefinite number of minor systems.

The major information systems include financial, personnel, and logistics. The basis of the financial system is the flow of dollars through the organization.[37] The personnel system is concerned with the flow of information about people working in the organization. It is assumed to be administered by the industrial relations officer. Finally, the logistics system is concerned with information about the physical flow of goods through an organization covering procurement, production, and distribution. Several separate logistic systems may be found in any one company. Dearden associates the financial system with Anthony's category of management control and the logistics system with operational control.

The minor systems, defined as those confined to a limited part of the organization, include mainly marketing, research and development, strategic planning, and executive observation. Some of these may be integrated into the three major systems or left separate. Dearden finally proposes a generalized organization chart for systems and data processing based on the vertical and horizontal framework just described.

Blumenthal Framework

Sherman Blumenthal presented his framework as a synthesis of the three concepts of information-decision-action suggested by Forrester, programmed and nonprogrammed decisions suggested by Simon, and the hierarchy of planning and control suggested by Anthony.[38] His major concern is the lack of consistent and uniformly applied approaches to the integration of related systems into larger entities of appropriate scope.

He starts with the activity center as being one of the basic organizational units in an organization under the common and direct supervision of a first-line manager. These activity centers are grouped into larger and complex organizational units known as decision centers, functional units, and management control centers. A decision center is defined as one or more management-level people who either prescribe the decision rules or make the decisions for the activity centers. A functional unit is an activity center and its decision center. A management control center is one or more management people together with their supporting staff, which acts as a decision center for a group of functional units or for a group of subordinate management control centers. The actions, carried by the same or different functional units, that regulate the inflow or outflow to or from sequences of levels as a group form an operational function.

Each of these organizational units may constitute groups to execute operational functions as action subsystems, decision subsystems, and information subsystems. The organization subsystems, the operational functions, and various modules constitute the main foundations of a management information system. Hence, a management information system is viewed as an operational function whose functional units are information subsystems of other operational functions. The modules are either operational or management control modules. An operational control module is viewed as that part of an information subsystem supporting the functional units of an operational function. A management control module is that part of an information subsystem supporting the management control centers of an operational function. Blumenthal concludes that a management information system is alternatively definable as an operational function whose parts are the management control modules and operational control modules of other operational functions.[39]

Blumenthal's framework has implications for management accounting. It advocates that the design and planning of any information system, including management accounting, be based on fundamental principles that refer to the effective use of systems resources, efficiency in systems life and performance, and organizational changes. The process advocated to ensure this objective consists of: (1) grouping the most elementary operational activities into identifiable and separate organizational units, (2) linking these activity centers to decision centers to form functional units, and (3) defining different modules (operational control module, management control module) as the basic components of the information system. This implies that both planning and control will take place at two levels.

THE BEHAVIORAL DIMENSION

Management accounting is built on behavioral foundations. Its explicit aim is to affect the behavior of individuals in a desirable direction. To accomplish this purpose, management accounting has to be adapted to the different characteristics that shape the "cognitive makeup" of individuals within an organization and affect their performance. In general, these characteristics pertain to three factors: (1) the perception by the individual of what should be the objective function or goals in the firm; (2) the various factors likely to motivate the individual to perform; and (3) the decision-making model most relevant to particular contexts and most preferred by the individual. Although these factors do not constitute an exhaustive list of the behavioral concepts likely to affect the performance of an individual within an organization, they have been identified in the literature of various disciplines as essential factors to be considered for an understanding of an individual behavior within an organization and the design of any information system.

Thus, management accounting requires a good grasp of the behavioral concepts, namely, the objective function in management accounting, motivation theories, and models of decision making. Each of these concepts identifies factors and situations that influence individual behavior and indicates avenues for management accounting to adapt its services.

The Objective Function in Management Accounting

Many authors in the field of complex organization define an organization as a social system that is created to achieve certain specific goals or objectives. For example, Amitai Etzioni defines organizations as "social units (or human groupings) deliberately constructed and reconstructed to seek specific goals."[40]

Richard Hall states: "An organization is a collectivity with a relatively identifiable boundary, a nonnative order, authority ranks, community systems, and membership coordinating systems; this collectivity exists on a relatively continuous basis in an environment and engages in activities that are usually related to a goal or a set of goals."[41]

The concept of organizational goal and/or objective has not, however, been clearly defined in the literature. The general goals refer to the intentions or wishes espoused by those persons who develop them. For example, V. Buck gives the following operational definition of organizational goals: "It is the decision to commit resources for certain activities and to withhold them from certain others that operationally defines the organization's goals. Verbal pronouncements are insufficient for defining goals; the speaker must put his resources where his mouth is if something is to be considered a goal."[42]

Different typologies of goals have also been proposed. First, J. D. Thompson differentiated between goals held for an organization and goals of an organization.[43] The former are held by persons who are not members of the organization but have a given interest in the activities of the firm, such as clientele, investors, action groups, and so on. The latter are held by persons who are part of the "dominant coalition" in terms of holding enough control to commit the organization to a given direction.

C. Perrow made a distinction between "official goals" and "operative goals."[44] Official goals refer to those objectives or general purposes stated either orally or in writing by key members. Operative goals refer to the designated objectives based on the actual operating policies of the organization. Etzioni refers to such goals as real goals. They constitute "the future states toward which a majority of the organizational means and major organizational commitments . . . are directed, and which, in cases of conflict with goals which are stated but command few resources, have clear priority."[45]

Each discipline conceives a different goal or objective in its examination of profit-oriented organizations. The discipline of economics, for example, in its neoclassical approach views profit maximization as the single determinant of behavior. Organizational and management theories have provided various behavioral theories of the firm. In management accounting, as in corporate finance, neither the economic model nor the behavioral model appears entirely suitable. In fact, both models have influenced three held views of business behavior applicable to management accounting: the shareholder wealth maximization model, the managerial welfare maximization model, and the social welfare maximization model.[46] Each of these models constitutes an acceptable objective of profit-oriented organizations in the field of management accounting. Because the scope and practice of management accounting is heavily influenced by these assumptions, each of them will be examined next.

The Shareholder Wealth Maximization Model

In most textbooks in the field of corporate finance and specifically in management accounting, authors operate on the assumption that management's primary goal is to maximize the wealth of its stockholders. This view is referred to as the shareholder wealth maximization (SWM) model. According to this model, the firm accepts all projects yielding more than the cost of capital, and in equity financing prefers retaining earnings to issuing new stocks. It also assumes that earnings are objectively determined to show the true financial position of the firm to its owners and other users. In fact, the SWM model translates into maximizing the price of the common stock. Management is assumed to use decision rules and techniques that are in the best interests of the stockholders. In a management accounting context, SWM implies an acceptance by management of budgeting and control standards, a rejection of slack budgeting or any suboptimizing behavior, and an adoption of management accounting techniques that are in the best interests of the owners of the firm. If management behaves otherwise, its right to manage may be either questioned or revoked, given that stockholders own the firm and elect the management team.

The Managerial Welfare Maximization Model

Another school of thought maintains that a different objective function other than shareholder wealth maximization exists for the firm—namely, that managers run firms for their own benefits. It is maintained that because the stock of most large firms is widely held, the managers of such firms have a great deal of freedom. This being the case, they may be tempted for personal benefits to pursue an objective other than shareholder welfare maximization. This school of thought is generally referred to as the managerial welfare maximization (MWM) model. So rather than maximizing profits, the managers may maximize sales or assets,[47] the rate of growth,[48] or managerial utility.[49] As a consequence, managers may engage in suboptimization schemes as long as they contribute to their own welfare. For example, an entrenched management may avoid risky ventures even though the returns to stockholders would be high enough to justify the endeavor. In a management accounting context, MWM implies a lesser acceptance by management of budgeting and control standards, a recourse to slack budgeting and any suboptimization behavior, a manipulation or avoidance within legality of full disclosure in order to present the firm's operation favorably (i.e., income smoothing), and, finally, adoption of management accounting techniques that are in the best interest of managers.

That managers may elect to substitute their own different interests raises the question of how goals within MWM are "determined" or "set" in decisions to commit the organization to a particular course of action. Three distinct models have been identified to represent the goal-setting processes: the bargaining model, the problem-solving model, and the coalition model.[50] Because they present good conceptualizations of the goal determination process under MWM, they are briefly presented next.[51]

The Bargaining Model. The bargaining model depicts goal determination as the result of an open-minded negotiation process among all interested parties leading to a series of tradeoffs and compromises. It is based on three important assumptions:

1. There is an active group of participants (internal or external) who impose demands on the organization.
2. These demands are conflicting; they cannot be accommodated simultaneously.
3. The individuals or groups are interdependent.[52]

The Problem-Solving Model. The problem-solving model describes goal determination as the result of successive decisions made by high-level administrators. It is based on three important assumptions:

1. Policy commitments are made within a set of constraints or requirements that are known to decision makers.

2. These constraints can be ranked and a preferred set accommodated.

3. The goals of different individuals or groups can be simultaneously satisfied.[53]

The Dominant Coalition Model. Given the existence of controlling interests in the firm, the dominant coalition model describes goal determination as the result of decisions made by those who control the ends to which policies and resources are committed, It is based on two assumptions:

1. There are many persons or groups who hold goals for an organization. These goals are frequently in conflict and cannot all be accommodated.

2. One individual or group does not have sufficient power alone to act unilaterally. Power is dispersed. Collective behavior is required to secure support for goals.[54]

The Social Welfare Maximization Model

The climate in which businesses operate is changing with the pressures on organizations to be more sensitive to the impact of behavior on society. In adopting a more socially responsible attitude and responding to the pressures of new dimensions—social, human, and environmental—organizations may have to alter their main objective, whether SWM or MWM, to include as an additional constraint the welfare of society at large. This view may be referred to as the social welfare maximization (SOWM) model. Under SOWM, the firm undertakes all projects that, in addition to the usual profitability objective, minimize the social costs and maximize social benefits created by the productive operations of the firm. Thus, under SOWM the firm is liable not only to the shareholders and managers, but also to the society at large. Given the different interest groups in the society at large, the organization may have to develop different corporate purposes. For example, it was reported that one group has defined eight corporate purposes: "profit, sensitivity to natural and human environment, growth, responsiveness to consumer needs, equitable distributions of benefits, dynamic business structure, fair treatment of employees, and legal and ethical behavior."[55]

In a management accounting context, SOWM implies the developing of a social reporting system oriented toward the measurement of social performance, including not only social costs but also special benefits. It suggests the development of a new concept of organization performance that will be more indicative of the firm's social responsibility than is provided by conventional accounting. For example, the AAA Committee on Measurement of Social Cost suggested a total organization performance, which is a function of "five outputs":

1. Net income, which benefits stockholders and provides resources for further business growth.

2. Human resource contribution, which assists the individual in the organization to develop new knowledge or skills.

3. Public contribution, which helps the organization's community to function and provides services for its constituency.

4. Environmental contribution (closely allied with public contribution), which affects "quality of life" for society.

5. Product or service contribution, which affects customer well-being and satisfaction.[56]

While a theory of social accounting is still emerging in the new public interest accounting paradigm, the proposed objectives and concepts for social accounting offer an interesting beginning.

However, regardless of the objective function adopted by managers, social reporting and particularly social reports are needed by management for relevant decision making and to comply with both social pressures and legal requirements.

Motivation Theories

Motivation is related to the intrinsic forces within the individual—namely, the motives and unsatisfied needs of the individual. More explicitly, motivation is concerned with "how behavior gets started, is energized, is sustained, is directed, is stopped, and what kind of subjective reaction is presented in the organization while all this is going on."[57] For this reason, motivation is important for an organization and for management accounting. It basically refers to an individual's needs or motives that make that individual act in a specific manner.

Motivation relates all aspects of individual behavior where a deliberate and conscious action is initiated in the organization to direct individuals so that they can satisfy their needs as much as possible while they strive to accomplish the objectives of the organization. These actions may be initiated either directly by the managers' actions or through the adoption of appropriate management accounting techniques. Thus, management accounting techniques necessitate a good grasp of motivation in organizations. The identification of the factors and situations that may influence and coordinate employee action allows the management accountant to adapt the services to the realities of human behavior. The literature on motivation identifies five theories of motivation: the need theory, the two-factor theory, the value/expectancy theory, the achievement theory, and the inequity theory. Each of these theories identifies what factors within the individual and his or her environment activate high performance, or attempts to explain and describe the process of how behavior is activated, what directs it, and how it is controlled and stopped.

Need Theory

Originally advanced by Abraham Maslow, need theory holds that people are motivated to satisfy a "hierarchy" of needs.[58] These needs are as follows (in ascending order of prepotency):

1. The physiological needs: food, shelter, warmth, and other bodily wants.
2. The safety needs: security and protection.
3. The need for love and belongingness: desire to both give and receive love and friendship.
4. The need for esteem: self-respect and the respect of others.
5. The self-actualization need: "What a man can be, he must be."

Thus, individuals strive to satisfy these needs in a sequential fashion, starting with the physiological needs. The process of deprivation-domination-gratification-activation continues until the self-actualization need has been activated. This suggests that once the basic physiological and safety needs are satisfied, individuals will respond better to rewards leading to self-respect and self-actualization than to economic rewards, which are primarily related to the satisfaction of lower-level needs. What this implies for management accounting is that assuming individuals in the organization are well paid, the emphasis should be on the introduction of management accounting techniques, in general, and control techniques, in particular, that are consistent with the satisfaction of higher-level needs. This view is also shared by E. H. Caplan when he states that "it may be more important to concentrate on the development of organizational structures, leadership practices, and control systems which are consistent with satisfaction of the higher level needs."[59]

Two-Factor Theory

In a series of studies, F. Herzberg and his associates developed the "motivation hygiene" theory.[60] Briefly, they found two factors affecting a job situation, which they labeled *satisfiers* and *dissatisfiers*. The satisfiers were related to the nature of the work itself and to rewards that flowed directly from the performance of that work: (1) perceived opportunity for achievement on the job, (2) recognition, (3) a sense of performing interesting and important work, (4) responsibility, and (5) advancement. The dissatisfiers were related to the context rather than the content of the job: (1) company policies that foster ineffectiveness, (2) incompetent supervision, (3) interpersonal relations, (4) working conditions, (5) salaries, (6) status, and (7) job security. The satisfiers were classified as "motivators" and the dissatisfiers as "hygiene" factors.

According to Herzberg, the satisfiers contribute very little to job dissatisfaction, and conversely, the dissatisfiers contribute very little to job satisfaction. Similarly, motivation to work is created by the satisfaction of the individual's needs for the satisfiers and not from an elimination of the dissatisfiers. The implications of Herzberg's theory for management accounting are twofold. First, to contribute to the motivation of employees, management accounting techniques should focus on better measurement and reporting of achievement, recognition, work, responsibility, and advancement. Second, given that the key to motivation is to make jobs more meaningful, management accounting techniques should focus on job enrichment. Job enrichment is the attempt by managers to design tasks in such a way as to affect employees' positive feelings about their job and to build in the opportunity for personal achievement, recognition, challenge, and personal growth. It gives the employees a greater amount of responsibility in carrying out complete tasks and insures a timely feedback on their performance.[61] Martin Evans suggests several steps to insure job enrichment of relevance to management accounting.[62]

1. Eliminating controls from the job while keeping accountability.

2. Increasing the individual's accountability for his or her job.

3. Providing each individual with a complete and natural work module (or elements of work).

4. Allowing greater job freedom for an individual's own work.

5. Providing timely feedbacks on performance to the employee instead of the supervisor.

6. Improving old tasks and introducing new tasks.

7. Assigning specific tasks so the employee can develop expertise in performing them.

Value/Expectancy Theory

The theories of Maslow, McClelland, and Herzberg are content theories in the sense of that they attempt to identify what factors within the individual and the individual's environment induce high performance. The value/expectancy theory is a process theory in the sense that it attempts to explain and describe the process of how behavior is initiated, maintained, and terminated.

Originally developed by K. Lewin,[63] and later specially applied to motivation to work by V. H. Vroom,[64] the basic tenet of the value/expectancy theory is that an individual chooses personal behavior on the basis of: (1) expectations that such behavior will result in a specific outcome, and (2) the sum of the valences—that is, personal utilities or rewards derived from the outcome. Vroom advances the following theoretical proposition:

The force on a person (motive) to perform a given act is based on the weighted value (or utility) of all the possible outcomes of the act multiplied by the perceived usefulness of the given act in the attainment of these outcomes. Whenever an individual chooses between alternatives that involve certain outcomes, it seems clear that his behavior is affected not only by his preferences among outcomes, but also by the degree to which he believes these outcomes to be probable."[65]

Hence, an individual's motivation may be expressed as:

$$M = \sum [(E\ O)\ (V)]$$

where:

E = Effort
O = Outcome
V = Values placed on the outcome

The above expression may be reformulated to include both an effort-performance linkage and a performance-rewarded linkage. The new model will include two expectancies. The first one refers to the probability that the effort will lead to a task accomplishment or performance. The second one refers to the probability that the task accomplishment will result in the desired outcomes. Hence, the individual's motivation may also be expressed as:

$$M = (E\ P)\sum[(P\ O)(V)]$$

where:

P = Performance

L. W. Porter and E. E. Lawler have extended the value/expectancy theory by arguing that poor performance may result if abilities are lacking and the individual's role perceptions are erroneous.[66] Thus, for preferences and expectations to affect performance, adequate ability and accurate role perceptions are necessary.

R. J Howse's formulation of the model can be expressed as follows:[67]

$$M = IV_b + P_i(IV_a + \sum P_{2i}\ EV_i)$$

where:

$I = 1, 2, \ldots, n$

M = Motivation to work

IV_a = Intrinsic valence associated with the successful performance of the task

IV_b = Intrinsic valence associated with the goal-directed behavior

EV_i = Extrinsic valences associated with the I extrinsic reward contingent on work-goal accomplishment

P_i = The expectancy that goal-directed behavior will accomplish the work goal (a given level of specified performance); the measure's range is $(-1, +1)$

P_{2i} = The expectancy that work-goal accomplishment will lead to the I extrinsic reward; the measure's range is $(-1, +1)$

This formulation shows some of the implications of expectancy theory for management accounting. Appropriate management accounting techniques may be chosen to affect the independent variables of the model in the following ways:

1. By determining what extrinsic rewards (EV_i) follow work-goal accomplishment.
2. By increasing through timely reports the individual's expectancy (P_2) that work-goal accomplishment leads to extrinsic rewards.
3. By increasing the intrinsic valence associated with work-goal accomplishment (IV_a) through a greater role of the individual in goal-setting and task-directed effort.
4. By recognizing and supporting the individual's effort, thereby influencing P_i.
5. By increasing the net intrinsic valences associated with goal-directed behavior (IV_b).

Achievement Theory

The concept of "achievement motive" was first introduced by McClelland, Atkinson, and their associates.[68] It is based on the desire of people to be challenged and to be innovative and adopt an "achievement-oriented behavior"—that is, a behavior directed toward meeting a standard of excellence. McClelland viewed the motive to achieve as distinct from acquisitiveness for money, except insofar as money is considered a symbol of achievement. Using the Thematic Apperception Test (TAT) to measure three distinct needs (need for achievement, need for power, and need for affiliation), he found the achievement level to be correlated with personality and cultural variables.

The achievement-oriented individual likes to assume responsibility for individual achievement, seeks challenging tasks, and takes calculated risks depending on the probabilities of success, Therefore, he will take small risks for tasks serving as stepping stones for future rewards, take intermediate risks for tasks offering opportunities for achievement, and will attempt to find situations falling somewhere between the two extremes, providing the highest probability of success, and hence maximizing his sense of personal achievement.

According to the theory, the individuals will particularly behave in an achievement-oriented way in situations that enable them to strive for a standard of excellence, require the use of skills, present a challenge, and allow the individuals to appraise their performance. Accordingly, Atkinson stated that the strength of one's tendency to succeed at a task (T_s)

is a multiplicative function of three variables: motive to achieve success (M_s) which is conceived as a relatively general and stable disposition of personality and measured in terms of need for achievement—and two other variables which represent the effect of the intermediate environment—the strength of expectancy (or subjective probability) that performance of a task will be followed by success (P_s) and the relative attractiveness of success of that particular activity, which is called the incentive of success (I_s). I_s assumed to be greater the more difficult the task.[69]

Another important contention of the theory is that all motives are learned, including the achievement motive. As a result, the high achiever is experienced in making maximizing decisions, is less affected by anxiety, and proceeds in an efficient way in any endeavor.

What these contentions imply for management accounting is: (1) the necessity of constructing ways of developing the achievement motive at all managerial levels, and (2) the need to introduce management accounting techniques and to report management accounting information that encourages and facilitates the performance of high achievers.

Inequity Theory

Elaine Walster, Stacey Adams, and their colleagues have advanced the theory that individuals in a relationship have two motives: to maximize their own gains and to maintain equity in the relationship.[70] Inequity results when a person's rewards from a relationship are not proportional to what that person has put into the relationship. More explicitly, inequity theory is based on the premise that when individuals compare their own situations with other situations and have a feeling of inequity, in terms of feeling either underrewarded or overrewarded for their contributions, they experience increased tension and strive to reduce it. Hence, overpaid workers will increase their efforts by producing more as a way of reducing inequity, while underpaid workers will produce less to achieve a contribution-reward balance. Other methods of restoring equity may be used also. Walster et al. state that individuals can restore actual equity by altering either their own payoffs or those of other participants. Similarly, a psychological equity can be restored when individuals change their perceptions of either rewards or contributions so that their contributions appear greater or lower than originally thought. They may also restore equity by quitting their jobs, severing relationships with comparison persons, or forcing comparison persons to leave the field.

The inequity theory suggests, then, that rewards must appear to the employees to be fair or equitable. An appeal to equity norms can be used to reduce conflict. The role of management accounting in restoring equity is in insuring correct and accurate measurement and reporting of performance and the corresponding rewards. To avoid creating feelings of inequity, the methods of measuring performance and rewards should be made public to the employees.

Models of Decision Making

Management accounting necessitates a good grasp of decision making in organizations. The identification of the decision-making models most relevant to particular contexts and most preferred by particular individuals allows the management accountant to adapt the services to offer to the realities of the decision situation. The literature on decision making identifies five main perspectives: the "rational" manager view, the "satisficing" process-oriented view, the organizational proceedures view, the political view, and the individual differences view.[71]

Before analyzing each of these models, it is appropriate to mention the excellent analysis of the Cuban missile crisis by G. T. Allison using three of these models: the rational actor view, the organizational procedures view, and the political view.[72] Addressing the central issues of the crisis from one of the three perspectives "lead[s] one to see, emphasize, and worry about quite different aspects of events."[73] By analogy, addressing management issues from any of the five perspectives leads one to have different perceptions and understanding of events and places on the management accountant different demands for services. Let us examine each of these models and its importance to management accounting.

The Rational View

The rational view of decision making is a normative model that refers to a consistent value-maximizing choice process in the presence of specific constraints. This process may be summarized as follows:

1. Individuals assume that there is a set of alternative acts or courses of action displayed before them in a particular situation.
2. They associate a set of possible outcomes or consequences with the set of possible acts.
3. They have a preference ordering over the consequences or payoff function that allows them to rank the consequences and select that act that ranks highest in their payoff function.

This view is used and relied upon as the model of the "economic man" in neoclassical economic theory and as the model of the "rational man" in game theory and statistical decision theory. Both make optimal choices in the presence of well-defined specific constraints.

As a defense of the rational view of decision making, one of the two assumptions has been made. On the one hand, there is the assumption of comprehensive rationality where individuals have perfect knowledge of all alternative acts, all the consequences, and the corresponding payoff function. On the other hand, there is the assumption of limited rationality with its inherent restricted claim on "optimal choice." Whatever the assumptions, the rational view of decision making requires the management accountant to define all the possibilities in terms of acts, consequences, and payoff function, and to evaluate the costs and benefits associated with rational decision making.

The rational view of decision making, although normative and rigorous, has been criticized as being descriptively unrealistic. H. A. Simon, in particular, advanced the principle of bounded rationality of the human decision maker:

When the limits to rationality are viewed from the individual's standpoint, they fall into three categories: he is limited by his values and conceptions of purpose, which may diverge from the organizational goals; he is limited by the extent of his knowledge and information. The individual can be rational in terms of the organization's goals only to the extent that he is able to pursue a particular course of action, he has a correct conception of the goal of the action, and he is correctly informed about the conditions surrounding his action. Within the boundaries laid down by these factors, his choices are rational-goal oriented.[74]

In replacement of the "economic man," Simon suggests the notion of the "administrative" or "satisficing" man as more representative of what is in decision making.

The Satisficing and Process-Oriented View

The satisficing and process-oriented view of decision making is a descriptive model that maintains that the administrative individual satisfices rather than optimizes when making most decisions. Thus, rather than searching the haystack for the sharpest needle, the objective of the administrative man is to find one sharp enough to sew with.[75] Simon summarizes the assumptions of the satisficer's theory as follows:

In actual organizational practice, no one attempts to find an optimal solution for the whole problem. Instead, various particular decisions, or groups of decisions, within the whole complex are made by specialized members or units of the organization. In making these particular decisions, the specialized units do not solve the whole problem but find a "satisfactory" solution for one or more subproblems, where some of the effects of the solution on other parts of the system are incorporated in the definition of "satisfactory."[76]

Thus, the satisficing man makes a decision-making choice in the context of a simplified view of the real situation. Simon introduces a concept of "subjective rationality" as a challenge to the concept of "objective rationality" advocated by the rational view of decision making. Subjective rationality depends on the individual's personal values. Thus, an objectively rational decision calls for a maximizing behavior, given values in a specific situation, while a subjectively rational decision calls for maximizing attainment relative to the actual knowledge of the individual.[77] To be able to satisfice, the individual's strategies will consist essentially of heuristics or rules of thumb that meet a subjective minimum standard with respect to the things being sought.

That managers satisfice rather than optimize, refer to subjective rather than objective rationality, and rely on their heuristics places distinctive demands on the management accountant. To be able to service managers and facilitate their decision-making process, an understanding of their heuristics is essential. It is not an insurmountable task, given the general evidence suggesting how simple and how few are the heuristics used by the managers. It also implies a good working relationship between managers and management accountants.

The Organizational Procedures View

The organizational procedures view of decision making is a descriptive model that maintains that individuals comply with an act according to a fixed set of standard operating procedures and programs. They make their choice in terms of goals and on the basis of expectations. R. M. Cyert and J. G. March perceive the organization as a coalition of individuals with different demands, priorities, goals, focus of attention, and competencies.[78] Decision making within the organization requires bargaining among the coalition members, resulting in de facto agreements and standard procedures for dealing with problematic situations.

Thus, individuals will act according to standard patterns of behavior established in their particular organizational unit to achieve its stated goals. What results in the organization is: (1) a permanent goal conflict between the units with possibly the dominant coalition imposing its independent constraints, (2) a quasi resolution of conflict marked by a sequential attention to problems, (3) uncertainty avoidance, (4) problematic search where the search is triggered by a specific problem and motivated to finding a solution to the problem, and (5) organizational learning leading to changes in goals, expectations, and standard procedures.

This process-oriented view of decision making has been applied with some success to simulate the working of a retail department store by Cyert and March,[79] the trust investment process used by officers in a bank by G. E. Clarkson,[80] the behavior of government units in municipal budgeting by John Crecine,[81] and the foreign investment decision process of businesses by Lair Aharoni.[82]

That managers may belong to coalitions that rely on programs and standard procedures places distinctive demands on management accountants. These coalitions and their standard procedures should be identified by management accountants to be able to service managers and facilitate their decision making. This implies that management accountants must be careful not to be identified with any of these coalitions, but as support agents providing the necessary information for an efficient resolution of problems. Following P. R. Lawrence and J. W. Lorsch's[83] suggestion for a balance between integration and differentiation within complex organizations, management accountants may act as integrating agents between the subunits of the organization.

The Political View

The political view of decision making is a descriptive model that maintains that decisions are due partly to political processes. In this process, different groups committed to different courses of action interact and arrive at decisions through the "pulling and hauling that is politics."[84] The differences between this view and the rational and process views are summarized by Allison as follows: "what moves the chess pieces is not simply the reasons that support a course of action or the routines of organizations that enact an alternative but the power and skill of proponents and opponents of the action in itself."[85] Thus each individual in the firm is a player in a competitive game called politics, where persuasion, accommodation, bargaining, and the constant search for support are the determinants of decision making. This may be justified because

managers [government leaders] have competitive, not homogeneous interests; priorities and perceptions are shaped by positions; problems are much more varied than straight-forward strategic issues; management of piecemeal streams of decisions is more important than steady state choices; making sure that management [the government] does what is decided is more difficult than selecting the preferred solution.[86] (Allison's original words are shown in brackets.)

This political view resulted in the concept of incremental change advanced mainly by C, W. Lindblom.[87] According to this view, labeled as "the art of the possible," managers attack rather than solve problems incrementally through "successive limited comparisons."

That managers may be motivated by political positions and disagree with other political positions in the firm, that they may favor managing through incremental muddling rather than comprehensive, satisfactory, or procedural choice is very relevant for the management accountant and should not be ignored. The acceptance and use of either management accounting techniques or information suggested by the management accountant is very much a function of the political dimensions existing in the firm.

The Individual Differences View

The individual differences view maintains that individuals have specific decision-making styles appropriate for some cases and less so for others. This view emerged from the recognition in psychology of the concept of cognitive style as a hypothetical construct to explain the mediation process between stimuli and responses. Five approaches have been reported for the study of cognitive style: authoritarianism, dogmatism, cognitive complexity, integrative complexity, and field dependence.[88]

1. Authoritarianism arose from the focus by T. W. Adorno et al. on the relationship between personality, antidemocratic attitudes, and behavior.[89] They were primarily interested in individuals whose way of thinking made them susceptible to antidemocratic propaganda. Two of the behavioral correlates of authoritarianism—rigidity and intolerance of ambiguity—were reflections of an underlying cognitive style. For example, J. Dermer investigated the relationship between intolerance of ambiguity and subjective cue usage.[90] His result showed a significant positive correlation between intolerance of ambiguity and the amount of information perceived to be important.

2. Dogmatism arose from M. Rokeach's efforts to develop a structurally based measure of authoritarianism to replace the content-based measure developed by Adorno and his colleagues.[91] His interest was in developing a measure of cognitive style that would be independent of the content of thought.

3. Cognitive complexity as introduced by G. A. Kelly[92] and J. Bieri[93] focuses on the psychological dimensions that individuals use to structure their environments and to

differentiate the behavior of others. The more cognitively complex individuals are assumed to have a greater number of dimensions available with which to construe the behavior of others than the less cognitively complex persons. Another clarification of decision makers in the literature is made in terms of two cognitive styles: heuristic and analytic. Based on terms and meanings used by Jan Huysmans,[94] they may be defined as follows: Analytic decision makers reduce problem situations to a more or less explicit, often quantitative, model as a basis for their decision. Heuristic decision makers refer instead to common sense, intuition, and unquantified feelings about future development as they apply to the totality of the situation as an organic whole rather than as built from clearly identifiable parts. Huysmans' findings show particularly that cognitive style may operate as an effective constraint on the implementation of operations research recommendations, and that operations researchers perceive their own analytic style as self-evident and tend to ignore the impact of cognitive style on the acceptance and use of analytic techniques. Similarly, in an experimental study of the relationship between different information structures, decision approaches, and learning patterns, T. Mock, T. Estrin, and M. Vasarhelyi[95] found that analytics significantly outperformed heuristics in terms of profit and decision time.

4. Integrative complexity as presented by O. J. Harvey et al.,[96] and later expanded by H. M. Schroder et al.,[97] results from the view that people engage in two activities in processing sensory input: differentiation and integration. Differentiation refers to the individual's ability to place stimuli along dimensions. Integration refers to the individual's ability to employ complex rules to combine these dimensions. Then a person low on both activities is said to be concrete, while a person high on both activities is said to be abstract. The continuum from concrete to abstract is referred to as an integrative or conceptual complexity. To the concept of integrative complexity is usually added the concept of environmental complexity and the level of information processing. It is expressed by the "U-Curve Hypothesis." As the level of information processing increases and reaches a maximum level at an optimal level of environmental complexity it begins to decrease.[98] H. M. Schroder et al. extended the concept of the inverted U-shaped curve to the study of integrative complexity. The more abstract the individual, the higher the maximum level of information processing.

5. Finally, field dependence as presented by H. A. Witkin and his associates is a measure of the extent of differentiation in the area of perception.[99] Field-dependent individuals tend to perceive the overall organization of a field and are relatively unable to perceive parts of the field as discrete. Field-independent individuals, however, tend to perceive parts of the field as discrete from organized parts rather than fused with it.

That managers have specific cognitive styles in terms of authoritarianism, dogmatism, cognitive complexity, integrative complexity, and field dependence, which give them specific styles of decision making, has strong implications for management accounting. First, management accounting reports should be compatible with the cognitive structures of the users. They should be designed on the basis of realistic assumptions about the users' decision styles. Second, the utilization and the acceptance of management accounting techniques and information depend on their suitability to the cognitive style of the users. Thus, management accountants should be aware of the cognitive style constraint in the implementation of management accounting. Quantitative-based management accounting techniques may be more attractive to the analytic rather than the heuristic decision makers. Finally, the analytic management accountants should not assume that all users are and should be like themselves.

THE STRATEGIC DIMENSION

Management accounting is built on strategic foundations. First, management accounting provides a framework and a language of discourse for the three stages of strategy: preenactment, resolution, and implementation. Second, the conduct of management accounting differs for different distinctions in the strategic process and the strategic decision-making process. Third, it works best when there is a consequence between the decision of management control systems and types of control strategies. Finally, the new area of strategic management accounting requires management accounting to its competitors and to monitor the firm's performance using strategic rather than tactical indicators.

Notions of Strategy

The Greeks refer to strategy as the "art of the general."[100] It evolved in the Harvard mold into an imaginative act of integrating numerous complex decisions.[101] A. D. Chandler, Jr. was the first to use strategy as a managerial tool.[102] He defined is as "the determination of the basic long-term goals and objectives of the enterprises and the adoption of courses of actions and the allocation of resources necessary for carrying out the goals."[103] The influence of this definition is clear in R. N. Anthony's depiction of strategic planning as "the process of deciding on objectives of the organization, or changes in these objectives, or the resources used to attain these objectives, and on the policies that are to govern the acquisition, use, and disposition of resources."[104] According to the last two definitions, the concern of strategy is the link between the organization and its environment through bold ends (objectives and goals) and means (courses of action and allocation of resources). Other theorists prefer to restrict strategy to only the objectives and goals and exclude the means to achieve them. C. W. Hofer and D. E. Schendel make the restriction by defining strategy as "the fundamental pattern of present and planned resource deployments and environmental interactions that indicates how the organization will achieve its objectives."[105] Another limitation is provided by M. E. Porter's concept of competition strategy as "the search for a favorable competitive position in an industry. . . . [It] aims to establish a profitable and sustainable position against the forces that determine industry competition."[106] This school of thought is more in line with the argument that firms act to create their own environments by making a strategic choice regarding markets, products, technologies, desired scale of production, and so on. K. E. Weick refers to this concept as *environmental enactment.*[107] This interpretive view of organization assumes that organizations are socially constructed systems of shared meanings. The environment is neither objective nor perceived but enacted through the social interaction process of the organizational participants. As summarized by L. Smirich and C. Stubbart, "theories involving objective or perceived 'environments' envision concrete, material 'organizations' that are within, but separate from real material 'environments'." The relationships between the two are expressed in terms of cause and effect. On the other hand, enactment theory abandons the idea of concrete, material "organizations/environments" in favor of a largely socially created symbolic world.[108] This view of enacted environment changes drastically the view of strategy and the role of the strategist from the old role of the one devoted to environmental scanning and data and fact collecting to a more imaginative and creative one best depicted as follows:

In the chaotic world, a continuous stream of ecological changes and discontinuities must be sifted through and integrated. Relevant and irrelevant categories of experience must be defined. People make sense of their situation by engaging in an interpretive process that forms the basis of their organized behavior. This interpretive process spans both intellectual and emotional realms. Managers can strategically influence this process. They can provide a vision to account for the streams of events and actions that occur—a universe within which organizational events and experiences take on meaning. The best work of strategic managers inspires splendid meanings.[109]

In any case, the identification of strategies is needed to impose order in whatever environment. The decisions selected to be interpreted are then infused with meanings. What may happen is that different organizations will assign different meanings to a particular environmental event, resulting in different responses to similar environmental events. As stated by Jane Dutton and Susan Jackson:

Meanings attached to strategic issues are imposed by categories that decision makers employ to describe an issue. Categories are engaged by using linguistic labels. Two labels most frequently applied to strategic issues are focused on: threat and opportunity. Once applied, labels initiate a categorization process that affects the subsequent cognition and motivations of the decision makers: these, in turn, systematically affect the process and content of organizational actions.[110]

Accounting plays a role in the three stages of strategic change: preenactment, resolution, and implementation. Accounting provides "a framework for a language of discourse [and] the power to establish and maintain the credibility of issue allocations through its authority structures, accountability measures, and performance evaluations."[111] Basically, strategies need to be framed in an accounting language and supported by the authority of accounting techniques, indicators, and reports.

Strategic Management Accounting

John Shank and Vijay Govindarajan predicted that strategic accounting will supplant managerial accounting as a decisional framework because managerial accounting lacks strategic relevance.[112] While cost analysis provides an assessment of the financial impact of managerial decision alternatives, strategic cost analysis will provide cost data for the development of the right strategy necessary to gain competitive advantage. As stated by Shank and Govindarajan, "a sophisticated understanding of a firm's cost structure can go a long way in the search for sustainable competitive advantage. This understanding is what [we] refer to as 'strategic cost analysis.' "[113]

Underlying Shank and Govindarajan's concern is the failure of management accounting to explicitly consider strategic issues and concerns. Only strategic management accounting in general and strategic cost analysis in particular can fill that void.

Strategic cost analysis is broader than conventional cost analysis by bringing into the analysis the strategic elements necessary to gain a competitive advantage. As a result, accounting information gains an expanded role in the four stages of the strategic process: (1) formulation of strategies and stages, (2) communication of strategies, (3) development of tactics, and (4) implementation. That role is defined as follows:

At *stage 1*, accounting information is the basis for financial analysis, which is one aspect of the process of evaluating strategic alternatives. Strategies that are not feasible or do not yield adequate financial returns cannot be appropriate strategies.

At *stage 2*, accounting reports constitute one of the important ways that strategy gets communicated throughout an organization. The things that are reported are the things people will pay attention to. Good accounting reports are those that focus attention on the factors that are critical to success of the strategy adopted.

At *stage 3*, specific tactics must be developed in support of the overall strategy and then carried through to completion. Financial analysis, based on accounting information, is one of the key elements in deciding which tactical programs are most likely to be effective in helping a firm to meet its strategic objectives.

Finally, at *stage 4*, monitoring the performance of managers or business units usually hinges partly on accounting information. The role of standard costs, expense budgets, and annual profit plans in providing one basis for performance evaluation is well accepted in businesses worldwide. These tools must be explicitly adapted to the strategic content of the firm if they are to be measurably useful.[114]

Another working definition of strategic management accounting is provided by M. Bromwich as "the provision and analysis of financial information on the firm's product markets and competitor's costs and cost structures and the monitoring of the enterprises' strategies and those of its competitors in these markets over a number of periods."[115] With such a definition focusing on the provision of information concerning the firm's markets and on its competitors, Bromwich was successful in offering the vertical supports for the involvement of accountants in strategic management accounting. The first theoretical support for the involvement of accountants in strategic management accounting is provided by Bromwich.[116] This theoretical support is derived from the economic theory that sees economic goods as being a bundle of attributes. The accountant is asked to cost these attributes and monitor their performance over time. Information about a number of demand and cost factors pertaining to these attributes is deemed important for optimal decision making. As stated by Bromwich:

Accountants may play a role here in costing the characteristics provided by goods and in monitoring and reporting on these costs regularly. Similarly, they may be involved in determining the cost of any package of attributes which is being considered for introduction in the market. However, where a strategic perspective is adopted by accountants, costs may have to be considered in the context of demand factors because of the likely interplay between costs and demand in determining successful strategic conduct when considering product attributes.[117]

The second theoretical support is derived from the theory of contestable markets that gives the conditions for a firm's price and output strategy to be sustainable in the face of potential competition.

Following contestable market theory precepts, and the recommendation for monitoring cost advantages over rivals, strategic management accounting is oriented toward not only the cost structure of the firm but also the cost structures of all firms in the market and those likely to enter the market.

What follows from this concern with strategic management accounting is a complete restructuring of the role of accounting toward an active role in the strategic process and an essential means to help achieving economic success. Consequently, Shank and Govindarajan suggest the following key management questions to ask about any accounting idea:

• Does it serve an identifiable business objective? (facilitate strategy formulation, . . . assess managerial performance).
• For the objective it is designed to serve, will the accounting idea enhance the chances of attaining the objective?
• Does the objective whose attainment is facilitated by the accounting idea fit strategically with the overall thrust of the business?[118]

In conclusion, management accounting needs to take the strategic concept into account to allow firms to achieve business success. It needs to adapt to various stages of the strategic process, the distinctions within the strategic process, the influence of strategic archetypes, and the new informational demands of strategic management accounting. As well stated by Bromwich,

There are good reasons why management accounting should be less introspectively concerned with enterprise costs and should adopt a more strategic perspective and become more concerned with markets and with the behavior of competitors. This is because costs and the other aspects of a firm's strategies are often highly inter-related and leaving corporate strategy to the strategists is likely not to capture the complete picture concerning enterprise strategic decisions.[119]

One way of implementing strategic management accounting is through the use of a balance scorecard, translating the firm's mission and strategy into a comprehensive set of performances that provides the framework for implementing the firm's strategy. The balance scorecard consists of four categories: learning and growth, internal/business processes, customer, and financial. The learning and growth category "identifies the infrastructure that an organization must hold to create long-term growth and improvement."[120] It includes as core outcomes measures such measures as employee education and skill levels, employee satisfaction scores, employee turnover rates, information systems availability, percentage of processes with advanced controls, percentage of employee suggestions implemented, and percentage of compensation based on individual and team incentives.[121]

The internal/business process measures focus on the internal processes that will have a major impact on customer satisfaction and achieving an organization's financial objectives. It includes as core outcomes measures such measures as:

• Innovation Process: In manufacturing, capabilities, number of new products or services, new product development times, and number of new patents.

• Operations Process: Yield, defect rates, time taken to deliver products to customers, percentage of on-time deliveries, average time taken to manufacture orders, set-up time, manufacturing downtime.

• Postal Service: Time taken to replace or repair defective products, hours of customer training for using the product.[122]

The customer perspective category contains customer and market-based measurement. It includes as core outcome measures such measures as market share, customer satisfaction, customer retention percentage, and time taken to fulfill customers' request.

The financial perspective category measures whether the firm's actions result in profits. It includes as core outcome measures such measures as operating income, revenue growth, revenues from new products, gross margin percentage, cost reductions in key areas, economic value added, return on investment.

The balance scorecard categories are assured to have specific relatives where an entire chain of cause-and-effect relationships can be established as a vertical vector through the four perspectives. Basically, the balance scorecard and framework predicts that (a) employee-related measures lead operations process measures, (b) operations process measures lead customer-related measures, and (c) customer-related measures lead financial measures.

THE ORGANIZATIONAL DIMENSION

Organizational Structure

Cost accounting rests not only on accounting but also on organizational foundations. It is this form of organizational structure that management often seeks to change to improve the organization's functioning. In turn, elements of the organizational structure may affect cost accounting—its techniques, approaches, and role in the firm. The strongest influences on cost accounting are the organizational chart, the line and staff relationships, and the role of the controller in the organization.

The *organizational chart* reflects the pyramidal system of relationships of an organization's staff. The chart results from deliberate, conscious planning of the areas of responsibility, specialization, and authority for each member of the organization. Each vertical level in the hierarchy depicts different levels of authority. Each horizontal dimension is differentiated by specialization. This process is *departmentalization*; employees are grouped into organizational units on the basis of similar skills and specialization. A firm may departmentalize horizontally by function, by location, by process, and by product. *Vertical differentiation* by authority and responsibility and *horizontal differentiation* through departmentalization lead to the creation of separate organizational units and necessitate provision for periodic planning and control. This need is met by the cost accounting system.

The lines connecting the organization units may imply either line or staff relationships. *Line authority* implies a basic relationship as defined by the chain of command. It is exerted downward by a superior over subordinates. *Staff authority* implies that part of the managerial task, of an advisory nature, has been assigned by an executive to someone outside the chain of command. *Functional authority* implies a basic relationship of command laterally and downward.

The authority relationships between the staff member and employees of the line at the same or lower levels may be one of four types: staff advice, compulsory advice, concurring authority, or limited company authority.

The concepts of line and staff influence cost accounting in the following ways. First, cost accounting is supportive by nature, providing services and assistance to other units in the organization. It is basically a staff function. Second, as a staff member, the cost accountant's authority may range from purely advisory to limited authority. Third, because of its great need for the cost accountant's specialized knowledge, the organization will likely position this person rather high in the organization. It any case, cost accounting is a *decision support system*.

Controllership

The manager in charge of the accounting department is known as the *controller*. A staff member of the top management team, the controller also has a line relationship within the department. The immediate supervisor is generally the vice president in charge of finance. As a staff person, the controller advises management in the areas of corporate reporting, planning, and control. The following are the controller's main activities:

1. Responsibility for the supervision of all facets of financial accounting leading to the publication of the annual reports.
2. Coordination of all the activities leading to the establishment of the master budget and long-term plan of the firm.
3. Maintenance of a system of control through proper circulation of performance reports.
4. Playing an essential part in the proper collection, dispersion, and channeling of pertinent and timely information as a designer and activator of the basic organizational communications system, the electronic data-processing system.

As business entities increase in size and complexity, as the use of planning and control techniques grows, and as most accounting attains a multidimensional scope, the importance of the controller in the organization also increases. The corporate controller has moved to center stage as the chief accounting executive.

As companies expand their operations, the duties and responsibilities of the accounting department increase, as does the size of the controller's staff. What may result is a flat organization, in which all subordinates report directly to the controller. Such a structure in the controller's department may benefit downward and upward communication between the controller and subordinates. Accuracy of upward and downward communication can increase because fewer people are in the vertical chain. This reduces the likelihood of perceptual error. Communication speed can increase. Finally, the controller can initiate more direct control communication and is able to obtain firsthand information about the department performance.

The flat organizational structure may also create downward and upward communication problems. There may be increased competition for the controller's time. Too much information may obscure the pertinent information. The controller may be unable to initiate timely control communication. These negative effects, however, may be reduced by the appointment of a staff assistant for the controller. This will make it easier for the controller to adopt a democratic rather than an autocratic approach to management.

The types of functions and responsibilities assigned to the controller are generally different from those assigned to the *treasurer*. To avoid the confusion and distinguish between the controller and treasurer functions, the Financial Executives Institute presented the following as job responsibilities for each area:

Controllership Functions

1. Planning and control
2. Reporting and interpreting
3. Evaluating and consulting
4. Tax administration
5. Government reporting
6. Production of assets
7. Economic appraisal

Treasurership Functions

1. Provision of capital
2. Investor Relations
3. Short-term financing
4. Bank and custody
5. Credits and collections
6. Investments
7. Insurance

The primary objective of the treasurer, then, is to deal with the financing function, whereas the primary objective of the controller is to deal with the information system. Note that the cost accounting is essential to the implementation of the controller's first three functions.

The controller and the heads of accounting for planning and control are involved in three major tasks: scorekeeping, attention directing, and problem solving. Notice that the role of these people goes beyond scorekeeping.

Supervising both the controller and the treasurer is the chief financial officer (CFO). The CFO is responsible for the areas of control, audit, task, treasury, risk management, and investor relations.

CONCLUSION

To meet the diverse needs of today's managers, cost (or management) accounting has evolved into a multidimensional area of inquiry resting on accounting, organizational, behavorial, and decisional foundations.

The accounting foundations consist of cost accounting concepts to guide the development of cost accounting techniques. The cost accounting concepts alleged to represent a necessary, if not a minimum, foundation for cost accounting's theoretical structure include measurement, communication, information, system, planning, feedback, control, and cost behavior.

The organizational foundations include the elements of the organizational structure that shape the techniques, approaches, and role of cost accounting in the firm: the organizational chart, the line and staff relationships, and the role of the controller in the organization.

The behavioral foundations of cost accounting include the motivation theories identifying the factors and situations that may influence and coordinate employees' actions. The main theories are the need theory, the two-factor theory, the value/expectancy theory, the achievement theory, and the inequity theory.

The decisional foundations of cost accounting are the different conceptual frameworks for viewing types of decisions and decision systems in an organization: Anthony's framework, Simon's framework, and the Gorry–Scott-Morton framework.

The strategic foundations replace management accounting by strategic management accounting.

NOTES

1. C.T. Horngren, G. Foster, and S.M. Datar, *Cost Accounting*, 10th ed. (Englewood Cliffs, NJ: Prentice-Hall, 1991), 10.

2. AAA Committee on Management Accounting, "Report of the 1958 Committee on Management Accounting," 210.

3. National Association of Accountants, *Definition of Management Accounting*, Statement Number IA (New York: NA, March 18, 1981), 4.

4. Ibid., 4–5.

5. AAA 1961 Committee on Management Accounting, "Report of the Management Accounting Committee," *The Accounting Review* (July 1962).

6. AAA Committee on Courses in Managerial Accounting, "Report of the Committee on Courses in Managerial Accounting," 6–7.

7. National Association of Accountants (NAA; NA), *Objectives of Management Accounting, Statement on Management Accounting IB* (NA, June 17, 1988), 2.

8. AAA Committee on Managerial Decision Models, "Report of the Committee on Managerial Decision Models," *The Accounting Review*, Supplement to Vol. 44 (1969): 47–58.

9. AAA, *Accounting Theory*, 51–55.

10. AAA Committee on Concepts and Standards—Internal Planning and Control, "Report of the Committee on Concepts and Standards—Internal Planning and Control," *The Accounting Review*, Supplement to Vol. 49 (1974): 83.

11. Ibid., 83.

12. AAA, *Accounting Theory*, 9.

13. Richard M. Cyert and H. Justin Davidson, *Statistical Sampling for Accounting Information* (Englewood Cliffs, NJ: Prentice-Hall, 1962), 49.

14. Ibid.

15. AAA Committee on Concepts and Standards—Internal Planning and Control, "Report," 91.

16. Wayne S. Boutell, *Computer Oriented Business Systems* (New York: Prentice-Hall, 1968), 152.

17. AAA Committee on Concepts and Standards—Internal Planning and Control, "Report," 91.

18. AAA Committee on Foundations of Accounting Measurement, "Report of the Committee on Foundations of Accounting Measurement," *The Accounting Review*, Supplement to Vol. 46 (1971): 3.

19. Claude E. Shannon and Warren Weaver, *The Mathematical Theory of Communication* (Urbana: University of Illinois Press, 1949), 95.

20. NAA, *Objectives of Management Accounting*, 3–4.

21. AAA Committee on Courses in Managerial Accounting, "Report on Courses in Managerial Accounting," 9–10.

22. R.N. Anthony, *Planning and Control Systems: A Framework for Analysis* (Cambridge, MA.: Harvard University Graduate School of Business Administration, Studies in Management Control, 1965).

23. Ibid., 24

24. Ibid., 27.

25. Ibid., 69.

26. H.A. Simon, *The New Science of Management Decision* (New York: Harper & Row, 1960).

27. Ibid., 5–6.

28. G.A. Gorry and M.S. Scott Morton, "A Framework for Management Information Systems," *Sloan Management Review* (Fall 1971): 55–70.

29. Henry C. Lucas, Jr., Kenneth W. Clowes, and Robert B. Kaplan, "Frameworks for Information Systems," *INFOR* (October 1974): 251.

30. Gorry Scott Morton, "A Framework for Management Information Systems," 67.

31. Ibid., 68.

32. P.G. Keen and M.S. Scott Morton, *Decision Support Systems*, Addison-Wesley Series on Decision Support (Reading MA.: Addison-Wesley, 1978), 92–93.

33. J.W. Forrester, *Industrial Dynamics* (Cambridge, MA: MIT Press, 1961).

34. Ibid., 94.

35. John Dearden, "How to Organize Information Systems," *Harvard Business Review* (March–April 1965): 66.

36. Ibid., 69.

37. It is assumed to be administered by the controller.

38. Sherman C. Blumenthal, *Management Information Systems: A Framework for Planning and Developmentt* (Englewood Cliffs, NJ: Prentice-Hall, 1969).

39. Ibid., 36.

40. Amitai Etzioni, *Modern Organizations* (Englewood Cliffs, NJ: Prentice-Hall, 1964), 3.

41. Richard H. Hall, *Organizations: Structure and Process* (Englewood Cliffs, NJ: Prentice-Hall, 1972), 9.

42. V. Buck, "The Organization as a System of Constraints," in *Approaches to Organization Design*, ed. J.D. Thompson (ed.) (Pittsburgh: University of Pittsburgh Press, 1966), 109.

43. J.D. Thompson, *Organizations in Action* (New York: McGraw-Hill, 1967), 128.

44. C. Perrow, "The Analysis of Goals in Complex Organizations," *American Sociological Review* 26 (1961): 854–66.

45. Etzioni, *Modern Organizations*, 7.

46. Chapman M. Findlay and G.A. Whitmore, "Beyond Shareholder Wealth Maximization," *Financial Management* (Winter 1974): 25–35.

47. W. Baumol, *Business Behavior, Value and Growth* (New York: Macmillan, 1964).

48. R. Marris, *The Economic Theory of Managerial Capitalism* (London: Macmillan, 1964).

49. A. Papandreou, "Some Basic Issues in the Theory of the Firm," in *A Survey of Contemporary Economics* ed. B. Haley (Homewood, IL: Richard D. Irwin, 1952). Also, O. Williamson, *The Economics of Discretionary Behavior: Managerial Objectives in the Theory of the Firm* (Englewood Cliffs, NJ: Prentice-Hall, 1964).

50. Francine S. Hall, "Organizational Goals: The Status of Theory and Research," in *Managerial Accounting: The Behavioral Foundations*, ed. J. Leslie Livingstone (Columbus, OH: Grid, 1975), 1–29.

51. For an excellent presentation of these models, the reader is advised to examine the article by Hall in ibid.

52. Ibid., 17.

53. Ibid., 20.

54. Ibid., 23.

55. American Accounting Association, Committee on Measurement of Social Costs, "Report of the Committee on the Measurement of Social Costs," *The Accounting Review*, Supplement to Vol. 69 (1974): 100.

56. Ibid., 101–2.

57. M.R. Jones (ed.), *Nebraska Symposium on Motivation* (Lincoln: University of Nebraska Press, 1955), 14.

58. A. Maslow, "A Dynamic Theory of Human Motivation," *Psychological Review* 50 (1943): 370–73.

59. E.H. Caplan, *Management Accounting and Behavioral Science* (Reading, MA: Addison-Wesley, 1971), 49.

60. F. Herzberg, B. Mausner, and B. Snyderman, *The Motivation to Work*, 2d ed. (New York: Wiley, 1959).

61. Jacques E. Powers, "Job Enrichment: How One Company Overcame the Obstacle," *Personnel* (May–June 1972): 8.

62. Martin G. Evans, "Herzberg's Two-Factor Theory of Motivation," *Personnel Journal* (January 1970): 33.

63. K. Lewin, *Field Theory and Social Science* (New York: Harper, 1951).

64. V.H. Vroom, *Work and Motivation* (New York: Wiley, 1964).

65. Ibid., 18.

66. L.W. Porter and E.E. Lawler, *Managerial Attitudes and Performance* (Homewood, IL: Irwin-Dorsey, 1968).

67. R.J. House, "A Path-Goal Theory of Leader Effectiveness," *Administrative Science Quarterly* 16 (September 1971): 321–38.

68. D.C. McClelland, *Personality* (New York: William Sloan, 1951); *The Achieving Society* (New York: Van Nostrand, 1961). Also, J.W. Atkinson, "Toward Experimental Analysis of Human Motivation in Terms of Motives, Expectancies, and Incentives," in *Motives in Fantasy. Action and Society*, ed. J.W. Atkinson (New York: Van Nostrand, 1958).

69 J.W. Atkinson, "Motivational Determinants of Risk Taking Behavior," *Psychological Review* 64 (1957): 14.

70. E. Walster, E. Berscheid, and G.W. Walster, "New Directions in Equity Research," *Journal of Personality and Social Psychology* 25 (1973): 151–76. Also, J.S. Adams, "Toward an Understanding of Inequity," *Journal of Abnormal and Social Psychology* 22 (1968): 1045–53.

71. Peter O. Keen and Michael S. Scott Morton, *Decision Support Systems: An Organizational Perspective*, Addison-Wesley Series on Decision Support (Reading, MA: Addison-Wesley, 1978), 62–63.

72. G.T. Allison, *Essence of a Decision* (Boston: Little, Brown, 1971).

73. Ibid., 5.

74. Herbert A. Simon, *Administrative Behavior*, 2d ed. (New York: Macmillan, 1957), 241.

75. J.G. March and H.A. Simon, *Organizations* (New York: Wiley, 1958), 141.

76. Simon, *Administrative Behavior*, 272.

77. Ibid., 76.

78. R.M. Cyert and J.G. March, *A Behavioral Theory of the Firm* (Englewood Cliffs, NJ: Prentice-Hall, 1963).

79. Ibid.

80. G.E. Clarkson, "A Model of Trust Investment Behavior," in *A Behavioral Theory of the Firm*, Cyert and March, chap. 10.

81. John P. Crecine, "Governmental Problem Solving," in *A Computer Simulation of Municipal Budgeting* (New York: Rand McNally, 1969).

82. Lair Aharoni, *The Foreign Investment Decision* Process (Boston: Harvard University Press, 1966).

83. P.R. Lawrence and J.W. Lorsch, *Organization and Environment* (Cambridge, MA: Division of Research, Harvard Business School, 1967).

84. Allison, *Essence of a Decision*, 144.

85. Ibid., 145.

86. Ibid., 146.

87. C.W. Lindblom, "The Science of Muddling Through," *Public Administration Review* (Spring 1959): 79–88.

88. Kenneth R. Goldstein and Sheldon Blackman, *Cognitive Style: Five Approaches and Relevant Research* (New York: Wiley, 1978), 12–13.

89. T.W. Adorno, E. Frenkel-Brunswick, D.J. Levinson, and R.N. Sanford, *The Authoritarian Personality* (New York: Harper & Row, 1950).

90. J. Dermer, "Cognitive Characteristics and the Perceived Importance of Information," *The Accounting Review* (January 1973): 511–19.

91. M. Rokeach, *The Open and Closed Mind* (New York: Basic Books, 1960).

92. G.A. Kelly, *The Psychology of Personal Constructs*, 2 vols. (New York: W.W. Norton, 1955).

93. J. Bieri, "Cognitive Complexity and Personality Development," in *Experience, Structure and Adaptability*, ed. O.J. Harvey (New York: Springer, 1966).

94. Jan H.B. Huysmans, "The Effectiveness of the Cognitive-Style Constraint in Implementing Operations Research Proposals," *Management Science* (September 1970): 94–95.

95. T. Mock, T. Estrin, and M. Vasarhelyi, "Learning Patterns, Decision Approach and Value of Information," *Journal of Accounting Research* (Spring 1972): 129–53.

96. O.J. Harvey, D.E. Hunt, and H.M. Schroder, *Conceptual Systems and Personality Organizations* (New York: Wiley, 1961).

97. H.M Schroder, M.J. Driver, and S. Streufert, *Human Information Processing* (New York: Holt, Rinehart & Winston, 1967).

98. Ibid., 37.

99. H.A. Witkin, R.B. Dyks, H.F. Faterson, D.R. Goodenough, and S.A. Karyn, *Psychological Differentiation* (New York: Wiley, 1962). Also, H.A. Witkin, H.B. Lewis, M. Hertzman, K. Machover, P.B. Meisner, and S. Wagner, *Personality through Perception* (New York: Harper, 1954).

100. B.H. Hart, *Strategy* (New York: Praeger, 1967).

101. K.R. Andrews, *The Concept of Corporate Strategy* (Homewood, IL: Richard D. Irwin, 1971).

102. A.D. Chandler, Jr., *Strategy and Structure* (Cambridge, MA: MIT Press, 1962), 13.

103. Ibid.

104. R.N. Anthony, *Planning and Control Systems: A Framework for Analysis* (Cambridge, MA: Harvard University Graduate School of Business Administration, 1965), 27.

105. C.W. Hofer and D.E. Schendel, *Strategy Formulation: Analytical Concepts* (New York: West, 1978), 75.

106. M.E. Porter, *Competitive Strategy: Techniques for Analyzing Industries and Competitors* (New York: Free Press, 1980), 1.

107. K.E. Weick, "Enactment Process in Organization," in *New Directions in Organizational Behavior*, ed. B.M. Staw and G.R. Slancik (Chicago: St. Clair Press, 1977).

108. L. Smirich and C. Stubbart. "Strategic Management in the Enacted World," *Academy of Management Review* (October 4, 1985): 727.

109. Ibid., 730.

110. Jane E. Dutton and Susan E. Jackson, "Categorizing Strategic Isues: Links to Organizational Action," *Academy of Management Review* (December 1, 1987): 77.

111. Jerry Dermer, "The Strategic Agenda: Accounting for Issues and Support," *Accounting, Organizations and Society* (February 1990): 74.

112. John K. Shank and Vijay Govindarajan, "Making Strategy Explicit in Cost Analysis: A Case Study," *Sloan Management Review* (Spring 1988): 19–22.

113. Ibid., 19.

114. John K. Shank and V. Govindarajan, *Strategic Cost Analysis: The Evolution from Managerial to Strategic Accounting* (Homewood, IL: Richard D. Irwin, 1985), xi–xii.

115. M. Bromwich, "The Case Study for Strategic Management Accounting: The Role of Accounting Information for Strategy in Competitive Markets," *Accounting, Organizations and Society* (February 1990): 27–46.

116. Ibid., 44.

117. Ibid.

118. Shank and Govindarajan, *Strategic Cost Analysis*, xii.

119. Michael Bromwich, *The Revolution in Management Accounting*, R.J. Chambers Research Lecture 1989 (Sydney: Accounting and Finance Foundation, 1985), 50.

120. R.S. Kaplan and N.P. Norton, *The Balance Scorecard—Translating Strategy into Action* (Boston: Harvard Business School Press), 28.

121. C.T. Horngren, G. Foster, and S.M. Datar, *Cost Accounting: A Managerial Emphasis* (Upper Saddle River, NJ: Prentice-Hall, 1999), 468.

122. Ibid.

SELECTED BIBLIOGRAPHY

Allison, G.T. *Essence of a Decision*. Boston: Little, Brown, 1971.

Blumenthal, Sherman C. *Management Information Systems: A Framework for Planning and Development*. Englewood Cliffs, NJ: Prentice-Hall, 1969.

Bromwich, M. "The Case for Strategic Management Accounting: The Role of Accounting Information for Strategy in Competitive Markets." *Accounting, Organizations and Society* (February 1990): 24–46.

Chapman, M. Frindlay, and G.A. Whitmore. "Beyond Shareholder Wealth Maximization." *Financial Management* (Winter 1974): 25–35.

Gorry, G.A., and M.S. Scott Morton. "A Framework for Management Information Systems." *Sloan Management Review* (Fall 1971): 55–70.

Simon, H.A. *The New Science of Management Decisions*. New York: Harper & Row, 1960.

2

Nature of the Control Process

INTRODUCTION

Control, like planning and organizing, is a vital function in the management process. For a while it was a neglected and misunderstood area of management activity. With the advent of the large, modern corporation and the need for efficient conduct of operations, it gained an input stature and the level of sophistication of the other management techniques. The various arrangements, contracts, and behaviors required within an organization necessitated mechanisms for ensuring an orderly conduct of operations and accountability of actions toward survival and growth of the corporation. Control and control techniques provided such mechanisms. Accordingly, it is the purpose of this chapter to elaborate on the nature of control process, the different basic control systems, and the framework for management control systems. It is important at the outset to point out that the scope of this chapter as well as this book is on the level of the more exhaustive management control rather than accounting control.

NATURE OF THE CONTROL PROCESS

Nature of Control

Organizations apply control. They require an ordered arrangement of individual human interactions. Control brings individuals to conform to such arrangement. Control as a concept has evolved over time from an early emphasis on power, followed by an emphasis on behavior, to an emphasis on multidimensional uses.

Control has been viewed first as power, as a process of intentionally influencing the behavior of others. Note the following:

... a person may be said to have power to the extent that he influences the behavior of others in accordance with his own intentions.[1]
... power is an actor's ability to induce or influence another actor to carry out his directives or any other norms he supports.[2]
... control is a cycle beginning with an intent on the part of one person, followed by an influence attempt addressed to another person, who then acts in some way that fulfills the intent of the first.[3]

The perception of control as an exercise of power may create strong emotional responses:

Control also has a psychological meaning or significance to the individuals involved. It may imply superiority, inferiority, dominance, submission, guidance, help, criticism, reprimand. It may imply (as some students of control argue) something about the manliness and virility of the individuals involved. The exercise of control, in other words, is charged emotionally.[4]

In spite of these emotional responses, control was traditionally perceived to be necessary to combat entropy, the movement toward disorder in the organization. The traditional concept of control as necessary power led to a constraining and directing of behavior, the development of task relationships, and the imposition of order. This traditional concept will only lead to dysfunctional and unintended rigid behavior. Fortunately, with the advent of the human relations approach, reference to social power or control was avoided because their connotations were inconsistent with the ideal of the harmonious, conflict-free organization. Control began to be viewed as a decision-making process intended to influence behavior toward what is best for the organization. A control system affects the direction, intensity, and duration of motivation. The importance of control in influencing behavior became a generally accepted theme. Note the following:

Control is seen as having one basic function: to help to ensure the proper behaviors of the people in the organization. These behaviors should be consistent with the organization's strategy, if one exists, which, in turn, should have been selected as the best path to take toward achievement of the organization's objectives.[5]

As soon as we considered the management control process as something that basically involved people and the reactions of people, it became evident that there were some useful things that could be said.[6]

The crucial aspect of any control system is its effect on behavior. . . . The system needs to be designed in a way that assists, guides, and motivates management to make decisions and act in ways that are consistent with the overall objectives of the organization.[7] [Control] systems exist primarily to improve the collective decisions within an organization. Because most decisions entail human behavior, our emphasis rightly belongs on human rather than technical considerations.[8]

With the advent of the large, modern corporation and its multidimensional facets, control evolved from the coercive nature of power and the focus on behavior to a multidimensional role and various uses. Control evolved in terms of their customary uses. As an example, William Travers Jerome III offered the following classification:[9]

1. *Controls used to standardize performance* in order to increase efficiency and to lower costs. Included might be time and motion studies, inspections, written procedures, or production schedules.

2. *Controls used to safeguard company assets* from theft, wastage, or misuses. Such controls would emphasize division of responsibilities, separation of operational, custodial, and accounting activities, and an adequate system of authorization and record keeping.

3. *Controls used to standardize quality* in order to meet the specifications of either customers or company engineers. Blueprints, inspection, and statistical quality controls would typify the measures employed to preserve the integrity of the product (or service) marketed by the company.

4. *Controls designed to set limits within which delegated authority can be exercised without further top management approval.* Organization and procedure manuals, policy directives, and internal audits would help to spell out the limits within which subordinates have a free hand.

5. *Controls used to measure on-the-job performance.* Typical of such controls would be special reports, output per hour or per employee, internal audits, and perhaps budgets or standard costs.

6. *Controls used for planning and programming operations.* Such controls would include sales and production forecasts, budgets, various cost standards, and standards of work measurement.

7. *Controls necessary to allow top management to keep the firm's various plans and programs in balance.* Typical of such controls would be a master budget, policy manuals, organization manuals, and such organization techniques as committees and the use of outside consultants. The overriding need for such controls would be to provide the necessary capital for current and long-run operations and to maximize profits.

8. *Controls designed to motivate individuals within a firm* to contribute their best efforts. Such controls necessarily would involve ways of recognizing achievement through such things as promotions, awards for suggestions, or some form of profit sharing.

Bases of Control

Control is based on some form of power. Each form of power dictates different control strategies, because each form of power differs in its ability to limit choices. Six types of power dictating different types of control strategies and tactics have been noted: reward power, coercive power, legitimate power, referent power, expert power, and integration of power.[10] They may be defined as follows:

Reward power is based on perceptions held by a person or a group that another person or another group has the ability to provide varying rewards for different performances.

Coercive power is based on perceptions held by a person or a group that another person or another group has the ability to inflict punishment.

Legitimate power is based on perceptions held by a person or a group that another person or another group has the right to influence the former's actions.

Referent power is based on perceptions held by a person or a group that another person or a group should be identified with by copying the latter's actions, style, and beliefs.

Expert power is based on perceptions held by a person or a group that another person or another group should be identified with because of the latter's knowledge and expertise.

Integration of power is a result of the use in any organization of all types of power, that is, reward power, coercive power, legitimate power, referent power, and expert power.

In fact, each type of power is effective only in specific situations. T. Burns and G. Stalker found that an "organic" management system is appropriate for firms operating in changing market environments, and mechanistic systems are more appropriate for firms operating in a relatively stable environment.[11] Hence, in an organic management system, characterized by more frequent changes of position and roles, less hierarchical structure, and more dynamic interplay between the various functions of an organization to deal with unstable and changing conditions, expert power and reward power may be more appropriate. However, in mechanistic management system, for firms operating in a relatively stable environment and with routine tasks, coercive power and legitimate power may be more dominant.

Stages of Control

The control process involves the following stages:

1. Setting of goals for the performance of the activity or function. These goals help direct and channel human efforts. "Organizational goals are the desired ends or states of affairs for whose achievement system policies are committed and resources allocated."[12]

2. Establishing standards of performance for each specified goal of the activity or function. Standards are basically statements of the results that will exist when performance is satisfactory.

3. Monitoring or measurement of actual performance. *Monitoring* can be expressed in

monetary and accounting terms such as profits, costs, and revenues; by other account-ing indicators such as rate of return on investment or residual income; and in non-monetary terms such as the quality of the product, the nature of the market response, or any other social indicator. *Measurement* is accomplished by human or mechanical means known as "sensors."

4. Reviewing and comparing the actual with the planned performance. This is also known as the "comparator process," which determines whether differences exist be-tween the activities and results that are taking place and what should be occurring.

5. Correcting the deviations and administering rewards to motivate and reinforce per-formance. This is known as the "evaluation/reward process."

Types of Control

Control is a central factor in the management of any organization. Various classification schemes have been proposed. Leonard Sayles listed four distinct types of control that serve very different functions for the manager:

1. *Reassurance to sponsors*, a high-level control, whereby stakeholders are informed of the efficient conduct of operations.

2. *Guidance to subordinates from managers*, a middle-level control, whereby the sub-ordinates are informed of what they should concentrate on.

3. *Guidance to lower-level management by higher management*, a middle-level control, whereby the managers are informed of where accomplishment is lagging and man-agement action is needed.

4. *Closing the loop*, a lower-level control, whereby the managers are informed that both technical and legal requirements have been met. They consist of checking procedures established to ensure that neither financial nor technical decisions are taken without adequate review and that no necessary step has been omitted. Examples include the following:

   • All expenditures over $500 have to be approved by the controller's office.

   • When "off-standard" temperature prevails for more than five minutes, written au-thorization from the chief engineer is required to continue processing procedures.

   • Storage of flammables within fifty feet of Building 209 requires the permission of the safety officer.

   • Any substitution of materials must be approved by the subsystem engineer, the functional manager, and a representative of the project office.[13]

A more operational classification is provided by W. H. Newman, who rec-ognized three types of control:

1. *Steering controls*, whereby management is provided signals indicating what will hap-pen if it continues its present operations. Steering controls enable management to take either a corrective or an adaptive response before the total operation is completed. A *corrective response* implies that the source of the error is inside the organization and

can be corrected. An *adaptive response* implies that the source of the error is outside the organization and cannot be corrected. In the latter case, the solution is to redesign the operations to adapt to the new environmental situations.

2. *Yes/no controls*, whereby management is provided rules indicating the conditions that must be met before work may proceed to the next step. Yes/no controls provide management with checkpoints at different levels of the total operation. The technique is a defensive strategy aimed at controlling the size of the errors to be made by lower-level management and subordinates in general. In other words, yes/no controls are comparable to safety devices.

3. *Postaction controls*, whereby management is provided with performance reports or scorecards upon completion of the operations, indicating the differences or variances between the actual and planned performance. In general, postaction controls and steering controls make use of the feedback mechanism for the correction of any deviations, except that the response in the steering controls comes before the completion of the total operation.[14]

A classification according to the object of control is provided by K. A. Merchant, who recognized three types of control:

• *Result controls*, where the focus is on results. It involves rewarding individuals or holding them accountable for accomplishing particular results or outcomes.
  They are feasible only if *all* of the following conditions are present:

  1. Knowledge exists as to what results are desirable.

  2. The desired result areas can be controlled (at least to some extent) by the individual(s) whose actions are being influenced.

  3. The controllable result areas can be measured effectively.[15]

  If the results are defined in monetary (usually accounting) terms, the result controls are labeled as financial accountability control.

• *Action controls*, where the focus is on actions. They are used when result controls are not feasible. They are intended to ensure that individuals take certain proper organizational actions. They may take the four following forms:

  1. *Behavioral constraint*, putting limits on the performance of specific acts. Centralization and separation of duties are two examples of behavioral constraints to ensure that certain tasks should not be completed.

  2. *Preaction review controls*, by observing the places or work of individuals being controlled before the activity and making necessary adjustments.

  3. *Action accountability*, by holding employees accountable for their actions.

  4. *Redundancy*, by increasing the number of people required to perform a given task that is theoretically required.

• *Personnel control*, where the emphasis is on personnel. They are intended to tap or encourage individual self-control or social control. Individual self-control, also known as "self-control," "intrinsic motivation," "ethics and morality," "trust and atmosphere," "loyalty," and "culture," is what naturally pushes people to perform adequately. Social control is a pressure exerted by the group and those who deviate from group norms or values.[16]

Another classification scheme, provided by W. G. Ouchi, describes three fundamentally different mechanisms of control. The three are referred to as "markets," "bureaucracies," and "clans." They are explicated as follows:

1. *Markets* may act as an efficient mechanism of contest. They deal with the control problem through their ability to measure and reward individual contributions. If the market fails as the mechanism of control, it is most often replaced by a bureaucratic form.
2. *Bureaucracies* are also used as mechanisms of control. They rely upon a mixture of close evaluation with a socialized acceptance of common objectives.
3. *Clans* are also used as mechanisms of control in the form of an informal social structure. They rely upon a relatively complete socialization process that effectively eliminates goal incongruence between individuals.[17]

While markets rely on prices, bureaucracies rely on rules. That creates important differences. Ouchi stated the point as follows:

In any case, rules differ from prices in the important sense that they are partial rather than complete bundles of information. A price implies that a comparison has taken place, a comparison between alternative buyers or sellers of the value of the object in question. A rule, however, is essentially an arbitrary standard against which a comparison is yet to be made. In order to use a rule (e.g., a budget, or cost standard), a manager must observe some actual performance, assign some value to it, and then compare that assigned value to the rule in order to determine whether the actual performance was satisfactory or not. All this consumes a great deal of administrative overhead. If the rule is expressed qualitatively rather than quantitatively, the cost of administration can be expected to be even higher.[18]

Markets, bureaucracies, and clans rely on both social requirements and information requirements. The social requirements include norm of reciprocity for markets, norm of reciprocity and legitimate authority for bureaucracy and norm of reciprocity, legitimate authority, and secured values and beliefs for clans. The information requirements include prices for markets, rules for bureaucracy, and traditions for clans.

Another classification, provided by Don Hellriegel and John Slocum, distinguishes between six strategies of control—human input control, reward-punishment system, formal structure, policies and rules, budgets, and mechanical controls.[19] They may be defined as follows:

1. *Human input control* is composed of means for controlling unwanted kinds of individual acts, especially their instability, variability, and spontaneity. Selection, training,

and even conditioning are some of the means intended to create unity without conformity.

2. *Reward-punishment system* is composed of three possible systems of rewards and punishments to help mold the individuals to the requirements of the organization. The three systems are identified as: (a) coercive, (b) utilitarian, and (c) normative. The coercive system puts the emphasis on punishment, the utilitarian system on extrinsic rewards, and the normative system on intrinsic rewards.

3. *Formal structures* are composed of the following major structural means for control: "(1) specification of the tasks and responsibilities in the position, (2) prescribing flows of communication, (3) use of special units to support or audit other units and positions, and (4) varying the span of control."

4. *Policies and rules* are the instruments used to exercise control.

5. *Budgets* may be used as a basis for control.

6. *Mechanical controls*, or machine controls, are used to extend the capability of people without the direct application of human energy, skill, intelligence, or control.[20]

In production activities, there has been a continuous shift toward machine control with respect to the nonhuman resources employed in the production process. With the advent of advanced mass-production technology, machines augmented other strategies for controlling production workers. Machines and the interdependencies between them serve as a form of control over the worker's exercise of discretion. A new threshold has been realized because machines control machines without direct application of human energy, skill, intelligence, or control.[21]

Sources of Control

Errors or variations are the sources of and causes for control. Because all errors or variations deserve to be controlled, various schemes have been proposed for a classification of the errors or variations.

A first scheme was proposed by Shahid Ansari.[22] It classifies variations along a nature dimension as either expected or unexpected variations and along an environmental origin dimension as either (a) internal (within a cost center), (b) external (from another cost center), or (c) exogenous (outside the organization). The six cells are used to classify variances using a digital code number referencing their cell classification.

A second scheme was proposed by Joel Demski.[23] He argued that one or more of five possible causes can lead to a difference between the actual and standard performance: implementation failure, prediction error, measurement error, model error, and random variation.

1. An *implementation failure* is a human or mechanical failure to obtain or maintain a specific obtainable action or standard. For example, the ordering or the use of the wrong quantity of a given input, material, labor, or overhead will result in an imple-

mentation failure. Given that the standard is assumed to be obtainable, the deviation caused by the implementation failure may be immediately corrected once its existence is known. The decision to correct such a variance depends on a comparison between the cost of correction and the resulting savings.

2. A *prediction error* is a failure to correctly predict one of the decision model's parameter values. Again, the decision to correct the variance depends on a comparison between the cost of resolving the model and the resulting cost savings.

3. A *measurement error* in determining the actual cost of operation occurs because of improper classification, recording, or counting. The correction of the variance involves improving the work habits of employees and motivating them to maintain proper records.

4. A *model error* results from an incorrect functional representation in the decision model. The decision to correct the variance depends on a comparison between the cost of reformulating the model and the resulting cost savings.

5. A *random deviation* results from minor variations in the input or output process. It arises from the stochastic operation of some correctly specified parameters. Random deviations are inevitable and need no corrective action.[24]

BASIC CONTROL SYSTEMS

There are three possible types of basic control systems: traditional, feedback, and feedforward.

Traditional Control System

A firm using a traditional control system establishes standards for each operational activity in a budget-setting phase. At the end of each period, it compares these standards with the actual results, using the variance-analysis techniques to assess (1) the nature of the obtained deviation, (2) the possibility of any corrective action, and (3) the provision of either rewards for satisfactory (good) behavior or negative sanction for unsatisfactory (bad) performance. Therefore, a proper selection of standards, the variance-analysis techniques, and the reward system is essential to the success of a traditional control system.

There are, however, a number of problems with the traditional control system. First, it is based on the scientific management school that separates planing from doing, whereby relevant goals and values are determined by X, who or which in turn causes Y to act in accordance with them. It does not allow for self-control—the coordination of planning and doing. Second, control is depicted as static rather than dynamic. The emphasis is on standard of performance and judgments about whether actual behavior is good or bad, satisfactory or unsatisfactory, or correct or incorrect. Third, individuals being controlled may resent the rigidity of the traditional control model. In effect, it implies a constraining, and directing of behavior, the development of task relationships, and the imposition of order.[25] The situation is found to lead potentially to an unintended rigidity of behavior, an excessive concern with being safe, and an avoidance of risk taking.[26] In addition, some consequences can also result. Chris Argyris, for example, has shown how budgets can be used as tools by authoritarian managements to control subordinates and how this usage can create pressure, hostility, tension, fear, and mistrust among subordinates.[27] The ultimate result can be intolerance, apathy, and an adverse effect on the accomplishment of long-range operational goals.[28]

Feedback Control System

In the traditional control system, costs are classified by responsibility, budgeted, and then compared at the end of the period with the actual results, using the techniques of standard cost-variance analysis. The traditional system does not include any monitoring system to detect and correct errors arising during the accounting period. It is an almost fatalistic approach in which the budget is perceived as a static rather than a continuous and dynamic process. A net separation between the budgeting and control phases dismisses the obvious complementarity of both operations.

One possible method of alleviating these shortcomings is the feedback control system, whereby an error in the system becomes the basis for the correction of the budget estimates. It is used after an error is detected and, therefore, represents a response to the error. As Exhibit 2.1 shows, the feedback control system consists of, first, an examination of a sample of operational activities; second, a feedback of observed errors or confirmation; and third, a revision of the budget in accordance with the deviation observed in the sample. Therefore, the feedback control system requires both the monitoring of errors and management action. R. N. Anthony and J. S. Reece observed:

Control reports are feedback devices, but they are only part of the feedback loop. Unlike the thermostat, which acts automatically in response to information about temperature, *a control report does not by itself* cause a change in performance. A change results only when managers take actions that lead to change. Thus, in a management control, the feedback loop requires both the control report *plus* management action.[29]

Various definitions of feedback control exist in various disciplines. A definition in terms of an information feedback system was provided by Jay Forrester: "An information-feedback [control] system exists when the environment leads to a decision that results in action which affects the environment and thereby influences future decisions."[30] A more specific definition is provided by the Committee of the American Institute of Electrical Engineers: "a feedback control system is a control system which tends to maintain a prescribed relationship of one system variable to another by comparing functions of these variables and using the difference as a means of control."[31] W. Jack Duncan made an interesting distinction between two types of feedback control: a self-correcting con-

Exhibit 2.1
Feedback Control System

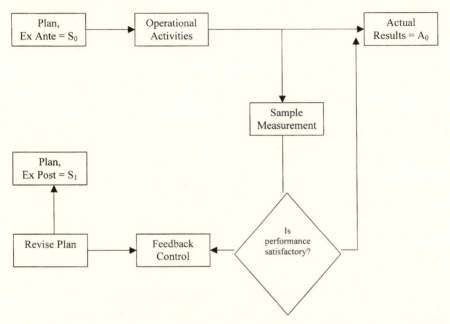

trol and a noncorrecting one.[32] A good example of self-correcting control, servomechanism, is the thermostat in a typical home that regulates itself. It is self-correcting in that it is not only automatic but does not require any corrective action to be taken. This may also be labeled an "adaptive (responsive) control system." The living organism is an example. The noncorrecting feedback control system provides the information necessary to take corrective actions but does not include self-correcting mechanisms. A good example is *statistical quality control*, which only indicates that a system is out of control and does not correct by itself. Somebody has to intervene to stop the process and make the necessary adjustments to bring the system back into control. Feedback control systems may be applied to any business operation. For example, in the control of the purchasing manager, the accountant examines the actual prices paid to the supplier (sensor) and compares them to the budgeted prices (controller). If a variance emerges, the purchasing manager is advised to revise the budgeted price (actuator) to correct the error.

J. S. Demski distinguished between three types of results: "1. The *ex ante budgeted performance* (the original budgeted estimates). 2. The *ex post budgeted performance* (the revised budgeted performance after the feedback). 3. The *observed performance* (the actual performance)."[33] The total traditional variance between the observed performance and the ex ante performance can be dichotomized as follows:

1. The difference between the ex ante and ex post results is a rough measure of the firm's forecasting ability. This is the difference between what the firm budgeted and what it should have budgeted.
2. The difference between the ex post and the observed results is a measure of the "opportunity cost to the firm" of not using its resources to maximum advantage.

Assuming

S_0 = Ex ante performance
S_1 = Ex post performance
A_0 = Observed performance

then

$$(A_0 - S_0) = (A_0 - S_1) + (S_1 - S_0)$$

where

$S_1 - S_0$ = Indicator of the efficiency of the planning process
$A_0 - S_1$ = "Opportunity cost of non-optimal capacity utilization"[34]

This feedback control system, also labeled the "ex post control system," when based on a linear programming formulation of the planning process was reported to have been applied successfully in conjunction with a petroleum-refinery model in an effort to examine the system's feasibility.[35]

Norton Bedford suggested the following five guidelines for feedback management control reports:

1. Feedback reports should reveal both accomplishment and responsibility.
2. Feedback reports should be rendered promptly at the end of regular periods or if any time variation exceeds a specified limit.
3. Feedback reports should reveal trends and relationships to trends of associated variables.
4. Feedback reports should reveal variations from standards (objectives), preferably supported by a probability measure that the variation is or is not normal or due to random fluctuations.
5. Feedback reports should be in standardized format wherever possible to facilitate communications.[36]

John C. Camillus suggested six broad approaches to implementing preventive management control:

- Indicators, both "leading" and "early warning"
- Contingency plans
- Trend analysis
- Adaptive mechanisms
- Congruent system design
- Policy directives[37]

Each of these approaches is assumed to function as a preventive control mechanism.

The feedback control system does have some operational limitations. First, it depends heavily on the success of the error-detection process. Second, there may be a time lag between the error detection, error confirmation, and error revision during which actual results may be changed again. The effectiveness of the feedback control system depends on the rapidity of the error-response process.

Feedforward Control System

Feedback control systems must sense a specific error from a specific standard result before initiating a correction, and the process always occurs after the fact. Feedforward control systems do not rely on the examination of errors to recommend a correction. Instead, any correction is based on the anticipation of an error. As Exhibit 2.2 shows, a feedforward control system consists of, first, an examination of a "related" activity based on the anticipation of a possible deviation between the standard and actual performance; second, the feedforward or confirmation of the possibility of such an error; and third, taking a compensatory action to maintain or adjust the operational activities. In other words, the information from the related activity acts as a surrogate for the operational activity and is fed forward to adjust the actual results through a compensatory action. Thus the feedforward control system implies the possibility of predicting the effects of future actions and the very existence of a related activity: "Anticipation of deviations from standards depends upon the correlation of two systems such as the change in one enables predictions of change in the other. A controlling activity, which we shall call the 'related activity,' is ahead of the primary activity 'feeds forward' information to it."[38] The important differences between feedforward and feedback control have been summarized as follows:

1. Feedforward control constitutes *ex ante*, that is, anticipatory control; whereas feedback control constitutes *ex post*, or follow-up control.
2. Feedforward control involves a forward flow of information; while feedback control involves both forward and backward flows of information.
3. Feedforward control is realized before the control variables function, that is, before the difference between anticipated and actual performance occurs.

Exhibit 2.2
Feedforward Control System

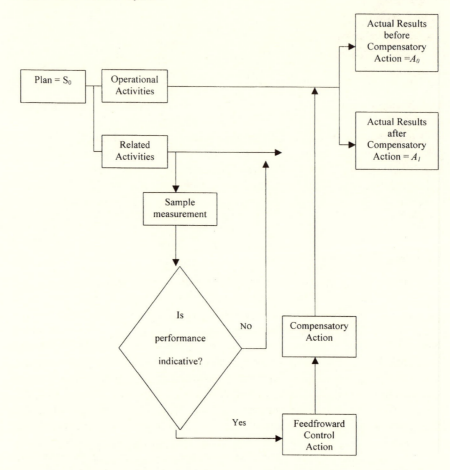

4. Feedforward control functions continuously in a given direction on the basis of the "command" of a set point and is established at the time the user first feeds data into the model. In contrast, the frequency and relative importance of the flow of feedback control is a function of the change in the controlled variables.[39]

Norbert Wiener, the father of cybernetics, recognized the limitations of feedback control systems. He pointed out that where there are lags in the system, corrections ("the compensator") must predict or anticipate errors. He referred to this system as an "anticipatory fecdback" system. In fact, feedforward control systems have been applied only to specialized engineering processes, mainly chemical processes.[40]

The related activity acts as a signal and surrogate for the possible future performance of the operational activity. For example:

In a business setting, a feedforward control system might be used to adjust levels for inventories, production volume, purchase schedules, and employment as sales volume increases or decreases. A change in sales volume could automatically adjust the prescribed levels in the other factors in order to maintain a predetermined relationship of costs and activities to income.[41]

The typical feedforward control system goes through the following stages. At $t - 1$, an internal or external disturbance is detected by the controller (sensor). Given certain implied business relationships, the impact of such a disturbance on an organizational member's behavior at time t is postulated (controller). Appropriate information is fed forward to the given member for confirmation, and a compensatory action is taken that affects and governs the actual results (actuator).

To put such a system into operation, three figures are needed: the ex ante budgeted performance results (the originally budgeted results), the observed performance results (the actual results possible *before* the compensatory action), and the ex post actual performance results (the actual results *after* the compensatory action).

Feedforward control systems apply to management control as long as management can be provided information on forthcoming trouble in time for correction. For example, feedforward control can be used in cash planning, inventory control, and new product development. Mathematical models of these decisions programmed into a computer may be necessary to trace readily the influence of changes of input variables on cash flow, inventory level, and product development.[42] However, before feedforward can be applied as successfully in management control as it has been in engineering, several guidelines must be followed:

1. Thorough planning and analysis is required. . . .
2. Careful discrimination must be applied in selecting input variables. . . .
3. The feedforward system must be kept dynamic. . . .
4. A model of the control system should be developed. . . .
5. Data on input variables must be regularly collected. . . .
6. Data on input variables must be regularly assessed. . . .
7. Feedforward control requires action.[43]

Akira Ishikawa noted the following limitations of the feedforward control system:

1. The feedforward process is an evaluation process and is concerned with the estimates of the uncertain future. This problem of uncertainty is likely to limit application of the concept.
2. It has only been recently that aspects of the systems science, especially system control

theory, have found application in business administration and/or accounting. It will take time for practitioners to accept the suggestion that feedforward control has application potential.

3. Study of the future (futuristics) is not well developed; neither are the tools that have potential for overcoming the problem of uncertainty.[44]

In fact, the feedforward and the feedback control systems can be linked together, thus reducing the limitations attributed to each system. The general control process of usual events falls under the feedforward control system, and the control process for unusual events will be handled by the feedback control system: "Technical discussions also emphasize that while feedforward systems are useful in dealing with events which may be anticipated, such systems are best linked with feedback systems to handle events which cannot be determined in advance."[45]

A conceptual framework for management control systems is needed as a good basis for viewing the type of control decisions and decision systems and the type of information needed: In effect, control of an organization is not possible without a clear depiction of the types of control decisions, the type of control decision systems, and information about what is occurring in that organization. Of the various frameworks proposed in the literature, two are particularly relevant in their clear definition of decisions and decision systems. They are R. N. Anthony's framework and H. A. Simon's framework, reviewed in Chapter 1.

CONCLUSIONS

This chapter examines, first, the nature of the control process in terms of its components: nature of control, bases of control, stages of control, types of control, and sources of control. What appears is that the control process is a complex process (a) having multidimensional uses, (b) being based on various forms of power, (c) proceeding through various stages, (d) being implemented in various types of forms, and (e) resting on various sources or types of errors.

Second, the chapter elaborates on the differences in the three known basic control systems, namely, (a) the traditional control model, (b) the feedback control model, and (c) the feedforward control model. A suggestion is made for an integration of the feedforward and feedback control systems, thus reducing the limitations attributed to each system. Thus, although feedforward systems are useful in dealing with events that may be anticipated, they are best linked with feedback systems.

NOTES

1. H. Goldhamer and E. A. Shils, "Types of Power and Status," *American Journal of Sociology* 45 (1939): 171.

2. A. Etzioni, *A Comparative Analysis of Complex Organizations* (New York: Free Press, 1961), 4.

3. A. S. Tannenbaum, *Control in Organizations* (New York: McGraw-Hill, 1968), 5.

4. A. S. Tannenbaum, "Control in Organizations: Individual Adjustment and Organizational Performance," *Administrative Quarterly* 8 (1962): 24.

5. Kenneth A. Merchant, *Control in Business Organizations* (Marshfield, MA: Pitman, 1985), 4.

6. R. N. Anthony, "Cost Concepts for Control," *The Accounting Review* 32 (April 1957): 229–30.

7. E. E. Lawler III and John G. Rhode, *Information and Control in Organizations* (Pacific Palisades, CA: Goodyear, 1976), 6.

8. C. T. Horngren, *Cost Accounting: A Managerial Emphasis* (Englewood Cliffs, NJ: Prentice-Hall, 1982), 318.

9. William Travers Jerome III, *Executive Control—The Catalyst* (New York: Wiley, 1961), 32–33.

10. J.R.P. French, Jr. and B. Raven, "The Bases of Social Power," in *Studies in Social Power*, ed. Dorwin Cartwright (Ann Arbor: University of Michigan, Institute for Social Research, 1959), 150–67.

11. T. Burns and G. Stalker, *The Management of Innovation* (London: Tavistock, 1964).

12. F. S. Hall, "Organizational Goals: The Status of Theory and Research," in *Managerial Accounting: The Behavioral Foundations*, ed. J. L. Livingston (Columbus, OH: Grid, 1975), 1–32.

13. Leonard Sayles, "The Many Dimensions of Control," *Organizational Dynamics* (Summer 1972): 22.

14. W. H. Newman, quoted in ibid., 23.

15. Merchant, *Control in Business Organizations*, 10.

16. Ibid., 13, 39.

17. William G. Ouchi, "A Conceptual Framework for the Design of Control Mechanisms," *Management Science* 25 (September 1975): 833–47.

18. Ibid., 831.

19. Don Hellriegel and John W. Slocum, Jr., *Management: A Contingency Approach* (Reading, MA: Addison-Wesley, 1973), 261.

20. Ibid., 266–67.

21. Ibid., 270.

22. Shahid L. Ansari, "Towards an Open System Approach to Budgeting," *Accounting, Organizations and Society* 4, No. 3 (1979): 151.

23. Joel S. Demski, *Information Analysis* (Reading, MA: Addison-Wesley, 1972), chap. 6.

24. Ibid.

25. D. Katz and R.L. Kahn, *The Social Psychology of Organizations* (New York: Wiley, 1966).

26. Robert K. Merton, "Bureaucratic Structure and Personality," in *Social Theory and Social Structure*, ed. Robert K. Merton, (New York: Free Press, 1957).

27. Chris Argyris, "Human Problems with Budgets," *Harvard Business Review* (January–February 1953): 97–110.

28. Michael E. Wallace, "Behavioral Considerations in Budgeting," in *Accounting and*

Its Behavioral Implications, eds. William J. Bums, Jr., and Don T. DeCoster (New York: McGraw-Hill, 1969), 321.

29. R.N. Anthony and J.S. Reece, *Management Accounting: Text and Cases* (Homewood, IL: Irwin, 1975), 78.

30. Jay W. Forrester, *Industrial Dynamics* (Cambridge, MA: Technology Press, and New York: Wiley, 1961), 14.

31. American Institute of Electrical Engineers, Committee Report, "Proposed Symbols and Terms for Feedback Control Systems," *Electrical Engineering* (October 1951): 909.

32. W. Jack Duncan, *Essentials of Management* (Hinsdale, IL: Dryden, 1975), 414–15.

33. J.S. Demski, "An Accounting System Structured on a Linear Programming Model," *The Accounting Review* (October 1967): 701–702.

34. Ibid., 704.

35. Ibid., 709.

36. Norton M. Bedford, "Managerial Control," in *Contemporary Management Issues and Viewpoints*, ed. Joseph W. McGuire (Englewood Cliffs, NJ: Prentice-Hall, 1974), 531.

37. John C. Camillus, "Six Approaches to Preventive Management Control," *The Financial Executive* (December 1980): 22–25.

38. A.C. Filley, R.J. House, and S. Kerr, *Managerial Processes and Organization Behavior* (Glenview, IL: Scott, Foresman, 1976), 441.

39. Akira Ishikawa, *Corporate Planning and Control Model Systems* (New York: New York University Press, 1975), 81.

40. E.C. MacMullen and F.G. Shinskey, "*Feedforward* Analog Computer Control of a Superfractionator," *Control Engineering*, No. 11 (1964): 69–74; F.G. Shinskey, "*Feedforward* Control of pH," *Instrumentation Technology*, No. 15 (1968), 65–69; and A.E. Nisenfield and T.M. Miyasaki, "Applications of Feedforward Control to Distillation Columns," *Proceedings IFAC* (June 1972): 1–7.

41. Filley, House, and Kerr, *Managerial Processes*, 443.

42. Harold Koontz and Robert W. Bradspies, "Managing through Feedforward Control," *Business Horizons* 15, No. 3 (June 1972): 25–36.

43. Ibid., 36–37.

44. Ishikawa, *Corporate Planning and Control Model Systems*, 91–92.

45. Filley, House, and Kerr, *Managerial Processes*, 463.

SELECTED BIBLIOGRAPHY

Amney, L.R. "Towards a New Perspective on Accounting Control." *Accounting, Organizations and Society* (March 1980): 247–58.

Ansari, Shahid L. "Towards an Open Systems Approach to Budgeting." *Accounting, Organizations and Society* 4, No. 3 (1979): 151.

Anthony, R.N. *Planning and Control Systems: A Framework for Analysis*. Boston: Graduate School of Business Administration, Harvard University, 1965.

Boland, R.J., Jr. "Control, Causality, and Information Systems Requirements." *Accounting, Organizations and Society* (March 1980): 259–72.

Daft, Richard L., and Norman B. Macintosh. "The Nature and Use of Formal Systems for Management Control and Strategy Implementation." *Journal of Management* 10, No. 1 (1984): 43–66.

Eilon, S. "A Classification of Administrative Control Systems." *Journal of Management Studies* (February 1966): 36–48.

Euske, Kenneth J. *Management Control: Planning, Control, Measurement, and Evaluation.* Reading, MA: Addison-Wesley, 1984.

Flamholtz, Eric. "Organizational Control Systems as a Managerial Tool." *California Management Review* (Winter 1979): 50–59.

French, J.R.P., Jr., and B. Raven. "The Bases of Social Power," in *Studies in Social Power*, ed. Dorvin Cartwright. Ann Arbor: University of Michigan, Institute for Social Research, 1959, 150–67.

Giglioni, Giovanni B., and Arthur G. Bedeian. "A Conspectus of Management Control Theory: 1900–1972." *Academy of Management Journal* (June 1974): 292–305.

Hofstede, Geert. "The Poverty of Management Control Philosophy." *Academy of Management Review* (July 1978): 450–61.

Ishikawa, Akira, and Charles H. Smith. "Feedforward Control in the Total Planning and Control System." *Cost and Management* (November–December 1972): 36–41.

———. "A Feedforward Control System for Organizational Planning and Control." *ABACUS* 8, No. 2 (1972): 163–80.

Jerome, William Travers, III. *Executive Control—The Catalyst.* New York: Wiley, 1961.

Koontz, Harold, and Robert W. Bradspies. "Managing through Feedforward Control." *Business Horizons* 15, No. 3 (June 1972): 25–36.

Lorange, Peter, and Michael S. Scott Morton. "A Framework for Management Control Systems." *Sloan Management Review* (Fall 1974): 41–56.

Merchant, Kenneth A. *Control in Business Organizations.* Marshfield, MA.: Pitman, 1985, Chaps. 1–5.

———. "The Control Function of Management." *Sloan Management Review* (Summer 1982): 43–55.

Michael, S.R. "*Feedforward* versus Feedback Controls in Planning." *Managerial Planning* (November–December 1972): 34–38.

Newman, William H. *Constructive Control: Design and Use of Control Systems.* Englewood Cliffs, NJ: Prentice-Hall, 1971.

Otley, D.T., and A.J. Berry. "Control, Organization, and Accounting." *Accounting Organizations and Society* (July 1980): 231–46.

Ouchi, William G. "A Conceptual Framework for the Design of Control Mechanisms." *Management Science* 25 (September 1975): 833–48.

———. "Markets, Bureaucracies, and Clans." *Administrative Science Quarterly* (March 1980): 129–41.

Ouchi, William G., and M.A. Maguire. "Organizational Control: Two Functions." *Administrative Science Quarterly* (December 1975): 559–69.

Sayles, Leonard. "The Many Dimensions of Control." *Organizational Dynamics* (Summer 1972).

Simon, H.A. *The New Science of Management Decision.* New York: Harper & Row, 1960.

Tocher, K.D. "Control." *Operational Research Quarterly* (June 1970): 159–80.

3

Linguistic Relativism in Management Accounting

INTRODUCTION

Speakers of different languages react differently to accounting phenomena, resulting in difficulties in interlinguistic communication internationally. Basically, the model in this chapter postulates that accounting may be perceived as a language and as a result of three theses: the linguistic relativity thesis, the sociolinguistic thesis, and the bilingual thesis. The linguistic characteristics of accounting dictate the judgment/decision process in accounting in general and management accounting in particular.

ACCOUNTING AS A LANGUAGE

Accounting textbooks routinely refer to accounting as a language and as a main vehicle for communicating information about a business.

As the language of business, accounting has many things in common with other languages. The various business activities of a firm are reported in accounting statements using accounting language, just as news events are reported in newspapers in the English language. To express an event in accounting or in English, we must follow certain rules. Without following certain rules diligently, not only does one run the risk of being misunderstood, but also risks a penalty for misrepresentation, lying, or perjury. Comparability of statements is essential to the effective functioning of a language whether it is in English or in accounting. At the same time, language has to be flexible enough to adapt to a changing environment.[1]

What makes accounting a language? Because language is generally defined in terms of lexical characteristics and grammar,[2] one answer to the question is to ascertain that accounting also includes the same two components of a language.

The symbols or lexical characteristics of a language are identifiable "meaningful" units or words. These symbols are linguistic objects used to identify particular concepts. Concerning this effect, Gerald Zaitman et al. state that concepts are located in the words of thought rather than in the world of actual things referred to here as objects, including linguistic objects commonly referred to as "terms."[3]

Symbolic representations do exist in accounting. For example, Daniel McDonald identifies numerals and words, and debits and credits, as the only symbols accepted and unique to the accounting discipline.[4]

The grammatical rules of a language reflect the syntactical arrangement existing in any given language. Such rules exist in accounting. They refer to the general set of procedures used for the preparation of financial statements of a firm.

Based on the existence of the two components of a language, lexical characteristics and grammatical rules, accounting may be viewed as a language. Therefore, the paradigmatic theses used in the study of language may be applied to accounting. These theses include the linguistic relativity thesis, the sociolinguistic thesis, and the bilingual thesis. These theses are the basis for the cultural relativism model in accounting.

LINGUISTIC RELATIVITY IN ACCOUNTING

The Sapir-Whorf Hypothesis of Linguistic Relativity

Anthropologists have always emphasized the study of language in their studies of culture. E. Sapir referred to the linguistic symbolism of a given culture. He perceived language as an instrument of thought and communication of thought. In other words, a given language predisposes its users to a distinct belief. All these premises led to the formulation of the principle of linguistic relativity: language is an active determinant of thought. Similarly, B. L. Whorf maintained that the ways of speaking are indicative of the metaphysics of a culture. Such a metaphysics consists of unstated premises that shape the perception and thought of those who participate in that culture and predisposes them to a given method of perception.[5]

Formulation of ideas is not an independent process, strictly rational in the old sense, but is part of a particular grammar, and differs, from slightly to greatly, between different grammars. . . . We are thus introduced to a new principle of relativity, which holds that all observers are not led by the same physical evidence to the same picture of the universe, unless their linguistic backgrounds are similar, or in some way may be calibrated.[6]

The linguistic relativity hypothesis is in fact preceded by a linguistic determinism hypothesis. Linguistic determinism implies that the structure of language determines the structure of thought. The deterministic aspect of such a position is well expressed by Whorf:

It was found that the background linguistic system (in other words, the grammar) of each language is not merely a reproducing instrument for voicing ideas but rather is itself the shaper of ideas, the program and guide for the individual's mental activity, for his analysis of impressions, for his synthesis of his mental stock and trade.

Formulation of ideas is not an independent process, strictly rational in the old sense, but is part of a particular grammar, and differs, from slightly to greatly, between different grammars. We dissect nature along lines laid down by our native languages. The categories and types that we isolate in the world of phenomena we do not find . . . because they stare every observer in the face; on the contrary, the world is presented in a kaleidoscopic flux by our minds—and this means largely by the linguistic system in our minds.[7]

These arguments were used to demonstrate the relativity of language. Whorf went even further by showing that in certain domains American Indian languages are superior to European languages:

It takes but little real scientific study of preliterate languages, especially those of America, to show how much more precise and finely elaborated is the system of relationship in many such tongues than ours. By comparison with many American languages, the formal systematic organization of ideas in English, German, French, or Italian is poor and jejeune. Why, for instance, do we not, like the Hopi, use a different way of expressing the relation of channel of sensation (seeing) to result in consciousness, as between "I see that it is red" and "I see that it is new"? We fuse the two different types of relationship into a vague sort of connection expressed by "that" whereas the Hopi indicates that in the first case seeing presents unspecified evidence from which is drawn the inference of newness. . . . Does the Hopi language show here a higher plane of thinking, a more rational analysis of situations, than our English? Of course, it does. In this field and in others, English compared to Hopi is like a bludgeon compared to a rapier.[8]

The basic view in the Sapir-Whorf hypothesis is that the characteristics of language have determining influences on cognitive processes. Basically monolingual individuals, speaking completely different languages in terms of structural, grammatical, and other characteristics, should adopt different mediated behaviors.

The [real world] is to a large extent unconsciously built up on the language habits of the group. The worlds in which different societies live are distinct worlds, merely the same world with different labels attached. We [as individuals] see and hear and otherwise experience very largely as we do because the language habits of our community predispose certain choices of interpretation.[9]

Thus, language is more than a communication vehicle about objective reality existing independently of language but instead represents an objective reality that man uses to organize the realities around him. The scheme used by speakers of different languages when speaking about the nonlinguistic world will differ drastically. As stated by Sapir, "Language does not as a matter of actual behavior stand apart from or run parallel to direct experience—but completely penetrates with it."[10] Or as stated by Whorf, "Observers are not led by the same picture of the universe, unless their linguistic backgrounds are similar or can in some way be calibrated."[11]

That the real world is to a large extent unconsciously built on the language of a given group and that the intellectual system embodied in each language shapes the thought of its speakers in a quite general way is the essence of the linguistic relativity hypothesis.

The categories and types we isolate from the world of phenomena we do not find . . . because they stare every observer in the face. On the contrary the world is presented in a kaleidoscopic flux of impressions which have to be organized in our minds. This means, largely, by the linguistic system in our minds.[12]

In its extreme position, the linguistic relativity hypothesis claims that cognitive organization is directly constrained by linguistic structure. J. A. Fishman explains this claim as follows:

Some languages recognize far more tenses than do others. Some languages recognize a gender of norms (and, therefore, also required markers of gender in the verb and adjective systems), whereas others do not. Some languages build into the verb system recognition of certainty or uncertainty of past, present, or future action. Other languages build into the verb system a recognition of the size, shape and color of norms referred to.[13]

In a summary of the linguistic relativity hypothesis, Roger Brown distinguishes two main hypotheses:[14]

I. Structural differences between language systems will, in general, be paralleled by nonlinguistic cognitive differences, of an unspecified sort, in the native speakers of two languages.

II. The structure of anyone's native language strongly influences or fully determines the world-view he will acquire as he learns the language.[15]

Paul Kay and Willett Kempton add a third hypothesis:

III. The semantic systems of different languages vary without constraint.[16]

The evidence on the three hypotheses is, however, mixed. "That the linguistic relativity hypothesis indicates that the characteristics of language have determining influences on cognitive processes generates both delight and horror. The delight resides in the knowledge that the mastery of the language is followed by the influence on our cognitive abilities." Fishman, however, mentions the horror:

The first is the *horror of helplessness*, since all of us in most walks of life and most of us in all walks of life are helplessly trapped by the language we speak. We cannot escape from it—and, even if we could flee, where would we turn but to some other language with its own blinders and its own vicelike embrace on what we think, what we perceive, and what we say. The second horror is the *horror of hopelessness*—for what hope can there be for mankind? What hope that our group will ever understand the other? What hope that one nation will ever communicate with the other?[17]

While these two horrors are exaggerated, the challenge remains to understand the full consequences of the linguistic relativity thesis in the social sciences in general and in accounting in particular.

Systematization of the Sapir-Whorf Hypothesis

Using a double dichotomy, Fishman systematized the Sapir-Whorf hypothesis as shown in Exhibit 3.1.[18] Fishman's model views the characteristics of language as either lexical or grammatical, and the behavior of the speaker as either verbal behavior per se (generally interpreted in terms of cultural themes, or *weltanschauung*) and individual behavior data that is nonverbal in nature. Four cells correspond to four levels of the Sapir-Whorf hypothesis of linguistic relativity.

Cell 1 corresponds to linguistic codifiability and cultural reflections. It implies a relationship between the lexical properties of a language and the speaker's linguistic behavior. Phenomena are codified differently in each language, which structures their verbal behavior. The absence of an English equivalent for German *gemütlichkeit* makes it easier for Germans to be aware of and to express the phenomena. The French use of one word for both "conscience" and "consciousness" is shown by R. Linderman to have led to a greater conceptual fusion between these two usages on the part of French philosophers than for English or German thinkers.[19] Because of the different codifications the linguistic behavior and communication will differ. For example, the fact that Arabs have different terms for horses and the Eskimos have different terms for snow makes it easier for Arabs to communicate about horses and Eskimos about snow. This analysis is applicable to R. D. Gastil's concept of polysemy that may be more easily expressible in one language than another.[20]

Languages differ as to the presence or absence of the field distinctions which they make. A language may be seen as a limited group of words and forms available for the use of a man thinking or expressing himself in the medium of that language. If he does not have the means to do a certain job of thinking or expressing, that job will not be accomplished as well as if he had such means.[21]

Exhibit 3.1
Fishman's Systematic Version of the Sapir-Whorf Hypothesis

Data about language Characteristics	Data of Speaker's Behavior	
	Linguistics Data	Nonlinguistic Data
Lexical Characteristic	1	2
Grammatical Characteristics	3	4

Cell 2 corresponds to linguistic codifiability and behavioral concomitants. It implies a relationship between lexical properties of a language and then on linguistic behavior of the users of a language. This level is more crucial than level 1 for the testing of the linguistic relativity hypothesis.

In order to find evidence to support the linguistic relativity hypothesis it is not sufficient merely to point to differences between languages and to assume that users of these languages have correspondingly different mental experiences. If we are not to be guilty of circular inference, it is necessary to show some correspondence between the presence or absence of a certain linguistic phenomenon and the presence or absence of a certain kind of non-linguistic response.[22]

The second level implies that speakers of a language that makes certain lexical distinctions will be able to perform certain nonlinguistic tasks better and more rapidly than the speakers of languages that do make these lexical distinctions. R. W. Brown and E. H. Lenneberg,[23] Lenneberg,[24,25] and De Lee Lantz and Volney Steffbre[26] showed a shorter response latency in naming culturally encoded colors (i.e., colors that can be named with a single word) than colors that are not culturally encoded.

Cell 3 corresponds to linguistic structure and its cultural concomitants. It implies a relationship between grammatical characteristics and linguistic behavior. In essence, the concern is with the relationship between language and worldview. It is best illustrated by Whorf's statement:

The background linguistic system (in other words, the grammar) of each language is not merely a reproducing instrument for voicing ideas, but rather is itself the shaper of ideas, the program and guide for the individual's mental activity, for his analysis of impressions, for his synthesis of his mental stock in trade. Formulation of ideas is not an independent process, strictly rational in the old sense, but is part of a particular grammar and differs, from slightly to greatly, between grammars.[27]

The thesis is best echoed by G. L. Trager:

Language as a whole has structure and all its parts and subdivisions also have structure. . . . [If] the rest of cultural behavior has been conditioned by language, then there must be a relationship between the structure of language and the structure of behavior.[28]

Basically the level of the hypothesis in cell 3 assumes that speakers of one language who use specific grammatical rules are predisposed to a given world-view different from the speakers of other languages. Whorf bases his conclusions on an analysis of Hopi and compares it with standard average European languages (SAE) (including English).[29] He highlights specific grammatical structures (absence of tenses, the classification of events by duration categories, the use of grammatical forms to indicate the type of validity intended by the speaker, etc.). H. Holier argued the same position by analyzing Navaho.[30] The work of Susan Erwin-Tripp on bilingualism may also be used to support this level of the linguistic relativity hypothesis.[31] Bilingual Japanese women married to U.S. servicemen were asked to converse in Japanese with the result that the context of their conversation was more typical of women in Japan. When asked to converse in English, the context was more typical of women in the United States.

Cell 4 corresponds to the linguistic structure and its behavioral concomitants. It implies a relationship between grammatical characteristics and nonlinguistic behavior. J. B. Carroll and T. S. Casagrande provide support for this level of the hypothesis.[32] They examined whether the speakers of a language that codes verbally for color, shape, and size, such as the Navaho language, will classify objects differently from the speakers of a language that codes verbally for tense, person, and number, as in English.

(a) . . . This feature of the Navaho language would affect the relative potency or order of emergency of such concepts as colour, size, shape or form, and number in the Navaho-speaking child (specifically that shape or form would develop earlier and increase more regularly with age, since this is the aspect provided for in the verb forms themselves), and (b) that he (i.e. the Navaho child) would be more inclined to perceive formal similarities (i.e. shape or form similarities) between objects than would English-speaking Navaho children of the same age.[33]

Systematization of the Linguistic Relativity Hypothesis in Accounting

Systematization of the linguistic relativity hypothesis in accounting can be accomplished by differentiating between the characteristics of an accounting language and the different data of cognitive behavior, where the characteristics of accounting language are the symbolic accounting representation and the manipulation rules and the data of cognitive behavior refer to a linguistic or non-linguistic behavior of users of accounting data. Such systematization leads to a fourfold analytic scheme as portrayed in Exhibit 3.2. Built on the evidence from

Exhibit 3.2
Belkaoui's Propositions of Linguistic Relativity in Accounting

Data about Accounting Characteristics	Data of User's Behavior	
	Linguistics Data	Nonlinguistic Data
Symbolic Representations	1	2
Manipulation Rules	3	4

linguistic and accounting research, Ahmed Belkaoui suggests four hypotheses corresponding to each of the four cells of Exhibit 3.2.[34]

1. Users who make certain lexical distinctions in accounting are enabled to talk and/or solve problems that cannot be easily solved by users who do not.
2. Users who make certain lexical distinctions in accounting are enabled to perform (nonlinguistic) tasks more rapidly or more completely than those users who do not.
3. Users who possess accounting (grammatical) roles are predisposed to different managerial styles or emphases than those who do not.
4. Accounting techniques may facilitate or render more difficult various (nonlinguistic) managerial behaviors on the part of users.[35]

While, with one exception,[36] these hypotheses are not explicitly tested, various evidence provided in the behavioral accounting and human processing literature may be explained in terms of the linguistic relativity hypothesis in accounting in general and these four hypotheses in particular.

THE SOCIOLINGUISTIC THESIS IN ACCOUNTING

Speech systems are generated, or controlled, by social relations. This role of language in defining communities and social relationships is the realm of sociolinguistics. It argues that the roots of social class are carried through a communication code that social class itself promotes.

If a social group, by virtue of its class relation, i.e., as a result of its common occupational function and social status, has developed strong communal bonds; if the work relations of this group offer little variety; little exercise in decision making; if asserting, if it is to be successful must be a collective rather than an individual act; if the work task requires physical manipulation and control rather than symbolic organization and control; if the diminished authority of the man at work is transformed into an authority of power at home; if the home is overcrowded and limits the variety of situations it can offer; if the children socialize each other in an environment offering little intellectual stimuli; if all these attributes are found in one setting, then it is plausible to assume that such a social setting will generate a particular form of communication which will shape the intellectual, social and affective orientation of the children.[37]

Exhibit 3.3
Role Systems

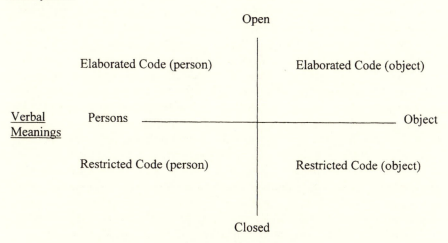

The linguistic thesis implies that different forms of social relations generate very different speech systems, linguistic repertoires, or communications codes.[38-41] In other words, people learn their social roles through the process of communication. Social role is best defined as follows: "A social role can then be considered as a complex coding activity controlling both the creation and organization of specific meanings and the conditions for their transmission and reception."[42]

Communication codes can be either elaborated or restricted, depending on whether it is difficult or easy to predict their linguistic alternatives. Similarly role systems are either open or closed, according to whether they permit or reduce the range of alternatives for realization of verbal meanings. Basil Bernstein used this simple dichotomy to identify the contextual nature of the use of repertoires and to show a causal connection between role systems, communication codes, and the realization of different orders of meaning and relevance. As shown in Exhibit 3.3, in distinguishing between object and person orders of meaning, an individual will use an elaborated or restricted code depending on whether the role system is closed and the verbal meanings are likely to be assigned or the role system is open and the verbal meanings are likely to be novel. As stated by Bernstein:

We can begin to see that in the area where the role system is open, there is an induced motivation to explore and actively seek out and extend meanings; where the role is closed, there is little induced motivation to explore and create novel meanings . . .

Where the role system is open, the individual child learns to cope with ambiguity and isolation in the creation of verbal meanings; where the role system is closed, the individual or child forges such learning. On the contrary, he learns to create verbal meanings in social contexts which are unambiguous and communalized.[43]

Thus the social role determines the communication code or linguistic repertoires used.

Accounting situations also involve different role relationships that result from a number of factors, including membership in different professional associations, difference in education levels and fluency in accounting, and difference in economic and social positions. These role relationships in turn determine either an elaborated accounting communication code if the role system is open or a restricted accounting communication code if the system is closed. In essence, the sociolinguistic thesis in accounting implies the existence of different linguistic repertoires in accounting as a result of the different social role relationships exposed by users and preparers of accounting information. For example, various professional affiliations in accounting create different linguistic repertoires or codes for intragroup communications and/or intergroup communications which lead to a differential understanding of accounting and social relationships.[44] Specifically, a select set of accounting concepts was subjected to analysis using multidimensional scaling techniques to evaluate the intergroup perceptual differences between three groups of users. A sociolinguistic construct was used to justify the possible lack of consensus on the meaning of accounting concepts. The dimensions of the common perceptual space were identified and labeled as conjunctive, relational, and disjunctive by analogy to the process of concept formation. The sociolinguistic thesis was verified for both the conjunctive and the disjunctive concepts.

THE BILINGUAL THESIS IN ACCOUNTING

The best tests of the Sapir-Whorf hypothesis can be provided by bilinguals as they are the only ones who can personally testify to the different *weltanschauungs* created by different languages. There are various expressions of the differential effect of the worldview imposed by different languages. Consider the following statement: "Language is so intimately interwoven with the whole of social behavior that a bilingual, for better or worse, is bound to differ from the monoglot."[45]

But bilingualism is not the only situation that may result in different worldviews created by different languages. Diglossia is another case. Diglossia occurs when a society uses two or more languages for intrasociety communication. It is basically manifested by the existence of stable and separable communication codes that depend on each other but serve different social functions. Basically some societies rely on separate dialects or functionally differentiated language varieties.[46] Fishman, in fact, makes the separation between high (H) language, used in conjunction with religion, education, and other aspects of high culture, and low (L) language used in conjunction with everyday aspects of society.[47] Charles A. Ferguson, who introduced the concept of diglossia, perceived H and L as superposed language.[48] Fishman distinguishes several different kinds of linguistic relationships between H and L languages as follows:

1. H is classical and L is vernacular, the two being genetically related, as in classical and vernacular Arabic, classical or classicized Greek (Katarevusa) and Demotiki, to name only a few.

2. H is classical and L is vernacular, the two not being genetically unrelated, as in Loshn Koydesh (textual Hebrew/Aramaic) and Yiddish.

3. H is written/formal spoken and L is vernacular, the two being genetically related to each other, as in Spanish and Guarani in Paraguay.

4. H is written/formal and L is vernacular, the two being genetically related to each other, as in High German and Swiss German.[49]

The important fact is that different social roles and relationships dictate the use of different languages or dialects resulting in different worldviews and attitudes: Where one set of behaviors, attitudes, and values supported, and was expressed in, one language, another set of behaviors, attitudes, and values supported and was expressed in the other. Both sets of behaviors, attitudes, and values were fully accepted as culturally legitimate and complementary (i.e., nonconflictual) and indeed, little if any conflict between them was possible in view of the functional separation between them.[50]

Both bilingualism and diglossia have an impact on the use of accounting language. Speakers of multiple languages or different dialects will experience different worldviews in their use of accounting languages from unilinguals. Different languages or dialect systems may provide cognitive enrichment or linguistic and perceptual confusion. Switching from one language or dialect to another may lead to better perception. In effect, language switching has been found to be related to higher levels of creativity and cognitive feasibility,[51] concept formation,[52] verbal intelligence,[53] and psycholinguistic abilities.[54] The three problems identified can affect the perception of accounting concepts by bilingual and unilingual speakers of languages or dialects. Janice Monti-Belkaoui and Ahmed Belkaoui conducted an experiment to evaluate the extent of these problems in accounting.[55] The findings supported the contention that unilingual speakers of separate languages differ from each other and from bilingual speakers in their perception of accounting concepts. Some of these findings also provided support for the contention that language switching may enhance understanding. The evidence suggests that fluency in more than one language aids in the uniform acquisition and comprehension of accounting concepts.

LINGUISTIC RELATIVISM IN MANAGEMENT ACCOUNTING: A MODEL

Management accounting may be represented as a language given the existence of the two components of symbolic representations and grammatical characteristics. The judgment/decision process in accounting is determined by the impact of language on behavior and attitudes as hypothesized by the linguistic relativity

Exhibit 3.4
Linguistic Relativism in Accounting: A Model

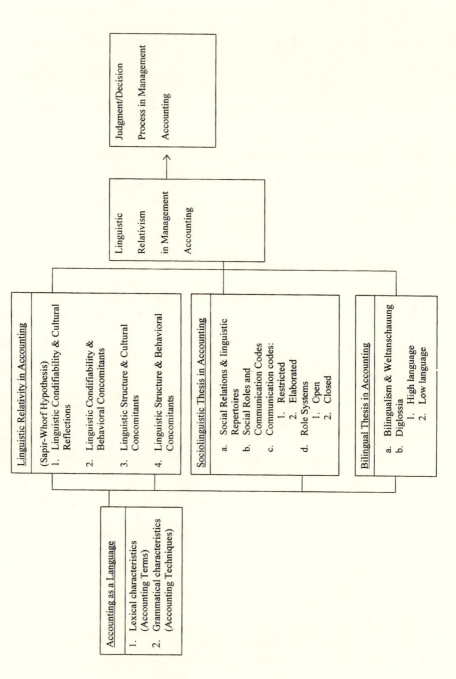

hypothesis, the sociolinguistic hypothesis, and the bilingual thesis. Basically the linguistic codifiability or structure of accounting language affects the linguistic and nonlinguistic behavior of users. The social roles created by different professional memberships, social classes, and education lead to different communication codes, either elaborated or restricted, that affect concept formation, understanding, and decision making in accounting. Finally, the use of different languages or dialects, as in bilingualism, or diglossia, provides speakers with a different understanding of accounting phemonena as well as different cognitive abilities. The three results contribute to a linguistic relativism model in accounting, as portrayed in Exhibit 3.4, which is assumed to determine the judgment/decision process in management accounting.

CONCLUSION

The essence of linguistic relativism in accounting is the presence of a linguistic process that is assumed to guide the judgment/decision process in management accounting. The model in this chapter postulates that management accounting as a language affects the judgment/decision process as result of the theory and findings underlying the Sapir-Whorf hypothesis of linguistic relativity, the sociolinguistic thesis, and the bilingualism, or diglossia, thesis.

NOTES

1. Yuji Ijiri, *Theory of Accounting Measurement*, Studies in Accounting Research No. 10 (Sarasota, FL: American Accounting Association, 1975), 14.

2. Leonard C. Hawes, *Pragmatics of Analoguing* (Reading, MA: Addison-Wesley, 1975).

3. Gerald Zaltman, C.R.A. Pison, and R. Angelman, *Metatheory and Consumer Research* (New York: Holt, Rinehart & Winston, 1973).

4. Daniel McDonald, *Comparative Accounting Theory* (Reading, MA: Addison-Wesley, 1972), 6.

5. E. Sapir, in D.G. Mandelbaum, ed., *Culture, Language and Personality: Selected Essays* (Cambridge, MA: MIT Press, 1956).

6. B.L. Whorf, *Language, Thought and Reality* (Boston: MIT Press, 1951).

7. Ibid., 214.

8. Ibid., 212.

9. Ibid., 84–85.

10. E. Sapir, "The Status of Linguistics as a Science," *Language* 5 (1929): 207–14.

11. B.L. Whorf, "Science and Linguistics," *Technological Review* 44 (1940): 229–31, 247, 248.

12. Ibid., 212.

13. J.A. Fishman, *The Sociology of Language* (New York: Newbury House, 1972), 156.

14. Roger Brown, "Reference: In Memorial Tribute to Eric Lenneberg," *Cognition* 4 (1976): 125–53.

15. Ibid., 128.

16. Paul Kay and Willett Kempton, "What Is the Sapir-Whorf Hypothesis?" *American Anthropologist* 86 (1984): 66.

17. J.A. Fishman, "A Systematization of the Whorfian Hypothesis," *Behavioral Science* 5/4 (1960): 332.

18. Ibid.

19. R. Linderman, *Der Begriff der Conscience in Franzosichen Denken* (Leipzig: Jena, 1938).

20. R.D. Gastil, "Relative Linguistic Determinism," *Anthropological Linguistics* 1/9 (1959): 24–38.

21. Ibid., 37.

22. J.B. Carroll and T.S. Casagrande, "The Function of Language Classification in Behavior," in *Readings in Social Psychology*, ed. E.E. Maccoby, T.M. Newcomb, and E.L. Hartley (New York: Holt, Rinehart & Winston, 1958), 13.

23. R.W. Brown and E.H. Lenneberg, "A Study in Language and Cognition," *Journal of Abnormal and Social Psychology* 49 (1954): 454–62.

24. E.H. Lenneberg, "Cognition in Ethnolinguistics," *Language* 29 (1953): 463–71.

25. E.H. Lenneberg, "A Probabilistic Approach to Language Learning," *Behavioral Science* 2 (1957): 1–12.

26. De Lee Lantz and Volney Steffbre, "Language and Cognition Revisited," *Journal of Abnormal and Social Psychology* 2 (1953): 454–62.

27. Whorf, "Science and Linguistics," 247.

28. G.L. Trager, "The Systematization of the Whorf Hypothesis," *Anthropological Linguistics* 1 (1959): 31–35.

29. Whorf, "Science and Linguistics."

30. H. Holier, "Cultural Implications of the Navaho Linguistic Categories," *Language* 27 (1951): 111–20.

31. Susan Erwin-Tripp, "Sociolinguistics," in *Advances in Experimental Social Psychology*, ed. L. Berkowitz (New York: Academic Press, 1969), 91–163.

32. J.B. Carroll and T.S. Casagrande, "Function of Language Classification in Behavior."

33. Ibid.

34. Ahmed Belkaoui, "Linguistic Relativity in Accounting," *Accounting, Organizations and Society* (October 1978): 97–124.

35. Ibid., 103.

36. Ahmed Belkaoui, "The Impact of Socio-Economic Accounting Statements on the Investment: An Empirical Study," *Accounting, Organizations and Society* (September 1980): 263–83.

37. Basil Bernstein, "A Sociolinguistic Approach to Socialization, with Some Reference to Educability," in *Directions in Sociolinguistics: Ethnography of Communication*, ed. John J. Gumperz and Dell Hymes (New York: Holt, Rinehart & Winston, 1972), 472.

38. Susan M. Erwin-Tripp, "An Analysis of the Interaction of Language, Topic and Listener," *American Anthropologist* 66/6 (1964): 86–102.

39. Erwin-Tripp, "Sociolinguistics," 91–165.

40. John J. Gumperz, "Linguistic and Social Interaction in Two Communities," *American Anthropologist* 66/6 (1964):137–54.

41. Dell Hynes, "Modes of the Interaction of Language and Social Setting," *Journal of Social Issues* 23/2 (1967): 8–28.

42. Bernstein, "Sociolinguistic Approach to Socialization, with Some Reference to Educability," 474.

43. Ibid., 478–79.

44. Ahmed Belkaoui, "The Interprofessional Linguistic Communication of Accounting Concepts: An Experiment in Sociolinguistics, *Journal of Accounting Research* (Fall 1980): 362–74.

45. Robert H. Lowie, "A Case of Bilingualism." *World* 1 (1945): 249–59.

46. J.A. Fishman, "Bilingualism with or without Diglossia; Diglossia with or without Bilingualism," *Journal of Social Issues* 2 (1967): 29–39.

47. Ibid., 30.

48. Charles A. Ferguson, "Diglossia," *World* 15 (1959): 325–40.

49. J.A. Fishman, "Bilingualism and Biculturalism, Individual and Social Phenomena," *Journal of Multilingual and Multicultural Development* 1 (1980): 3–15.

50. Fishman, "Bilingualism with or without Diglossia; Diglossia with or without Bilingualism," 29–30.

51. E. Peal and W.E. Lambert, "The Relationship of Bilingualism to Intelligence," *Psychological Monographs* 1 (1962): 76–84.

52. W.W. Liedke and L.D. Nelson, "Concept Formation and Bilingualism," *Alberta Journal of Educational Research* 2 (1968): 4–20.

53. W.E. Lambert and G.R. Tucker "The Benefits of Bilingualism," *Alberta Journal of Educational Research* (September 1973): 115–22.

54. M.C. Casserby and A.P. Edwards, *Detrimental Effects of Grade One Bilingualism Programs: An Exploratory Study*, paper presented at the annual conference of the Canadian Psychological Association, Toronto, 1979.

55. Janice Monti-Belkaoui and Ahmed Belkaoui, "Bilingualism and the Perception of Professional Concepts," *Journal of Psycholinguistic Research* 12/2 (1983): 111–27.

SELECTED BIBLIOGRAPHY

Belkaoui, Ahmed. "The Impact of Socio-Economic Accounting Statements on the Investment Decision: An Empirical Study." *Accounting, Organizations and Society* (September 1980): 263–83.

———. "The Interprofessional Linguistic Communication of Accounting Concepts. An Experiment in Sociolinguistic." *Journal of Accounting Research* (Fall 1980): 362–74.

———. "Linguistic Relativity in Accounting." *Accounting, Organizations and Society* (October 1978): 97–124.

Bernstein, Basil. "A Sociolinguistic Approach to Socialization, with Some Reference to Educability." In *Directions in Sociolinguistics: The Ethnography of Communication*, ed. John J. Gumperz and Dell Hymes. New York: Holt, Rinehart & Winston, 1972, 472.

Brown, R.W., and E.H. Lenneberg. "A Study in Language and Cognition." *Journal of Abnormal and Social Psychology* 49 (1954): 454–62.

Brown, Roger. "Reference: In Memorial Tribute to Eric Lenneberg." *Cognition* 4 (1976): 3–18.

Carroll, J.B., and T.S. Casagrande. "The Function of Language Classification in Behavior." In *Readings in Social Psychology*, ed. E.E. Maccoby, T.M. Newcomb, and E.L. Hartley. New York: Holt, Rinehart & Winston, 1958.

Casserby, M.C., and A.P. Edwards. "Detrimental Effects of Grade One Bilingualism Programs: An Exploratory Study." Paper presented at the annual conference of the Canadian Psychological Association, Toronto, 1979.

Erwin-Tripp, Susan. "An Analysis of the Interaction of Language, Topic and Listener." *American Anthropologist* 66/6 (1964): 86–102.

———. "Sociolinguistics." In *Advances in Experimental Social Psychology*, ed. L. Berkowitz. New York: Academic Press, 1969, 91–165.

Ferguson, Charles A. "Diglossia." *World* 15 (1959): 325–40.

Fishman, J.A. "Bilingualism and Biculturalism, as Individual and Social Phenomena." *Journal of Multilingual and Multicultural Development* 1 (1980): 3–15.

———. "Bilingualism with or without Diglossia; Diglossia with or without Bilingualism." *Journal of Social Issues* 2 (1967): 29–39.

———. *The Sociology of Language.* New York: Newbury House, 1972.

———. "A Systematization of the Whorfian Hypothesis." *Behavioral Science* 514 (1960): 332.

Gastil, R.D. "Relative Linguistic Determinism." *Anthropological Linguistics* 1/9 (1959): 24–38.

Grumperz, John J. "Linguistic and Social Interaction in Two Communities." *American Anthropologist* 66/6 (1964): 137–54.

Hawes, Leonard C. *Pragmatics of Analoguing.* Reading, MA: Addison-Wesley, 1975.

Hoijer, H. "Cultural Implications of the Navaho Linguistic Categories." *Language* 27 (1951): 111–20.

Hynes, Dell. "Modes of the Interaction of Language and Social Setting." *Journal of Social Issues* 2312 (1967): 8–28.

Ijiri, Yuji. *Theory of Accounting Measurement.* Studies in Accounting Research No. 10. Sarasota, FL: American Accounting Association, 1975.

Kay, Paul, and Willett Kempton. "What Is the Sapir-Whorf Hypothesis?" *American Anthropologist* 86 (1984):66.

Lambert, W.E., and G.R. Tucker. "The Benefits of Bilingualism." *Alberta Journal of Educational Research* (September 1973): 115–22.

Lantz, De Lee, and Volney Steffbre. "Language and Cognition Revisited." *Journal of Abnormal and Social Psychology* 2 (1953): 454–62.

Lenneberg, E.H. "Cognition in Ethnolinguistics." *Language* 29 (1953): 463–71.

———. "A Probabilistic Approach to Language Learning." *Behavioral Science* 2 (1957): 1–12.

Liedke, W.W., and L.D. Nelson. "Concept Formation and Bilingualism." *Alberta Journal of Educational Research* 2 (1968): 4–20.

Linderman, R. *Der Begriff Conscience in Franzosichen Denken.* Leipzig: Jena, 1938.

Lowie, Robert H. "A Case of Bilingualism." *World* 1 (1945): 249–59.

McDonald, Daniel. *Comparative Accounting Theory.* Reading, MA: Addison-Wesley, 1972.

Monti-Belkaoui, Janice, and Ahmed Belkaoui. "Bilingualism and the Perception of Professional Concepts." *Journal of Psycholinguistic Research* 1212 (1983): 111–27.

Peal, E., and W.E. Lambert. "The Relationship of Bilingualism to Intelligence." *Psychological Monographs* 1 (1962): 76–84.

Sapir, E. *Culture, Language and Personality: Selected Essays*. Ed. D.G. Mandelbaum. Cambridge, MA: MIT Press, 1956.

———. "The Status of Linguistics as a Science." *Language* 5 (1929): 207–14.

Trager, G.L. "The Systematization of the Whorf Hypothesis." *Anthropological Linguistics* 1 (1959): 31–35.

Whorf, B.L. *Language, Thought and Reality*. Boston: MIT Press, 1951.

———. "Science and Linguistics." *Technological Reality* 44 (1940): 229–31, 247, 248.

Zaltman, Gerald, C.R.A. Pison, and R. Angelman. *Metatheory and Consumer Research*. New York: Holt, Rinehart & Winston, 1973.

4

Cultural Relativism in Management Accounting

INTRODUCTION

Cultural relativism in management accounting implies that people from different cultures construct, and/or use differently, management accounting concepts and practices. Basically, the model in this chapter postulates that culture, through its components, elements, and dimensions, dictates the organizational structures adopted, the microorganizational behavior, the management accounting environment, and the cognitive functioning of individuals faced with a management accounting phenomenon.

HISTORY OF THE THEORIES OF CULTURE

By the middle of the eighteenth century, efforts were being made to develop scientific theories of cultural differences. Cultural differences were then attributed to the different degrees of intellectual and moral progress achieved by different peoples. Scholars such as Adam Smith,[1] Adam Ferguson,[2] Jean Turgot,[3] and Denis Diderot[4] held this view of progress in defining different cultures. The nineteenth century saw the emergence of the concept of *cultural evolution*, which posited that cultures move through various stages of development. Scholars such as Auguste Comte,[5] Georg Wilhelm Friedrich Hegel,[6] and Lewis Henry Morgan[7] held this view of progression of cultures from one state to another. Morgan's stages were savagery, barbarism, and civilization.[8] In the case of Comte they included theological, metaphysical, and positivistic modes of thought.[9] In all these schemes culture was viewed as evolving in conjunction with the evolution of human biological types and races, an idea started with social philosophers such as Thomas Malthus[10] and Herbert Spencer[11] and espoused by Charles Darwin.[12] The resulting movement, called social Darwinism, postulates that cultural and biological progress results from the free play of competitive forces in the struggle of individual against individual, nation against nation, and race against race. Karl Marx also espoused the nineteenth-century evolution-and-progress paradigm of culture.[13] In his case the stages were primitive capitalism, slave society, feudalism, capitalism, and communism. The idea was also expressed by Friedrich Engels.[14]

The early twentieth century saw the emergence of various challenges to the evolutionism theory of culture. One challenge, introduced by Franz Boas,[15] is known as historical particularism. Boas viewed each culture as having a long and unique history that offers the best way to understand it. In addition, cultural relativism holds that there are no higher or lower forms of culture and that the stages proposed by the evolutionists merely reflect their ethnocentrism. Another challenge to evolutionism, known as diffusionism, holds that cultural differences and similarities are merely the result of people imitating and borrowing from other cultures. However, diffusionism fails to recognize that similarities between societies may be caused by the effects of similar environments.[16] British challenges to evolutionism were functionalism and structural functionalism. Functionalism advocates the descriptions of recurrent functions of customs and institutions rather than the origin of cultural differences and similarities.[17,18] All attempts to study the origin of cultural differences were viewed as speculative history. This new opposition, coupled with Freud's interpretation of cultures in psychological terms, shifted the emphasis to culture and personality theories, where cultural beliefs and practices were related to individual personality.[19,20]

More recently, dissatisfaction with antievolutionism has led to a return to some of the evolutionary theories of culture, a phenomenon spurred by Leslie White's linking of energy to the evolution of culture.[21] His basic law governing the evolution of culture is as follows: "Other factors remaining constant, culture evolves as the amount of energy harnessed per year is increased, or as the efficiency of the means of putting energy to work is increased."[22] This new evolutionism movement gave rise to the cultural ecology approach, advocated by Julian Steward, who identified the causes of cultural differences and similarities as the interaction of natural conditions with cultural factors.

With the popularity of dialectical materialism, which stresses the internal contradictions of sociocultural systems, and "dialectical" revolutions toward communism,[23] the new evolutionism led to the emergence of cultural materialism, which attributed cultural differences to the material constraints or conditions affecting the conduct of life in each society. The French contribution to the debate, advanced by Claude Levi-Strauss, is known as structuralism.[24] It stresses the similarities among cultures as a product of the structure of the human brain and of the unconscious thought processes, a structure characterized by binary contrasts.

Finally, despite the overwhelming evidence that culture is encoded in the brain rather than the genes, the units of biological heredity, there are still some racial determinism theories being offered to explain cultural differences. With the realization that most intelligence tests are culture-bound, and with increasing evidence of environmental influences, these theories do not constitute a dominant paradigm.

CONCEPTS OF CULTURE

The concept of culture has been subjected to various interpretations. In fact, some anthropologists have stated that culture in the abstract can be explained only by reference to specific cultures.[25] Anthropologists approach culture in at least three different ways: (1) the cultural universals approach, (2) the value systems approach, and (3) the systems approach.[26] The cultural universals approach focuses on identifying certain universals common to all cultures, which does allow an examination of cultures in terms of how they contribute to these variables. An example of such a list is provided by G. P. Murdock.[27]

The value systems approach focuses on classifying cultures according to value systems. Instruments used to assess values among cultures include the Allport, Vernon, and Lindzey instrument,[28] Morris's "way of life" instrument,[29] Kluckhohn and Strodtbeck's value theory,[30] Sarnoff's human value index,[31] and Rokeach's value survey.[32]

The systems approach focuses on the systems that make up a given culture. P. R. Harris and R. T. Moran identified eight subsystems in a culture: kinship, education, economy, politics, religion, association, health, and recreation.[33] Some anthropologists view culture as information doubly coded—once chemically in the brain as memory, and once externally as a language, behavior, material, or document, and as a cultural pool from which each individual, each dyad, each group draws its particular culture.[34]

In short, culture remains the basis of anthropological research. Anthropologists differ as to what the concept of culture means, although they generally agree that it is learned rather than logically transmitted, that it is shared by the members of a group, and that it is "the foundation of the human way of life."[35] There is also a consensus on the issue of cultural utility in the sense that cultural practices have "functions" or reflect a society's "adaptations" to its environment.

[C]ulture is man's primary mode of achieving reproductive success. Hence particular sociocultural systems are arrangements of patterned behavior, thought, and feeling that contribute to the survival and reproduction of particular social groups. Traits contributing to the maintenance of a system may be said to have *a positive function* with respect to that system. Viable systems may be regarded as consisting largely of positive-functioned traits, since the contrary assumption would lead us to expect the system's extinction.[36]

[C]ustoms which diminish the survival chances of a society are not likely to persist. . . . Those customs of a society that enhance survival chances are *adaptive* and are likely to persist. Hence we assume that, if a society has survived to be described in the annals of anthropology, much if not most of its cultural repertoires is adaptive, or was at one time.[37]

That cultural customs can be explained in practical materialist terms is well explained by anthropologist Marvin Harris in his popular *Cows, Rigs, Wars and Witches: The Riddles of Culture.*[38]

Various concepts of culture exist in anthropology suggesting different themes for accounting research.[39]

1. Following Malinowski's functionalism,[40] culture may be viewed as an instrument serving biological and psychological needs. Applying this definition to accounting research suggests the perception of accounting in each culture as a specific social instrument for task accomplishment and the analysis of cross-cultural or comparative accounting.

2. Following Radcliffe-Brown's structural functionalism,[41] culture may be viewed as an adaptive regulatory mechanism that unites individuals with social structures. Applying this definition to accounting research suggests the perception of accounting in each culture as an adaptive instrument existing by process of exchange with the environment and the analysis of an accounting culture.

3. Following Goodenough's ethnoscience,[42] culture may be viewed as a system of shared cognitions. The human mind thus generates culture by means of a finite number of rules. Applying this definition to accounting suggests that accounting may be viewed as a system of knowledge that members of each culture share to varying degrees and the analysis of accounting as cognition.

4. Following Geertz's symbolic anthropology,[43] culture may be viewed as a system of shared symbols and meanings. Applying this definition to accounting research suggests that accounting may be viewed as a pattern of symbolic discourse or language and the analysis of accounting as language.

5. Following Levi-Strauss's structuralism,[44] culture may be viewed as a projection of the mind's universal unconscious infrastructure. Applying this definition to accounting suggests that accounting may be viewed in each culture as the manifestation of unconscious processes and the analysis of unconscious processes in accounting.

CULTURAL RELATIVISM IN MANAGEMENT ACCOUNTING

The Cultural Relativism Model

Edward T. Hall has stated that "culture is man's medium; there is not one aspect of human life that is not touched and altered by culture. This means personalities, how people express themselves (including show of emotions), the way they think, how they move, how problems are solved, how their cities are planned and laid out, how transportation systems function and are organized, as well as how economic and government systems are put together and function."[45] This point applies well to accounting where culture can be viewed as accounting's medium. Culture in essence determines the judgment/decision process in accounting. The model, as illustrated in Exhibit 4.1, postulates that culture, through its components, elements, and dimensions, dictates the organizational structures adopted, the microorganizational behavior, and the cognitive func-

Exhibit 4.1
Cultural Relativism in Accounting

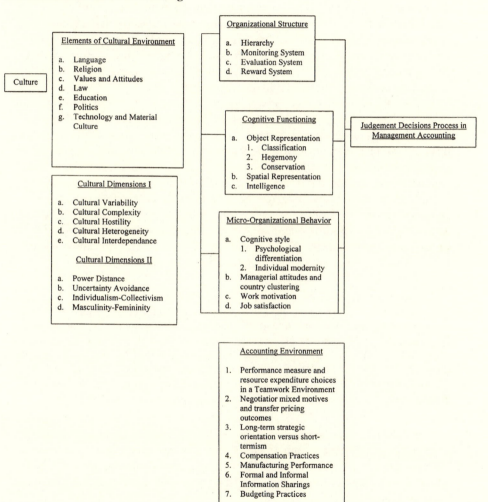

tioning of individuals, in such a way as to ultimately affect their judgment/ decision process when they are faced with a management accounting phenomenon.

Operationalization of Culture

This model avoids the two main problems that had beset earlier operationalization and use of culture: the equating of culture with nations and the ad hoc use of culture as a residual factor in explaining the variations that had not been explained by other factors.[46] Culture is viewed as collective mental programming,[47] that is, an ideological system forming the backdrop for human activity and providing people with a theory of reality.[48] This backdrop is composed of distinct elements and includes definite dimensions.

Those cultural elements generally assumed to affect the conduct of international business—language, religion, values and attitudes, law, education, politics, technology and material culture, and social organization—are assumed in this cultural relativism model to have the potential of dictating the organizational structures adopted, the cognitive functioning of individuals, and microorganizational behavior that may shape the judgment/decision process in accounting.

Cultures vary along five dimensions: cultural variability, cultural complexity, cultural hostility, cultural heterogeneity, and cultural interdependence.[49] The first three dimensions refer to conditions within cultures while the latter two refer to conditions among cultures. These dimensions may be seen as potential sources of problems for the multinational corporation:

(1) *Cultural variability* generates uncertainty, which calls for organizational flexibility and adaptability; (2) *Cultural complexity* raises the difficulty of understanding, which necessitates organizational and individual contexting and preparation; (3) *Cultural hostility* threatens goal attainment and survival, which demands the maintenance of social acceptability; (4) *Cultural heterogeneity* hinders centralized decision making with information overload, which calls for decentralization; and (5) *Cultural independence* increases the vulnerability of an organization to intergroup conflict, which necessitates less autonomy for individual subsidiaries and more system-wide coordination.[50]

This cultural relativism model assumes that differences in these five dimensions generate different cultural environments that have the potential of dictating the organizational structures adopted, the cognitive functioning of individuals, and the microorganizational behavior that may shape the judgment/decision process in accounting.

Cultures also vary along four dimensions that reflect the cultural orientations of a country and explain 50 percent of the differences in value systems among countries:[51] (1) individualism versus collectivism, (2) large versus small power distance, (3) strong versus weak uncertainty avoidance, and (4) masculinity versus femininity.

Individualism versus collectivism is a dimension that represents the degree of integration a society maintains among its members or the relationship between an individual and his/her fellow individuals. While individualists are expected to take care of themselves and their immediate families only, collectivists are expected to remain emotionally integrated into in-groups, which protect them in exchange for unquestioning loyalty.

Large versus small power distance represents the extent to which members of a society accept the unequal distribution of power in institutions and organizations. In large power distance societies, there is a tendency for people to accept a hierarchical order in which everybody has a place that needs no justification, whereas in small power distance societies, people tend to live for equality and demand justification for any existing power inequalities.

Strong versus weak uncertainty avoidance is a dimension that represents the degree to which the members of a society feel uncomfortable with uncertainty and ambiguity. In strong uncertainty avoidance societies, people are intolerant of ambiguity and try to control it at all costs, whereas in weak uncertainty avoidance societies, people are more tolerant of ambiguity and tend to live with it.

Masculinity versus femininity is a dimension that represents the nature of the social divisions of sex roles. Masculine roles imply a preference for achievement, assertiveness, making money, sympathy for the strong, and the like. Feminine roles imply a preference for warm relationships, modesty, care for the weak, preservation of the environment, concern for the quality of life, and so on.

This cultural relativism model assumes that differences among these four dimensions create different cultural arenas that have the potential of dictating the organizational structures adopted, the type of cognitive functioning, and the microorganizational behavior that may shape the judgment/decision process in accounting.

Cultural and Organizational Structure

The cultural relativism model assumes that culture, through its elements and dimensions, dictates the type of organizational structure. The idea was first advanced by J. Child, who stated that culture affects the design of organizational structure,[52] refuting the "culture free" contingency theory of organizational structure proposed by D.J. Hickson and colleagues.[53–55] In fact, A. Sorge argued that all facts that bear upon organizational practices do so in the form of cultural constructs, and that organizations develop through a "nonrational" process of experimentation that is wholly cultured.[56]

There is no culture-free context of organization, because even if organizational solutions of contexts are similar, they are always culturally constructed and very imperfectly interpreted as the reaction to a given constraint. Culture enters organization through artful, unselfconscious, piecemeal experimentations with alternatives in business policy, finance, work/organization, industrial relations, education and training, and many other factors.[57]

Uma Sekaran and Carol R. Snodgrass carry the argument one step further by offering ideas on how specific cultural dimensions affect particular structural elements.[58] More specifically, they attempt to match the four structural aspects of the organization—hierarchy, monitoring system, evaluation system, and reward system—with the four cultural dimensions identified by Hofstede to synchronize with the preferred modes of behavior of organizational members.

Hierarchies refer to how organizations distribute power among their members while power distance refers to how a society accepts the fact that power in institutions and organizations is unequally distributed. It follows that the situation for large power distance culture groups calls for centralized and rigid hierarchies followed by emergent behavior of dependence and counterdependence while the situation for low power distance cultural groups calls for decentralized and fluid hierarchies followed by a behavior of independence.

The monitoring system refers to the process of collection and dissemination of information on performance, while uncertainty avoidance refers to the certainty of an unknown future and the difference in the way people react to it by experiencing different levels of anxiety. It follows that the situation for weak uncertainty avoidance calls for a simplistic monitoring system, while the situation for high uncertainty avoidance calls for a complete and comprehensive monitoring system followed by low levels of anxiety.

The evaluation system refers to the process of appraising the effectiveness and efficiency of organizational individual performance. Individual collectivism refers to the type of relationship between a group and one of its members. It follows that a situation for individualistic cultural groups calls for an evaluation system based on individual achievement followed by a calculative behavior while a situation for collectivistic cultural groups calls for an evaluation system based on organizational performance followed by a moralistic behavior.

The reward system refers to the process of bestowing rewards for organizational or individual performance while masculinity-femininity refers to the nature of the social division of sex roles. It follows that a situation for "masculine" cultural groups calls for a reward system based on money, power, individual recognition and promotion, challenging assignments, status symbols, and the like, and catering to their machismo ideals, while a situation for "feminine" cultural groups calls for a reward system based on good quality of work life, security, a sense of belonging, a cooperative work system, and catering to their androgynous ideals.

Microorganizational Behavior and Culture

Cross-cultural research on microorganizational behavior has examined various issues including cognitive style, work motivation, job satisfaction, and other important managerial attitudes and behavior, and has highlighted the differences across various cultures.[59]

Research on cognitive style focuses on cultural differences in the structural aspects of an individual's cognitive system. It relies on the concept of psychological differentiation introduced by Witkin, Dyk, Faherson, Goodenough, and Karp[60] and used by Witkin and Berry,[61] for an understanding of the effects of subjective culture on individual behavior. Known as the theory of psychological differentiation, it relies on field dependence and field independence measures to categorize people along the dimension of field of articulation. Cultural differences were found in the level of field articulation among cultural groups in several countries.[62] Besides the concept of field dependence, the cognitive style approach known as individual modernity was used in cross-cultural research to explain how cultures change from traditional to modern.[63]

Research on attitudes and values focuses on cultural differences rather than similarities in personal, work-related, and ancestral values and attitudes. Various studies focus on a clustering of countries in terms of managerial and worker attitudes and values. Simcha Ronen and Oded Shenkar present a review of the published literature on country clustering and propose a map that integrates and synthesizes the available data.[64] The variables examined in these clustering studies include work goal importance, need deficiency, fulfillment and job satisfaction, managerial and organizational variables, and work role and interpersonal orientation. The resulting clusters discriminate on the basis of language, religion, and geography. Well-defined clusters are the Anglo, Germanic, Nordic, Latin-European, and Latin American ones. Ill-defined clusters are those describing the Far East and Arab countries as well as countries described as independent (e.g., Israel and Japan). Areas in Africa have not been studied at all while those in the Middle East and Far East have not been studied sufficiently. The review is, however, criticized by Peter Blunt[65] for alleged ethnocentrism and technocentrism, defined as a lack of interdisciplinary approach in organizational studies.

Research on work motivation examines cross-cultural differences in motivation using one of the following theoretical bases: Atkinson's expectancy theory,[66] McClelland's achievement motivational theory,[67] vocation- and achievement-related motivation,[68] and Adam's equity theory.[69]

Research on job satisfaction focuses on cross-cultural differences in the relationships between satisfaction and other variables of interest, such as absenteeism or productivity. These studies rely on the following theoretical bases: Maslow's need theory,[70] the importance of various job dimensions,[71] frame reference theory,[72] environmental theory,[73] Herzberg's two-factor theory,[74] and the alienation hypothesis.[75]

Cognitive Functioning

How people learn and think represents the study of human cognition. Cultural differences in cognitive functioning have also been subject to debate. Do people from different cultures perform differently on tasks that require certain cognitive skills? Two general hypotheses have been proposed. One maintains that cognitive processes are similar in individuals in different cultures; the other that cognitive processes are subject to cultural differences.[76,77] Evidence has been presented in support of both positions.[78,79] A third "situationist" hypothesis argues that cultural differences depend on the particular situation in the sense that "cultural differences in cognition reside more in the situations in which particular cognitive processes are applied than in the existence of a process in one cultural group and its absence in another."[80]

The debate needs to be continued in accounting research to determine whether people from different cultures will perform differently on tasks that require certain cognitive skills. Certain conditions need to be met in order to be able to usefully interpret potential cultural differences in cognitive functioning in an accounting context.

When we consider intellectual growth or style in different cultures, we are confronted by three requirements. We need to obtain . . . some picture of skills common to people from many backgrounds, as well as skills that differentiate among them. At the same time, we need to find the features of milieu that may account for the similarities and differences in skills. And finally, . . . we have to ask as we transpose a task from one culture to another whether the same answer means the same thing in both worlds.[81]

To meet these requirements, two conditions need to be met. One is to insure the absence of ambiguous communication between the participants of the experiment and the preparers of the tasks, as differences in the way people perform may reflect different understandings of the requirements rather than differences in cognitive functioning. The second is to insure that the participants are truly representative of their respective cultures.

Are there any differences in the cognitive strategies used by people from different cultures when they represent information about objects? To answer this question, various studies have examined potential differences in classification, memory, and conservation.

There may be cultural differences in the way people classify objects, through the use of different attributes. Cultural differences in classification tasks have been observed although the variation may be attributable in some cases to differences in education and differences in familiarity with the items to be classified.[82] Similarly, cultural differences in ability to abstract or to think in generalities have been observed in sorting tasks. However, in constrained classification tasks where the subjects learn to identify objects consistently on the basis of some feature, the skill in performing the task increases with age[83] and with education level.[84]

The recall of information from memory and its relation to culture is another research question of interest to object representation. In most experiments assessing the potential for cultural differences in the recall of information, age and education level were better related to the ways people from different cultures assess their memories.[85–87]

The concept of conservation, as introduced in Piaget's theory, refers to the ability of people to recognize the identity of objects or substances in spite of changes in their appearance. Cultural differences in the performance of conservation tasks are another research question of interest to object representation. While there are some obvious common problems due to differences in testing and scoring methods, age range of subjects, amount and kind of verbalization elicited from subjects, and language of testing, the results of experiments confirm the existence of a similar sequence of conservation across cultures and the existence of a "lag" in development of conservation among some cultures.[88–90] Education, although not necessarily formal, and familiarity with the task are also associated with differences in conservation performance.

Are there any differences in the cognitive strategies used by people from different cultures when they organize and use spatial information? Various studies have examined the potential for cultural difference in spatial reference systems. Different spatial reference systems were found to be used by Puluwat sailors navigating among the islands in the Western Pacific[91] and the Ternme in West Africa.[92] Other studies determined that cultural differences in the degree of field dependence are a result of differences in child rearing and other socialization practices.[93] The evidence tends toward the existence of cultural differences in the organization and use of spatial information. More evidence is needed, however, to insure that the participants are more representative of their culture and are more familiar with tasks they can relate to.

There are also potential cultural differences in competence in cognitive behavior, which is equivalent to the Western notion of intelligence. A good definition follows:

Intelligence, a concept within the area of individual differences, reduces itself to two essentials, the power of the mind, and the skills through which this power expresses itself. The former aspect comes nearest to what the man in the street means by intelligence. It can be defined as "the ability to learn, "the capacity for understanding," "the ability to perceive essential relations between things," "insight into the nature of things." The "machines" through which this power expresses itself provide the foundation of abilities—from the highest abilities such as the solving of mathematical equations, right down to the simplest such as tying one's bootlaces.[94]

Attempts to provide possible cultural bases for differences in general intelligence have been criticized for a number of reasons: (1) most tests of intelligence are culture-specific; (2) conceptual abilities are used as the skills to be assessed as intelligence while members of non-European cultures are known to think concretely;[95] (3) the environmental conditions between different cultural groups are not necessarily identical,[96] (4) contact with Western culture, familiarity with test materials, and conditions of testing affect the results;[97–99] (5) rural versus urban environment, educational level, and early nutrition can also affect general intellectual development, a phenomenon known as the deficit hypothesis.[100] Berry, however, emphasizes that one must accept that it is clever to do different things in different cultural systems, and if inferences about intelligence are made, the original observations must be based upon an adequate sample of what people are able to do in their own cultural system.[101] A similar point is made by Bernon:

We must try to discard the idea that intelligence (i.e. intelligence b) is a kind of universal faculty, a trait which is the same (apart from variations in amount) in all cultural groups. Clearly, it develops differently in different physical and cultural environments. It should be regarded as a name for all the various cognitive skills, which are developed in, and valued by, the group. In Western civilization it refers mainly to grasping relations and symbolic thinking, and this permeates to some extent all the abilities we show at school, at work, or in daily life. We naturally tend to evaluate the intelligence of other ethnic groups on the same criteria, though it would surely be more psychologically sound to recognize that such groups require, and stimulate, the growth of different mental as well as physical skills for coping with their particular environments, i.e., that they possess different intelligences.[102]

Culture and Management Accounting Environment Variables

Culture is an important variable affecting a country's management accounting environment. It has been argued that accounting is in fact determined by the culture of a given country.[103] The lack of consensus among different countries on what constitutes proper accounting methods because the purpose of accounting is cultural not technical.[104] Various approaches examining the impact of culture in the accounting environment have been taken.

1. One study examined the effects of a key attribute of national culture—individualism/collectivism—on employee preference for individual versus team-based performance measures and pay in a team-based work setting and examined employee resource expenditure decisions under different degrees of team-based performance measures and pay, when faced with a self versus team interest tradeoff.[105] The results of the laboratory experiment indicated that contrary to expectations the U.S. subjects rather than the Chinese subjects chose sure team-based performance when they perceived a higher level of task interdependence. The importance of these findings was stated as follows:

   These findings are significant because they suggest that difference[s] in work-related national culture may not be insurmountable obstacles to the import and export of management practices. Rather, individuals possess self-insight and resourcefulness and can take actions, including voluntarily placing restrictions on themselves, to adapt to the demands of new management practices and work environments.[106]

2. One study relied on the predictions of the Dual Concern Model on negotiator mixed motives to empirically examine the effects of accountability and performance evalu-

ation schemes on transfer pricing negotiation behavior and outcome in two cultural settings.[107] The Dual Concern Model predicts that two elements are available in a negotiating setting:

1st: Concern about others' outcomes as either high or low.

2nd: Concern about our outcomes as either high or low.

Four strategies may result from the combination of the two elements:

1: *In action* if both elements are low.

2: *Yielding* if element one is high and element two is low.

3: *Contending* if element one was low and element two was high.

4: *Problem solving* if both elements are higher. The results of the experiment providing empirical support for the effects of negotiator concern for self and for the other party in negotiation goal setting and negotiation outcomes are stated as follows.

When analyzed separately, high accountability and division-based performance evaluation scheme were limited to higher targeted profits but only firm-based performance evaluation was associated with higher joint profits. When their effects were confirmed, negotiators' concern for self (influenced by accountability) was positively moderated by their concern for the other party (influenced by performance evaluation scheme) to facilitate a case of convergence of interests where mutual efforts were exchanged in search of integrative (i.e., win-win) solutions.[108]

3. Based on the notion that differences in strategic approaches are shaped by context and culture, one study contrasted, through case studies, strategic decision-making styles in Britain, Germany, the United States, and Japan.[109] The examination of specific formal strategic and financial appraisal techniques, and subsequent control approaches, confirmed the longer-term strategic orientation of German and Japanese companies and our Anglo-American short-termism. It points to the difficulty of exporting or generalizing strategic styles. As stated by the authors:

The evidence there provides powerful support for those who point to the impact of national context and culture in establishing strategic management styles and financial approaches. In the absence of such understanding of context and culture, the U.S. styles cannot be assumed to translate appropriately to context as different as Germany and Japan.[110]

4. Labor cost is a major determinant of the competitiveness of firms in the global economy. Research to date reveals a wide range of compensation practices in different countries within the same industries.[111–115] These variations in compensation practices can be an important factor in firms' decisions on new investments on their production and/or distribution facilities, favoring countries in the lower compensation practices. An understanding of the international differences in compensation practices can be useful for multinational corporations in meeting employees' expectations about pay equity. Townsend et al.[116] show that the differences in pay policies being dependent on culture based on the cultural cluster model has some merits in segmenting countries into culturally related groups for purposes of understanding work values and the relationship of culture to those values; however, the author's theory fails to account for the intracultural differences that make every nation a specific subcultural entity.[117] Accordingly, Riahi-Belkaoui[118] examined the international differences in compensation practices and related these differences to cultural dimensions. The results sup-

ported the cultural determinism thesis in setting compensation practices and contributed practices. Basically, cultural difference in the level of compensation from one country to another is significant. The results show also that there are differences in the cost of labor between countries within a culture depending on the level of the cultural dimensions of individualism, uncertainty avoidance, and masculinity. The results refute the assertion that employment practices are only marginally affected by cultural affiliation.[119] This cultural determinism is not to be taken, however, as permanent. In the long run, people, irrespective of their culture, may be compelled to provide similar levels of compensation to comply with similar imperatives of industrialization.[120] The competing hypothesis, generally labeled the convergence hypothesis, argues for the convergence of managerial practices and stages of industrial development.[121] It calls for an investigation of the relationships between the changes in the level of compensation and changes in industrial development internationally. Another worthwhile avenue of research is to investigate the combined effect of cultural and economic variables on compensation practices internationally.

5. Manufacturing performance has been linked to culture. One school of thought maintains that the Asian firms' superior manufacturing performance was primarily attributable to the national culture of their employees and the design of management control based on that culture.[122-124] For example, Asian culture may be characterized as group rather than individual oriented, a collective approach leading to specific management approaches such as teams, participative decision making, and quality circles.[125] This raises the question of whether the noted Asian firms' superior manufacturing performance is caused by their management control systems, the national culture of their employees, or the interaction of these two factors. Accordingly, Chow et al.[126] provided a direct control system on manufacturing performance. The results of their experiment were consistent with cultural individualism and management controls having independent, but not interactive, effects on manufacturing performance.

6. The conduct of planning and control curtails information processing and information sharing.[127] Such open sharing of information is crucial to the process of:

   a. benchmarketing[128]

   b. managing the value chain[129]

   c. networking[130]

   d. total quality management[131]

   e. organizational learning[132]

   Both formal and informal mechanisms are involved in the open sharing of information among organizational members. Formal mechanisms do not differ drastically among cultures as they consist of conventional accounting information systems. Informal mechanisms that include interpersonal communications in the context of meetings and conventions, direct observations, and informal reports are likely to be affected by culture. In effect, Chow et al.[133] examined cultural factors that may facilitate or impede the sharing of information in the context of face-to-face meetings in Chinese as compared to Anglo-American organizations. The choice of the cultural groups was motivated by the three attributes assumed to be different between the Anglo-American and Chinese-based cultures:

   a. The individualism in the Anglo-American culture versus the collectivism in the Chinese counterpart.

b. The concern with maintaining face in the Chinese culture.

c. The importance of power distance in the Chinese culture, which is the degree to which people accept interpersonal inequality in power and the organizational institutionalization of such inequality.[134]

The results of Chow et al.'s study point to the focus on individual differences, individual assertiveness, and corporate culture in influencing informal information sharing in Australia, and the tradeoff between collective interests, respect in hierarchical statues, and concern with face in Taiwan.[135]

7. Various studies examined the impact of culture in budgeting practices. Hawkins[136] reported that U.S. firms encouraged greater participation from a larger percentage of division heads while preparing operational budgets, resorted to less long-range planning, and attached more importance to the use of accounting data in performance evaluation than their Japanese counterparts. The Japanese managers were also found to be more inclined to develop long-range budgets and resort to slack budgeting.[137] Some aspects of the budget control process are likely to be influenced by culture. They are: (1) communication and coordination processes resorted to in budget planning; (2) planning time horizons long range—long-range versus short-term planning; (3) structuring of budgetary processes in terms of formalized rules and procedures; (4) budget slack, or the extent to which slack is built into the budget; (5) controllability of budgets, or the extent to which managers are charged or credited only for such items as are within their control; and (6) budget performance evaluation time horizons—i.e., short-term and long-term evaluation time frames.[138] Ueno and Sekaran examined the influence of culture on these six aspects of budget control practices in the United States and Japan.[139] The results of their study indicate that the U.S. culture, while high on individualism, predisposes U.S. companies to use more communication and coordination, build more slack in the budget, and resort to short-term performance evaluations more than the Japanese counterparts. The verifications of the results are stated as follows:

All in all, there is strong indication that the individualism-collectivism dimension is a good predictor of budget planning practices and processes in the two cultures. How does this knowledge help managers of U.S. and Japanese companies as they engage in collaborative efforts? For one, managers in each culture will have a better understanding of why differences in preferences for communication and coordination patterns exist and the reason why short-term performance evaluation is desired in the U.S., but long-term evaluation is preferred in Japan. Such understanding will help managers in both cultures to be non-judgmental about the other set of managers and work through any needed adjustments in a non-evaluative and reasonable manner. The Japanese managers will tend also to be less suspicious when more slack is seen as being "padded" in the building of budgets in the U.S. With misunderstandings, misperceptions, and misinterpretations being considerably reduced, both parties can work together more amicably and effectively in their joint ventures.[140]

Participation has also generally been found to have an effect in the relation between budget-emphasis in superior evaluative style and subordinates' related attitudes. More specifically, it was generally hypothesized that subordinates would develop favorable predisposition to high budget emphasis evaluative styles only if they had participated in the budget construction.[141] Is this result generalizable across cultures? Harrison[142] hypothesized that participation's effect will be the same in low power distance/high individualism and high power distance/low individualism cultures, using respondent samples from Australia and Singapore as proxy nations. The findings show that the effects of participation on the relation between budget emphasis and superior evaluative study and the dependent variable of job-related tension and job satisfaction can be generalized across nations that have cultural dimensions in confirmation of high power distance/low individualism and low power distance/high individualism. As stated by the authors: "In particular, matching increasing levels of budget emphasis with increasing levels of participation was found to be associated with reduced job related tension in the part of the subordinates in both cultures, but not associated with job satisfaction in either culture."[143]

Frucot and Shearon[144] examined the impact of budgeting participation and locus of control on Mexican managerial performance and job satisfaction, where the locus of control classifies individuals as (1) externals, believing that events are controlled by fate, luck, chance, or powerful others, or (2) internals, believing that they have more control over events. The results were consistent with other findings on the positive impact of participation and locus of control on managerial performance; the impact of locus of control on managerial satisfaction was not significant, a reflection of an ostensible difference in culture. Another interesting result was that the effect of locus of control on the performance of high-level managers was significantly stronger than the impact on the performance of lower-level managers.

Various studies evaluated the impact of culture in various aspects of management control systems. First, Birnberg and Snodgrass [145] compared the perceptions of management control systems that are held by U.S. and Japanese workers. The findings are summarized as follows:

The overall findings are consistent with the view that the presence of a culture which is homogeneous and possesses the critical dimension of cooperation would lead to less emphasis being placed on the "enforcing" of management's wishes. In turn, a greater emphasis and resources can be spent on communicating across organizational levels and directing information to the proper individual or work group. The Japanese firms are able to do this because in the U.S. a significant proportion of the resources and effort embodied in the accounting information (and control) system is directed toward achieving behavioral congruence through bureaucratic rules and incentive systems. Those aspects of the control system [were shown] not to be necessary in a homogeneous culture with positive work attributes.[146]

Second, Chow et al.[147] investigated the effects of national culture on firms' design of and employees' preference for management controls. The seven management controls examined included (a) decentralization, (b) structuring of activities, (c) participative budgeting, (d) standard tightness, (e) participative performance evaluation, (f) controllability filters, and (g) performance-contingent financial rewards. The results were generally consistent with national culture affecting firms' design of and employees' preference for the seven management controls. Third, a review of the current state of cross-cultural research in management control systems design identified the four following major weaknesses:

(i) a failure to consider the totality of the cultural domain in theoretical exposition, (ii) a tendency to consider explicitly the differential intensity of cultural norms and values across nations, (iii) a tendency to treat culture simplistically both in the form of its representation as a limited set of aggregate dimensions, and in the assumption of a uniformity and unidimensionality of those dimensions; and (iv) an excessive reliance on the value dimensional conceptualization of culture, which has produced a highly restricted conception and focus on culture, and placed critical limits on the extent of understanding derived from resource to date.[148]

CONCLUSION

The essence of cultural relativism in management accounting is the presence of a cultural process that is assumed to guide the judgement/decision process in management accounting. The model in this chapter postulates that culture, through its components, elements, and dimensions, dictates the organizational structures adopted, the microorganizational behavior, the management accounting environment, and the cognitive functioning of individuals faced with a management accounting phenomenon.

NOTES

1. Adam Smith, *An Inquiry into the Nature and Causes of the Wealth of Nations* (London: J. Maynard, 1811).

2. Adam Ferguson, *An Eye on the History of Civil Society* (New York: Garland, 1971).

3. Anne Robert Jacques Turgot, *Reflections on the Formation and Distribution of Rides* (New York: A.M. Welly, 1963).

4. Denis Diderot, *Pensees Philosophiques* (Geneva: E. Droz, 1950).

5. Auguste Comte, *A General View of Positivism* (London: Rutledge, 1907).

6. Georg Wilhelm Friedrich Hegel, *Lectures on the Philosophy of World History: Introduction* (New York: Cambridge University Press, 1975).

7. Lewis Henry Morgan, *Ancient Society* (New York: Holt, Rinehart & Winston, 1877).

8. Ibid.

9. Comte, *General View of Positivism.*

10. Thomas R. Malthus, *An Essay on the Principle of Population* (London: T. Bensley, 1803).

11. Herbert Spencer, *Education: Intellectual, Moral and Physical* (New York: D. Appleton, 1961).

12. Charles Darwin, *The Descent of Man* (New York: H.M. Caldwell, 1874).

13. Karl Marx, *Capital* (Chicago: Encyclopedia Britannica, 1955).

14. Friedrich Engels, *The Origin of the Family, Private Property and the State* (New York: International, 1979).

15. Franz Boas, *Anthropology and Modern Life* (New York: W.W. Norton, 1928).

16. R.J. Earner, "Population Pressure and Ten Social Evolutions of Agriculturalists," *South Western Journal of Anthropology* 26 (1970): 67–86.

17. Bronislaw Malinowski, *Argonauts of the Western Pacific* (New York: Dutton, 1950).

18. A.R. Radcliffe-Brown, *Structure and Function in Primitive Society* (London: Cohen & West, 1961).

19. Ruth Benedict, *Patterns of Culture* (New York: Houghton Mifflin, 1934).

20. Margaret Mead, *Coming of Age in Samoa: A Psychological Study of Primitive Youth for Western Civilization* (New York: Morrow, 1961).

21. Leslie White, *The Science of Culture* (New York: Grove Press, 1949).

22. Ibid., 368–69.

23. In the words of Karl Marx: "The mode of production in material life determines the general character of the social, political and spiritual processes of life. It is not the consciousness of men that determines their existence, but on the contrary, their social existence determines their consciousness" (*A Contribution to the Critique of Political Economy* [New York: International, 1970], 21).

24. Claude Levi-Strauss, *Le Cru and Le Cult* (Paris: Pbon, 1964).

25. White, *Science of Culture.*

26. Simcha Ronen, *Comparative and Multinational Management* (New York: Wiley, 1986), 20–27.

27. G.P. Murdock, "Common Denominator of Cultures," *The Science of Man in the World Crises*, ed. R. Linten (New York: Columbia University Press, 1945), 12–42.

28. G.W. Allport, P.E. Vernon, and Q. Lindzey, *A Study of Values* (Boston: Houghton Mifflin, 1960).

29. C. Morris, *Varieties of Human Value* (Chicago: University of Chicago Press, 1956).

30. F.R. Kluckhohn and F. Strodtbeck, *Variations in Value Orientations* (Westport, CT: Greenwood Press, 1961).

31. I. Sarnoff, *Society with Tears* (Secaucus, NJ: Citadel Press, 1966).

32. J. Rokeach, *The Nature of Human Values* (New York: Free Press, 1966).

33. P.R. Harris and R.T. Moran, *Managing Cultural Differences* (Houston: Gruff, 1979).

34. Paul Bohannan, "Rethinking Culture: A Project for Current Anthropologists," *Current Anthropology* 14/4 (October 1973): 357–65.

35. Harris and Moran, *Managing Cultural Differences*, 8.

36. Marvin Harris, *Culture, Man and Nature* (New York: Thomas Y. Crowell, 1971), 141.

37. Carol R. Ember and Melvin Ember, *Cultural Anthropology*, 3d ed. (Englewood Cliffs, NJ: Prentice-Hall, 1981), 32.

38. Marvin Harris, *Cows, Rigs, Wars and Witches: The Riddles of Culture* (New York: Vintage Books, 1974).

39. Linda Smirich, "Concepts of Culture and Organizational Analysis," *Administrative Science Quarterly* 28 (1983): 339–58.

40. B. Malinowski, *A Scientific Theory of Culture* (Chapel Hill: University of North Carolina Press, 1944).

41. A.R. Radcliffe-Brown, *Structure and Function in Primitive Society* (New York: Free Press, 1968).

42. Ward H. Goodenough, *Culture, Language and Society* (Reading, MA: Addison-Wesley, 1971).

43. Clifford Geertz, *The Interpretation of Cultures* (New York: Basic Books, 1973).

44. Claude Levi-Strauss, *Structural Anthropology* (Chicago: University of Chicago Press, 1983).

45. E.T. Hall, *Beyond Culture* (Garden City, NY: Anchor Books, 1977), 16–17.

46. J. Child, "Culture, Contingency and Capitalism in the Cross-National Study of Organizations," in *Research in Organizational Behavior*, Vol. 3, eds. L.L. Cummings and B.M. Staw (Greenwich, CT: JAI Press, 1981), 303–56.

47. G. Hofstede, *Culture's Consequences: International Differences in Work-Related Values* (Beverly Hills, CA: Sage, 1980).

48. Uma Sekaran and Carol R. Snodgrass, "A Model for Examining Organizational Effectiveness Cross-Culturally," *Advances in International Comparative Management*, Vol. 2 (Greenwich, CT: JAI Press, 1986), 213.

49. Ven Terpstra, *The Cultural Environment of International Business* (Cincinnati: South Western, 1978), xvii.

50. Ibid., xxii.

51. G. Hofstede, "Dimensions of National Cultures in Fifty Countries and Three Regions," in *Explications in Cross-Cultural Psychology*, ed. J.B. Deregowski, S. Dziuarawiec, and R.S. Annis (Lise, The Netherlands: Soviets & Zeilinger, 1983) 335–55.

52. Child, "Culture, Contingency and Capitalism in the Cross-National Study of Organizations," 313.

53. The argument that context-structure relations will be stable across societies is stated as follows: "This hypothesis implicitly rests on the theory that there are imperative, or causal relationships, from the resources of customers, of employees, of materials and finance, etc., and of operating technology of an organization, to its structure, which take effect whatever the surrounding societal differences" (pp. 63–64), in D.J. Hickson et al., "The Culture-Free Context of Organizational Structure: A Tri-National Comparison," *Sociology* 8 (1974).

54. D.J. Hickson, et al., "Grounds for Comparative Organizational Theory: Quicksands or Hard Core?" in C.J. Lammers and D.I. Hickson, eds., *Organizations Alike and Unlike* (London; Rutledge & Kegan Paul, 1979), chap. 2.

55. J.H.K. Inkson, D.J. Hickson, and D.S. Pugh, "Administrative Reduction of Variance in Organization and Behavior: A Comparative Study," in *Organizational Behavior in Its Context: The Aston Programme III*, ed. D.S. Pugh and R.L. Payne (Farnborough, Hants: Sasoon House, 1977), chap. 2.

56. A. Sorge, "Cultured Organization" (discussion paper 80–56, Berlin: International Institute of Management, 1980).

57. Ibid.

58. Sekaran and Snodgrass, "Model for Examining Organizational Effectiveness Cross-Culturally," 216–20.

59. Rabi S. Bhagat and Sara I. McQuaid, "Role of Subjective Culture in Organizations: A Review and Directions for Future Research," *Journal of Applied Psychology Monograph* (October 1982): 653–85.

60. H.A. Witkin et al., *Psychological Differentiation* (Potomac, MD: Erlbaum, 1974).

61. H.A. Witkin and J.W. Berry, "Psychological Differentiation in a Cross-Cultural Perspective," *Journal of Cross-Cultural Psychology* 6 (1975): 4–87.

62. L.W. Gruenfeld, "Field Dependence and Field Independence as a Framework for the Study of Task and Social Orientations in Organizational Leadership," in *Management Research: A Cross-Cultural Perspective*, ed. D. Graves (Amsterdam, The Netherlands: Eisener North Holland Biomedical Press, 1973).

63. A. Inkeles and D.H. Smith, *Becoming Modern: Individual Change in Six Developing Countries* (Boston: Harvard University Press, 1974).

64. Simcha Ronen and Oded Shenkar, "Clustering Countries on Attitudinal Dimensions: A Review and Synthesis," *Academy of Management Review* 10/3 (1985): 435–54.

65. Peter Blunt, "Techno and Ethnocentrism in Organization Studies: Comment and Speculation Prompted by Ronen and Shenkar," *Academy of Management Review* 11/4 (1986): 857–59.

66. J.W. Atkinson, "Motivational Determinants of Risk Taking Behavior," *Psychological Review* 64 (1957): 359–72.

67. D.C. McClelland, *The Achieving Society* (Princeton, NJ: Van Nostrand, 1961).

68. P.C. Smith, L.M. Kendal, and C.L. Hulin, *The Measurement of Satisfaction in Work and Retirement: A Strategy for the Study of Attitudes* (Chicago: Rand McNally, 1965).

69. J.C. Adam, "Toward an Understanding of Inequity," *Journal of Abnormal and Social Psychology* 67 (1963): 422–36.

70. A. Maslow, *Motivation and Personality* (New York: Harper & Row, 1954).

71. F. Sahili, "Determinants of Achievement Motivation for Women in Developing Countries," *Journal of Vocational Behavior* 14 (1974): 297–305.

72. 167. H. Soliman, "Motivation-Hygiene Theory of Job Satisfaction: An Empirical Investigation and an Attempt to Reconcile Both the One- and Two-Factor Theories of Job Attitudes," *Journal of Applied Psychology* 54 (1970): 452–61.

73. Ibid.

74. F. Herzberg, B. Mausner, and B. Snyderman, *The Motivation to Work* (New York: Wiley, 1959).

75. C.L. Hulin and M.R. Blood, "Job Enlargement, Individual Differences and Worker Responses," *Psychological Bulletin* 69 (1968): 41–55.

76. M. Cole, J. Gray, J. Glick, and D. Sharp, *The Cultural Context of Learning and Thinking* (New York: Bane Books, 1971).

77. B.B. Lloyd, *Perception and Cognition: A Cross-Cultural Perspective* (Middlesex, England: Penguin, 1972).

78. H.C. Triandis, R.S. Malpass, and A.R. Davidson, "Psychology and Culture," *Annual Review of Psychology* 24 (1973): 356.

79. J. Kagan, M.M. Haith, and F.J. Morrison, "Memory and Meaning in Two Cultures," *Child Development* 44 (1973): 356.

80. Cole et al., *Cultural Context of Learning and Thinking*.

81. J. Goodnow, "Problems in Research on Culture and Thought," in *Studies in Cognitive Developments*, ed. D. Ekland and J. Flavell (New York: Oxford University Press, 1969).

82. P.M. Greenfield, "Comparing Dimensional Categorization in Natural and Artificial Contents: A Developmental Study among the Zimacantecos of Mexico," *Journal of Social Psychology* 93 (1974): 157–71.

83. A.C. Mundy-Castle, "An Experimental Study of Prediction among Ghancian Children," *Journal of Social Psychology* 73 (1967): 161–68.

84. M. Cole, J. Gray, and J. Glick, "Some Experimental Studies of Kjello Quantitative Behavior," *Psychonomic Monographs Supplement* 2 (1968): 173–90.

85. D.A. Wagner, "The Development of Short-Term and Incidental Memory: A Cross-Cultural Study," *Child Development* 45 (1974): 389–96.

86. S. Scribner, "Development Aspects of Categorized Recall in a West African Society," *Cognitive Psychology* 6 (1974): 475–94.

87. J.A. Meacham, "Patterns of Memory Abilities in Two Cultures," *Developmental Psychology* 11/1 (1975): 50–53.

88. P.R. Dasen, "Cross-Cultural Piagetian Research: A Summary," *Journal of Cross-Cultural Psychology* 3 (1972): 23–39.

89. P.R. Dasen, "The Influence of Ecology, Culture and European Contact in Cognitive Development in Australian Aborigines," in *Culture and Cognition: Readings in Cross-Cultural Psychology*, ed. J. Berry and P. Dasen (London: Methuen, 1974).

90. P.R. Dasen, "Concrete Operational Development in Three Cultures," *Journal of Cross-Cultural Psychology* 6/2 (1975): 156–72.

91. T. Gladwin, *East Is a Big Bird* (Cambridge, MA.: Harvard University Press, 1970).

92. J. Littlejohn, "Cultural Relationism," *Anthropological Quarterly* 36, (1963): 1–17.

93. H.A. Witkin et al., *Psychological Differentiation* (New York: Wiley, 1962).

94. S. Biesheuvel, "The Nature of Intelligence: Some Practical Implications of Its Measurement," in *Culture and Cognition: Readings in Cross-Cultural Psychology*, ed. J.B. Jeffrey (London: Methuen, 1974), 221.

95. A.G.J. Cryrs, "African Intelligence: A Critical Survey of Cross-Cultural Intelligence Research in Africa South of the Sahara," *Journal of Social Psychology* 57 (1962): 283–301.

96. S. Biesheuvel, "Psychological Tests and Their Applications to Non-European People," in *The Yearbook of Education*, ed. J.B. Jeffrey (London: Evans, 1949).

97. E.T. Abiola, "The Nature of Intelligence in Nigerian Children," *Teacher Education* 6 (1965): 37–58.

98. J.M. Faverge and J.C. Falmagne, "On the Interpretation in Intercultural Psychology: A Page Written in Recognition of the Work Done in This Field by Dr. S. Biesheuvel," *Psychologia Africana* 9 (1962): 22–36.

99. P.E. Vernon, "Administration of Group Intelligence Tests to East African Pupils," *British Journal of Educational Psychology* 37 (1967): pt. 3, 251–82.

100. M. Cole and J. Bruna, "Cultural Differences and Influences about Psychological Processes," *American Psychologist* 26 (1971): 867–76.

101. J.W. Berry, "Radical Cultural Relativism and the Concept of Intelligence," in *Culture and Cognition: Readings in Cross-Cultural Psychology*, eds. J. Berry and P. Dasen (London: Methuen, 1974).

102. P.E. Bernon, *Intelligence and Cultural Environment* (London: Methuen, 1969), 10.

103. William, J. Violet, "The Development of International Accounting Standards: An Anthropological Perspective," *International Journal of Accounting Education and Research* (Spring 1983): 1–13.

104. Geert Hofstede, "The Cultural Contact of Accounting," in *Accounting and Culture*, ed. B.B. Cushing (Sarasota, FL: American Accounting Association, 1987), 1–11.

105. Vidya N. Awasthi, Chee W. Chow and Anne Wu, "Performance Measure and Resource Expenditure Choices in a Teamwork Environment: The Effects of National Culture," *Management Accounting Research* 9 (1998): 119–138.

106. Ibid., 121.

107. Chris W. Chan, "Transfer Pricing Negotiation Outcomes and the Impact of Negotiation Mixed-Motives and Culture: Empirical Evidence from the U.S. and Australia," *Management Accounting Research* 9 (1998): 139–61.

108. Ibid., 138.

109. Chris Carr and Cyril Tomkins, "Content, Culture and the Role of the Finance Function in Strategic Decisions: A Cognitive Analysis of Britain, Germany, the U.S.A. and Japan," *Management Accounting Research* 9 (1998): 213–39).

110. Ibid., 232.

111. R. Tung, "Patterns of Motication in Chinese Industrial Enterprises," *Academy of Management Review* 6, no. 3 (1981): 69–75.

112. M. White, *Payment Systems in Britain* (Alderhot, UK: Gaver, 1981).

113. N. Hashimoto and J. Raisian, "Employment Tenure and Earnings Profiles in Japan and the United States," *American Economic Review* (September 1985): 721–35.

114. J. Nelson and J. Reeder, "Labor Relations in China," *California Management Review* 27 no. 4 (1985): 13–32.

115. A. Bowey and R. Terope, *Payment Systems and Productivity* (New York: St. Martin's, 1986).

116. A.M. Townsend, K.D. Scott, and S.E. Markham, "An Examination of Country and Culture-Based Differences in Compensation Practices," *Journal of International Business Studies* 211, no. 4 (1990): 667–78.

117. S. Ronen and O. Shankar, "Clustering Countries in Additional Dimensions: A Review and Synthesis," *Academy of Management Review* 10 (1985): 435–54.

118. Ahmed Riahi-Belkaoui, "Cultural Determinism and Compensation Practices," *International Journal of Commerce and Management* 2, no. 4 (1994): 76–83.

119. A. Neghandi, "Cross-Cultural Studies: Too Many Conclusions," in *Modern Organizational Theory*, ed. A. Neghandi (Ohio: Kent, 1975).

120. L. Kelly, A. Whatley, and R. Worthley, "Assessing the Effects of Culture on Managerial Attitudes: A Three Culture Test," *Journal of International Business Studies* (Summer 1987): 17–31.

121. F. Harlison and C.A. Myers, *Management in the Industrial World* (New York: McGraw-Hill, 1959).

122. R. Cole, *Work Nobility and Participation: A Comparative Study of American and Japanese Industry* (Berkeley: University of California Press, 1979).

123. R. Pascale and A. Athos, *The Art of Japanese Management* (New York: Simon & Schuster, 1981).

124. W. Ouchi, *Theory 2: How American Companies Can Meet the Japanese Challenge* (Reading, MA: Addison-Wesley, 1981).

125. J. Lincoln and K. McBride, "Japanese Industrial Organization in Comparative Perspective," *Annual Review of Sociology* 10 (1987): 49–61.

126. Chee W. Chow, M.D. Shields, and Y.K. Chan, "The Effects of Management Controls and National Culture on Manufacturing Performance: An Experimental Investigation," *Accounting Organizations and Society* 16, no. 3 (1991): 209–26.

127. N.B. Macintosh, *Management Accounting and Control Systems* (New York: Wiley, 1994).

128. M. Smith, *New Tools for Management Accountants* (Melbourne: Longman Professional Publishing, 1994), 72.

129. A.J. Nanni, Jr., J.A. Dixon, and T.E. Vollman, "Integrated Performance Measurement: Management Accounting to Support the New Manufacturing Realities," *Journal of Management Accounting Research* 4 (1992): 3.

130. G., Fairthough, "Organizing for Innovation: Components, Competencies, and Networks," *Long Range Planning* 27 (1994): 85.

131. R. Chenhall, "Contemporary Performance Measurement," *Accounting Communique* 39, (1992): 4.

132. D.A. Levinthal and J.G. March, "The Myopia of Learning," *Strategic Management Journal* 14 (1993): 96.

133. Chee W. Chow, Craeme L. Harrison, Jill L. McKinnon, and Anne Wu, "Cultural Influences on Informal Information Sharing in Chinese and Anglo-American Organizations: An Exploratory Study," *Accounting, Organizations and Society* 24 (1999): 561–82.

134. Ibid., 564.

135. Ibid., 561.

136. C.E. Hawkins, *A Comparative Study of the Management Accounting Practices of Individual Companies in the United States and Japan* (Ann Arbor, MI: University Microfilms, 1983).

137. L. Daley, J. Jimbalvo, G.L. Sundem, and Y. Kondo, "Attitudes toward Financial Control Systems in the United States and Japan," *Journal of International Business Studies* (Fall 1985): 91–110.

138. S. Ueno and U. Sekaran, "The Influence of Culture in Budget Control Practices in the USA and Japan: An Empirical Study," *Journal of International Business Studies* 23–24, (1992): 660–61.

139. Ibid.

140. Ibid., 672.

141. P. Brownell, "Participation in the Budgeting Process: When It Works and When It Doesn't," *Journal of Accounting Literature* 7 (1982): 124–53.

142. G.L. Harrison, "The Cross-Cultural Generalizability of the Relation between Participation, Budget Emphasis and Job Related Attitudes," *Accounting Organizations and Society* 17, no. 1 (1992): 1–15.

143. Ibid., 13.

144. Veronique Frucot and Winston T. Shearon. "Budgetary Participation, Locus of Control, and Mexican Managerial Performance and Job Satisfaction," *The Accounting Review* (January 1991): 80–99.

145. Jacob G. Birnberg and Coral Snodgrass, "Culture and Control: A Field Study," *Accounting, Organizations and Society* 13 (1998): 447–64.

146. Ibid., 460.

147. Chee W. Chow, Michael D. Shields, and Anne Wu, "The Importance of National Culture in the Design of and Preference for Management Controls for Multi-National Operations," *Accounting, Organizations and Society* 24 (1999): 441–61.

148. Graeme Harrison and Jill McKinnon, "Cross-Cultural Research in Management Control Systems Design: A Review of the Current State," *Accounting, Organizations and Society* 24 (1999): 483.

SELECTED BIBLIOGRAPHY

Acheson, J. "Accounting Concepts and Economic Opportunities in a Tarascon Village: Emic and Etic Views." *Human Organization* (Spring 1972): 83–91.

Adam, J.C. "Toward an Understanding of Inequity." *Journal of Abnormal and Social Psychology* 67 (1963): 422–36.

Adler, Nancy. "A Typology of Management Studies Involving Culture." *Journal of International Business Studies* (Fall 1983): 24–47.

Allport, G.W., P.E. Vernon, and Q. Lindzey. *A Study of Values*. Boston: Houghton Mifflin, 1960.

Atkinson, J.W. "Motivational Determinants of Risk Taking Behavior." *Psychological Review* 64 (1957): 359–420.

Belkaoui, A. "Cultural Determinism and Professional Self-Regulation in Accounting." *Research in Accounting Regulation*. Forthcoming.

———. "Managerial, Academic and Professional Influences and Disclosure Adequacy: For Empirical Investigation." *Advances in International Accounting*. Forthcoming.

———. "Is Disclosure Adequacy a Cultural or Technical Purpose?" Discussion paper, College of Business Administration, University of Illinois at Chicago, 1989.

———. *The New Environment in International Accounting*. Westport, CT: Greenwood Press, 1988.

———. *International Accounting*. Westport, CT: Greenwood Press, 1985, chap. 2.

———. "Economic, Political and Civil Indicators and Reporting and Disclosure Adequacy: Empirical Investigations." *Journal of Accounting and Public Policy* (Fall 1983): 16–23.

Belkaoui, A., A. Kahl, and J. Peyrard. "Informational Needs of Financial Analysts: An International Comparison." *International Journal of Accounting Education and Research* (Fall 1977): 19–27.

Benedict, Ruth. *Patterns of Culture*. New York: Houghton Mifflin, 1934.

Berry, J.W. "Introduction to Methodology." In *Handbook of Cross-Cultural Psychology*, vol. 2, ed. H.C. Triandis and J.W. Berry. Boston: Allyn & Bacon, 1980.

———. "Radical Cultural Relativism and the Concept of Intelligence." In *Culture and Cognition: Readings in Cross-Cultural Psychology*, ed. J. Berry and P. Dasen. London: Methuen, 1974.

———. "On the Cross-Cultural Comparability." *International Journal of Psychology* 4/2 (1969): 119–28.

Bhagat, Rabi S., and Sara J. McQuaid. "Role of Subjective Culture in Organizations: A Review and Directions for Future Research." *Journal of Applied Psychology Monograph* (October 1982): 653–85.

Biesheuvel, S. "The Nature of Intelligence: Some Practical Implications of Its Measurements." In *Culture and Cognition: Readings in Cross-Cultural Psychology*. London: Methuen, 1974.

———. "Psychological Tests and Their Applications to Non-European People." In *The Yearbook of Education*, ed. J.B. Jeffrey. London: Evans, 1949.

Blunt, Peter. "Techno and Ethnocentrism in Organization Studies: Comment and Speculation Prompted by Ronen and Shenkar." *Academy of Management Review* 11144 (1986): 857–59.

Boas, Franz. *Anthropology and Modern Life*. New York: W.W. Norton, 1928.

Bohannan, Paul. "Rethinking Culture: A Project for Current Anthropologists." *Current Anthropology* 1414 (October 1973): 357–67.

Chang, L.S., and K.S. Most. "An International Comparison of Investor Uses of Financial Statements." *International Journal of Accounting Education and Research* (Fall 1981): 43–60.

Chevalier, G. "Should Accounting Practices Be Universal?" *Chartered Accountant Magazine* (July 1977): 47–50.

Child, J. "Culture, Contingency and Capitalism in the Cross-National Study of Organizations." In *Research in Organizational Behavior*, vol. 3, ed. L.L. Cummings and B.M. Staw. Greenwich, CT: JAI Press, 1981, 303–56.

Cleary, T.A., and T.L. Hilton. "An Investigation of Item Bias." *Educational and Psychological Measurement* 28 (1968): 61–75.

Cole, M., and J. Bruna. "Cultural Differences and Influences about Psychological Processes." *American Psychologist* 26 (1971): 867–76.

Cole, M., J. Gray, J. Glick, and D. Sharp. *The Cultural Context of Learning and Thinking*. New York: Bane Books, 1971.

———. "Some Experimental Studies of Kjello Quantitative Behavior." *Psychonomic Monographs Supplement* 2 (1968): 173–90.

Comte, Auguste. *A General View of Positivism*. London: Routledge, 1907.

Cronbach, L.J., G.C. Gleser, H. Nanda, and N. Rajaratnam. *The Dependability of Behavioral Measurements*. New York: Wiley, 1972.

Cronbach, L.J., and P.E. Meehl. "Contrast Validity in Psychological Tests." *Psychological Bulletin* 52 (1955): 281–302.

Cryrs, A.G.J. "African Intelligence: A Critical Survey of Cross-Cultural Intelligence Research in Africa South of the Sahara." *Journal of Social Psychology* 57 (1962): 283–301.

Da Costa, R.C., J.C. Bourgeois, and W.M. Lawson. "A Classification of International Financial Accounting Practices." *International Journal of Accounting Education and Research* (Spring 1978): 73–85.

Darwin, Charles. *The Descent of Man*. New York: H.M. Caldwell, 1874.

Dasen, P.R. "Concrete Operational Development in Three Cultures." *Journal of Cross-Cultural Psychology* 6/2 (1975): 156–72.

———. "The Influence of Ecology, Culture and European Contact in Cognitive Development in Australian Aborigines." In *Culture and Cognition: Readings in Cross-Cultural Psychology*, ed. J. Berry and P. Dasen. London: Methuen, 1981.

———. "Cross-Cultural Piagetian Research: A Summary." *Journal of Cross-Cultural Psychology* 3 (1972): 23–39.

Diderot, Denis. *Pensees Philosophiques*. Geneva: E. Droz, 1950.

Ember, Carol R., and Melvin Ember. *Cultural Anthropology*. 3d ed. Englewood Cliffs, NJ: Prentice-Hall, 1981.

Engels, Friedrich. *The Origin of the Family, Private Property and the State*. New York: International, 1979.

Faverge, J.M., and J.C. Falmagne. "On the Interpretation in Intercultural Psychology: A Page Written in Recognition of the Work Done in This Field by Dr. S. Biesheuvel." *Psychologia Africana* 9 (1962): 22–36.

Fons, J.R., and Ype H. Poortinga. "Cross-Cultural Generalization and Universality." *Journal of Cross-Cultural Psychology* (December 1982): 387–408.

Frake, C.O. "Cultural Ecology and Ethnography." In *Language and Cultural Description; Essays by Charles O. Frake*, ed. S.A. Dil. Stanford, CA: Stanford University Press, 1980, 18–25.

Frank, W.G. "An Empirical Analysis of International Accounting Principles." *Journal of Accounting Research* (Fall 1979): 593–605.

Geertz, Clifford. *The Interpretation of Cultures*. New York: Basic Books, 1973.

———. "The Impact of the Concept of Culture on the Concept of Man." In *New Views on the Nature of Man*, ed. J.R. Platt. Chicago: University of Chicago Press, 1965.

Gladwin, T. *East Is a Big Bird*. Cambridge, MA: Harvard University Press, 1970.

Goodenough, Ward H. *Culture, Language and Society*. Reading, MA: Addison-Wesley, 1971.

Goodnow, J. "Problems in Research on Culture and Thought." In *Studies in Cognitive Developments*, ed. D. Ekland and J. Flavell. New York: Oxford University Press, 1969.

Goodrich, P.S. "Accounting and Political Systems." Discussion paper no. 109, School of Economic Studies, University of Leeds, 1982.

Gray, S.J. "Towards a Theory of Cultural Influence on the Development of Accounting Systems Internationally." *ABACUS* (March 1988): 1–15.

Greenfield, P.M. "Comparing Dimensional Categorization in Natural and Artificial Contents: A Developmental Study among the Zimacantecos of Mexico." *Journal of Social Psychology* 93 (1974): 157–71.

Gruenfeld, L.W. "Field Dependence and Field Independence as a Framework for the Study of Task and Social Orientations in Organizational Leadership." In *Management Research: A Cross-Cultural Perspective*, ed. D. Graves. Amsterdam, The Netherlands: Eisener North Holland Biomedical Press, 1973.

Hall, E.T. *Beyond Culture*. Garden City, NY: Anchor Books, 1977.

Harner, R.J. "Population Pressure and Ten Social Evolutions of Agriculturalists." *South Western Journal of Anthropology* 26 (1970): 67–86.

Harris, Marvin. *Cultural Materialism: The Struggle for a Science of Culture*. New York: Random House, 1979.

———. *Cows, Rigs, Wars and Witches: The Riddles of Culture*. New York: Vintage Books, 1974.

———. *Culture, Man and Nature*. New York: Thomas Y. Crowell, 1971.

Harris, P.R., and R.T. Moran. *Managing Cultural Differences*. Houston: Gruff, 1979.

Hegel, Georg Wilhelm Friedrich. *Lectures on the Philosophy of World History: Introduction*. New York: Cambridge University Press, 1975.

Herzberg, F., B. Mausner, and B. Snyderman. *The Motivation to Work*. New York: Wiley, 1959.

Hickson, D.J., C.R. Hinings, C.J. McMillan, and J.P. Schmitter. "The Culture-Free Context of Organizational Structure: A Tri-National Comparison." *Sociology* 8 (1974): 59–80.

Hickson, D.J., C.J. McMillan, K. Azumi, and P. Horvath. "Grounds for Comparative Organizational Theory: Quicksands or Hard Core?" In *Organizations Alike and Unlike*, ed. C.J. Lammers and D.J. Hickson. London: Rutledge and Kegan Paul, 1979, chap. 2.

Hofstede, Geert. "The Cultural Context of Accounting." In *Accounting and Culture*, ed. B.E. Cushing. Sarasota, FL: American Accounting Association, 1987, 1–11.

———. "Dimensions of National Cultures in Fifty Countries and Three Regions." In

Explications in Cross-Cultural Psychology, ed. J.B. Deregowski, S. Dziuarawiec, and R.S. Amis. Lisse, The Netherlands: Soviets and Zeilinger, 1983, 335–55.

————. *Culture's Consequences: International Differences in Work-Related Values*. Beverly Hills, CA: Sage, 1980.

Hulin C.L., and M.R. Blood. "Job Enlargement, Individual Differences and Worker Responses." *Psychological Bulletin* 69 (1968): 41–55.

Inkson, J.H.K., D.J. Hickson, and D.S. Pugh. "Administrative Reduction of Variance in Organization and Behavior: A Comparative Study." In *Organizational Behavior in Its Context: The Aston Programme III*, ed. D.S. Pugh and R.L. Payne. Farnborough, Hants: Sasoon House, 1977, chap. 2.

Irvine, S.H., and W.K. Carroll. "Testing and Assessment across Cultures: Issues in Methodology and Theory." In *Handbook of Cross-Cultural Psychology*, vol. 2, ed. H.C. Triandis and J.W. Berry. Boston: Allyn & Bacon, 1980.

Jaggi, B.L. "Impact of Cultural Environment on Financial Disclosure." *International Journal of Accounting Education and Research* (Spring 1982): 75–84.

Kagan, J., M.M. Haith, and F.J. Morrison. "Memory and Meaning in Two Cultures." *Child Development* 44 (1973): 356.

Kluckhohn, F.R., and F. Strodtbeck. *Variations in Value Orientations*. Westport, CT: Greenwood Press, 1961.

Lennie, R.A. *Culture, Behavior and Personality*. Chicago: Aldine, 1973.

Levi-Strauss, Claude. *Structural Anthropology*. Chicago: University of Chicago Press, 1983.

————. *Le Cru and Le Cult*. Paris: Pbon, 1964.

Littlejohn, J. "Cultural Relativism." *Anthropological Quarterly* 36 (1963): 1–17.

Lloyd, B.B. *Perception and Cognition: A Cross-Cultural Perspective*. Middlesex, England: Penguin, 1972.

Lonner, Walter J. "The Search for Psychological Universals." In *Handbook of Cross-Cultural Psychology*, ed. H.C. Triandis and W.W. Lambert. Boston: Allyn & Bacon, 1980, 46, 147–48.

McClelland, D.C. *The Achieving Society*. Princeton, NJ: Van Nostrand, 1961.

Malinowski, Bronislaw. *Argonauts of the Western Pacific*. New York: Dutton, 1950.

————. *A Scientific Theory of Culture*. Chapel Hill: University of North Carolina Press, 1944.

Malthus, Thomas R. *An Essay on the Principle of Population*. London: T. Bensley, 1803.

Marx, Rad. *A Contribution to the Critique of Political Economy*. New York: International, 1970.

————. *Capital*. Chicago: Encyclopedia Britannica, 1955.

Meacham, J.A. "Patterns of Memory Abilities in Two Cultures." *Developmental Psychology* 11/1 (1975): 50–53.

Mead, Margaret. *Coming of Age in Samoa: A Psychological Study of Primitive Youth for Western Civilization*. New York: Morrow, 1961.

Mierles, A., and D.H. Smith. *Becoming Modern: Individual Change in Six Developing Countries*. Boston: Harvard University Press, 1974.

Monroe, R.L., and R.H. Monroe. "Perspectives Suggested by Anthropological Data." In *Handbook of Cross-Cultural Psychology*, ed. H.C. Triandis and W.W. Lambert. Boston: Allyn & Bacon, 1980.

Morey, Nancy C., and Fred Luthans. "An Emic Perspective and Ethnoscience Methods for Organizational Research." *Academy of Management Review* 9/1 (1984): 27–36.

Morgan, Lewis Hay. *Ancient Society*. New York: Holt, Rinehart & Winston. 1877.

Morris, C. *Varieties of Human Value*. Chicago: University of Chicago Press. 1956.

Mueller, C.W. *International Classification of Financial Reporting*. New York: Croom Helm, 1984.

Mundy-Castle, A.C. "An Experimental Study of Prediction among Ghancian Children." *Journal of Social Psychology* 73 (1967): 161–68.

Murdock, G.P. "Common Denominator of Cultures." In *The Science of Man in the World Crises*, ed. R. Linten. New York: Columbia University Press, 1945, 12–22.

Nair, R.D., and W.G. Frank. "The Impact of Disclosure and Measurement Practices on International Accounting Classifications." *The Accounting Review* (July 1980): 426–35.

Nobes, C.W. *International Classification of Financial Reporting*. New York: Croom Helm, 1984.

———. "A Judgmental International Classification of Financial Reporting Practices." *Journal of Business Finance and Accounting* (Spring 1983): 1–19.

Parsons, Talcott, and Edward A. Shils, eds. *Toward a General Theory of Action*. Cambridge, MA: Harvard University Press, 1950.

Pelto, P.J. *Anthropological Research: The Structures of Inquiring*. New York: Harper & Row, 1970.

Perera, M.H.B., and M.R. Mathews. "The Interrelationship of Culture and Accounting with Particular References to Social Accounting." *Advances in international Accounting*. Forthcoming.

Pike, K.L. *Language in Relation to a Unified Theory of the Structure of Human Behavior*. 2d ed. The Hague: Moulton, 1967.

Radcliffe-Brown, A.R. *Structure and Function in Primitive Society*. New York: Free Press, 1968.

———. *Structure and Function in Primitive Society*. London: Cohen & West, 1961.

Radebaugh, L.H. "Environmental Factors Influencing the Development of Accounting Objectives, Standards and Practices in Press." *International Journal of Accounting Education and Research* (Fall 1985): 6–16.

Rokeach, J. *The Nature of Human Values*. New York: Free Press, 1966.

Ronen, Simcha. *Comparative and Multinational Management*. New York: Wiley, 1986.

Ronen, Simcha, and Oded Shenkar. "Clustering Countries on Attitudinal Dimensions: A Review and Synthesis." *Academy of Management Review* 1013 (1985): 435–54.

Sahili, F. "Determinants of Achievement Motivation for Women in Developing Countries." *Journal of Vocational Behavior* 14 (1974): 297–305.

Sarnoff, I. *Society with Tears*. Secaucus, NJ: Citadel Press, 1966.

Scribner, S. "Development Aspects of Categorized Recall in a West African Society." *Cognitive Psychology* 6 (1974): 475–94.

Sekaran, Uma, and Carol R. Snodgrass. "A Model for Examining Organizational Effectiveness Cross-Culturally." *Advances in International Comparative Management*, vol. 2. Greenwich, CT: JAI Press, 1986, 213, 216–20.

Witkin, H.A., and J.W. Berry. "Psychological Differentiation in a Cross-Cultural Perspective." *Journal of Cross-Cultural Psychology* 6 (1975): 4–87.

Witkin, H.A., R.B. Dyk, H.F. Faherson, D.R. Goodenough, and S.A. Karp. *Psychological Differentiation*. Potomac, MD: Erlbaum, 1974.

———. *Psychological Differentiation*. New York; Wiley, 1962.

Zeff, S.S. *Forging Accounting Principles in Five Countries: A History and an Analysis of Freud*. Houston: Stipes, 1972.

5

Cognitive Relativism in Management Accounting

INTRODUCTION

What happens when people make decisions about an accounting phenomenon, amid the pressures, constraints, dangers, and opportunities of today's business environment?[1] This chapter presents a model that focuses on the cognitive process employed by a decision maker attempting to use his/her judgment to make a decision about an accounting phenomenon. Basically, both judgment and decision are the products of a set of social cognitive operations that include the observation of information on the accounting phenomenon and the formation of a schema to represent the accounting phenomenon that is stored in memory and later retrieved when needed to allow the formation of a judgment and a decision. Before we present the model, an elaboration on the notion and use of schemata in cognitive psychology and accounting is necessary.

SCHEMATA IN COGNITIVE PSYCHOLOGY

The Notion of Schema-Guided Processes

The schema theory as developed by F.C. Bartlett[2] served as the stimulus for all schema theories. As defined by Bartlett, a schema is "an active organization of past reactions, or past experiences, which must always be supposed to be operating in any well-adapted organic response."[3] Schemata are complex unconscious knowledge, as "masses of organized past experiences."[4] They are generic cognitive representations, in the sense that they constitute a process that can deal with an indefinitely large number of new instances.

Modern views of schemata refer generally to cognitive structures that represent organized knowledge about a given concept or a given stimulus and that serve as mechanisms for the interaction of old knowledge and new knowledge in perception, language, thought, and memory.

Schemata are generally regarded as fundamental elements upon which all information processing depends. They constitute a theory about knowledge: how knowledge is represented, and how that representation facilitates the use of knowledge in numerous ways. As stated by D.E. Rumelhart, "Schemata are employed in the process of interpreting sensory data, in retrieving information from memory, in organizing actions, in the determining of goals and sub-goals, in the allocation of resources and generally in guiding the flow of processing in the system."[5] In fact, useful analyses of schemata suggested by Rumelhart include plays, theories, procedures, and parsers.[6] Properties of schemas include the following:

1. A schema represents a prototypical abstraction of the complex concept it represents.
2. A schema is induced from past experiences with numerous exemplars of the complex concept it represents.
3. A schema can guide the organization of incoming information into clusters of knowledge that are "instantiations" of the schema itself.
4. When one of the constituent concepts of a schema is missing in the input, its features can be inferred from "default values" in the schema.[7]

Schemata versus Categories

Jean Mandler[8] made an unusual distinction between two types of representations—categories and schemata. Categories are denoted by verbal or nonverbal symbols (i.e., "names") and are represented by a set of features that serve as the basis for inferring membership in it. Schemata, on the other hand, are cognitive representations whose features, like those of categories, are organized according to specific a priori spatial, temporal, or logical criteria." Categories and schemata function differently. As Robert S. Wyer and S.E. Gordon note:

Information about a set of attributes processed by the members of a particular category may not spontaneously activate this category unless either (a) the attributes are very strongly and uniquely associated with it, (b) one has a specific objective that leads the object being described to be classified, or (c) a category and its characteristic features are already activated at the time the information is received . . . In contrast, information that describes the characteristic features of a schema may become more inclined to activate the schema spontaneously.[9]

Schema Growth and Change

In considering schema growth and change the evidence favors a perseverance effect whereby generic schemata are resistant to change even in the face of contrary evidence.[10-11] In fact, people may even interpret exceptions as proving a given schema, unless they are asked to counterargue it, to explain why their favorite theory might be wrong.[12]

Schemata are developed from experience with instances of the category in question and become more complex, more abstract, and more organized with experience. With increasing experience a schema becomes more mature and more complex. Hence, the schemata of experts contain more informational elements than those of novices, are more organized, contain more links, and may have a more complex hierarchy.[13-15]

Sources of Activation for Schemata

D. G. Bobrow and D. A. Norman[16] distinguish between two basic sources of activation for schemata: conceptually driven and data-driven processing. In conceptually driven processing, an activated schema in turn activates a subschema with the expectation that this will account for some portion of the input data. In data-driven processing, the activated subschema causes the activation of the various schemata of which it is a component. Data-driven processing goes from the part to the whole. In another source of activation, known as schema-directed processing, the activation is assumed to go in both directions. It proceeds as follows:

Some events occur at the sensory system. The occurrence of this event "automatically activates certain low level" schemata (such schemata might be called "*feature detectors*"). The low level schemata, in turn, activates (in a data driven fashion) certain of the "higher level" schemata (the most probable ones) of which they are constituents. These "higher level" schemata then initiate conceptually driven processing by activating the subschemata not already activated in an attempt to evaluate their goodness of fit.[17]

Encoding of Information in a Schema

For W. F. Brewer and G. V. Nalsamura, the interaction of old knowledge with new knowledge involves two processes: one refers to the modification of the generic knowledge in the relevant schema, while the other refers to the construction of a specified instantiated memory representation, where the instantiated schema is the cognitive structure that results from the interaction of the old information and the new information from the episodic unit.[18]

The encoding of information is in fact subject to at least two interpretations. First, the interpretation proposed by R.S. Woodswork and H. Schlosberg[19] postulates that once a schema is activated by incoming episodic information, features that are inconsistent with the implications of this schema are appended to the representation of information as "corrections." A second conceptualization, proposed by A. C. Graesser, S. E. Gordon, and J. D. Sawyer,[20] known as the "script-pointer-plus-tag" formulation, postulates that when people receive information that is interpretable in terms of a prototypic event schema (script), they do not retain the information itself but retain a "pointer" to the general script, along with an indication of the values of the information that instantiate the script variables. If features of the information do not match attributes of the generic script, and thus cannot be reconstructed, they are appended to the representations as "tags." Basically, new information is represented by a series of "pointers" to prototypic event schemata that can be used to understand or describe the event, accompanied when necessary by "tags" denoting objects or events that cannot be derived from the event schemata alone.

Social Schema Research

Social schema research investigates self-schemata, person schemata, script or event schemata, and person-in-situation schemata.[21]

The self-schema contains cognitive generalizations about the self that are derived from past experiences. People are generally self-schematic on dimensions that are of importance to them, on which they perceive themselves as extreme, and on which they perceive the opposite to be untrue.[22] They are schematic on those dimensions perceived to be of lesser importance to them.

Research on perception shows that people who are schematic on a particular dimension recognize and filter rapidly incoming information about the dimension, notice the dimension in other people, and think harder about kinds of schema-relevant information.[23]

Research on memory shows that self-schematic people remember schema-relevant information, are difficult to change, have more accessible knowledge about others because of the sheer familiarity of self-knowledge, and are more affect-laden in knowledge about others, especially unfamiliar individuals.[24,25]

Research on inference shows that people make rapid predictions about their own behavior that are consistent with their self-schemata.[26] Under certain circumstances these predictions take longer than for aschematics,[27] especially if the judgment is novel.

The person-schema contains cognitive generalizations about traits and behavior information common to certain groups or types of people.

Research on perception shows that categories for people, like categories for objects, are organized hierarchically.[28] Research on memory shows that schemata for people's traits and goals typically help the perceiver to remember schema-consistent information in more detail than would be possible without the schemata. Research on inference shows that person schemata affect subsequent inferences.

The evidence on person schemata is summarized as follows:

Person schemata include protypical representations of traits such as extroversion and introversion, as well as notions of what behavior is consistent with a given goal. Person schemata of all sorts shape the processes of perception, memory, and inference to conform to our general assumptions about other people. The effects of schemata on perception, memory and inference are not necessarily well suited to accuracy in identifying individual instances. Schemata are used by the mind to manage such processes economically, if not accurately.[29]

The script or event schema contains cognitive generalizations that describe the appropriate sequence of events in a given situation.[30] Research on script or event schemata is summarized as follows:

Script or event schemata describe sequences of activity from everyday life. They contain props, roles and sequence rules. Scripts also may be subdivided into segments (scenes). Like other schemata, scripts guide the perception of ambiguous information and often shape memory toward schema consistent information. Inferences can be seen as filling in gaps where information was missing, and gap filling appears to be exaggerated by repeated encounters with the script. Most of the functions of scripts echo those of other schemata, in their focus on relevant—and usually on consistent—information in perception, memory and inference.[31]

The person-in-situation or role schema contains cognitive generalizations about people in situations or scripts for behavior in situations. Role schemata not only help perception, memory, and inference but may be a way to account for stereotyping.

Research on perception shows that categorization instantiates the stereotypic content of the schema whether or not the person fits the category and in the process minimizes the amount of variability and complexity that may exist in the category.[32,33] In addition to minimizing variability and complexity, a schema slants perception of the content of what a person does.

Research on memory shows that the role schema shapes memory in a schema-consistent fashion. In addition, the categorical information seems to override the details of the specific instance.[34] Schema-discrepant information is, however, likely to receive added attention at input, if task conditions allow. Attentional processes can facilitate remembering inconsistent information.[35]

SCHEMA-BASED RESEARCH IN ACCOUNTING

Cognitive Research in Accounting and Auditing

The cognitive revolution in social psychology has created strong interest in the knowledge structure in memory in general and how people learn in particular. This research paradigm also affects accounting and auditing. Given that the difference between declarative knowledge and procedural knowledge is equivalent to the difference between content knowledge and the use of that knowledge or between "knowing what" and "knowing how," W.S. Waller and W.L. Felix used the concepts to propose a model of how an ordinary person learns from experience.[36] Basically, its thesis is that learning from experience involves the formation and development of generalized cognitive structures that organize experience-based declarative and procedural knowledge in long-term memory. Declarative knowledge is organized by categories, which depend on similarity of class membership relations, and schemata, which depend on spatial and/or temporal relations. Procedural knowledge is organized into production systems, i.e., hierarchies of condition-action pairs.[37]

What the model implies is that schemata are developed through a gradual process of abstracting domain-specific knowledge on the basis of experience. The difference between the expert and the novice's knowledge structure is therefore the result of difference in experience. What is apparent from the research on novices and experts is that longer chunks of information are taken and stored by experts than novices at any point in time and for a particular task;[38, 39] pieces of information are better clustered into meaningful categories within a single chunk by experts;[40] and the recall of experts is based on conceptual representations for information while the novices' is based on functional relationships.[41–44]

The findings in accounting so far parallel those in psychology. More specifically, R. Weber found that expert auditors clustered internal control cues according to their control categories significantly more than novices did.[45] D. M. Frederick and R. Libby found that expert auditors clustered financial statement errors by transaction cycles.[46]

Propositions about Knowledge Structures in Accounting

The notion of schemata (knowledge structures or templates) was used by Michael Gibbins to make general propositions, corollaries, and hypotheses about the psychological operations of professional judgment in the "natural" everyday settings experienced by public accountants.[47] Professional judgment in public accounting was described as a five-component process:

- schemata or knowledge structures accumulated through learning or experience
- a triggering event or stimulus
- a judgment environment
- a judgment process
- a decision/action

The list of propositions, corollaries, and hypotheses is proposed. While it awaits empirical validation, the list constitutes one general descriptive theory of professional judgment in public accounting, where auditor judgment is viewed as a responsive, continuous, unconscious, instrumental process of sequentially matching cues to knowledge structures to generate preferences and responses based on experience.[48] Preliminary findings on these propositions are provided by Gibbins,[49] Gibbins and Emby,[50] and Emby and Gibbins.[51]

A COGNITIVE VIEW OF THE JUDGEMENT/DECISION PROCESS IN MANAGEMENT ACCOUNTING

In this section a model of the judgment/decision process in accounting is proposed as an exercise in social perception and cognition, requiring both formal and implicit judgment.[52] The primary input to this process is an accounting problem or phenomenon that needs to be solved and requires a judgment preceding either a preference or a decision. The model consists of the following steps:

1. Observation of the accounting phenomenon by the decision maker
2. Schema formation or building of the accounting phenomenon
3. Schema organization or storage
4. Attention and recognition process triggered by a stimulus
5. Retrieval of stored information needed for the judgment decision
6. Reconsideration and integration of retrieved information with new information
7. Judgment process
8. Decision/action response

Observation of the Accounting Phenomenon by the Decision Maker

The decision maker is assumed to have the opportunity to observe the accounting phenomenon. To understand the accounting phenomenon, the decision maker may be given some information that is deemed diagnostic. If this information is not provided, the decision maker may seek the information and test available information judged most relevant to the phenomenon. Following H. H. Kelly's approach to causal attribution,[53] the search behavior may concentrate on these types of available information:

1. *Consensus information*: how this accounting phenomenon and other accounting phenomena were rated or performed on given dimensions
2. *Distinctiveness information*: how this accounting phenomenon was rated or performed on various other dimensions
3. *Consistency information*: how this accounting phenomenon was rated or performed on important dimensions in the past

Evidence shows that subjects tend to focus more on distinctiveness or consistency information than on consensus information.[54] Studies examining search behavior in reaction to an accounting phenomenon are very limited.

The search behavior is not misguided. It is fair to assume that the decision maker has some expectations about the accounting phenomenon that may determine the type of information sought. These expectations are termed *preconceived notions* in A. S. De Nisi et al.'s model.[55] They result from the decision maker's previous experiences with the accounting phenomenon. These expectations or preconceived notions may bias the decision maker toward choosing some information rather than other information. Providing background information prior to observation contributes to this phenomenon.[56, 57] R. S. Wyer and T. K. Srull maintain that prior information predisposes the subject to select one of a number of frames of references.[58] Bias is a result of the tendency to seek evidence confirming preconceived notions rather than neutral or disconfirming evidence.[59–61]

Schema Formation or Building

Once the accounting phenomenon has been observed, the relevant information is encoded in the sense that it is categorized on the basis of experience and organized in memory along schemata or knowledge structures. As put by R. E. Nisbett and L. Ross:

Few, if any, stimuli are approached for the first time by the adult. Instead, they are processed through pre-existing systems of schematized and abstracted knowledge—beliefs, theories, propositions and schemas. These knowledge structures label and categorize objects and events quickly and, for the most part, accurately. They also define a set of expectations about objects and events and suggest appropriate responses to them.[62]

A schema can be simply an update of templates that existed prior to the occurrence of a known accounting phenomenon or a new template generated by the occurrence of a new accounting phenomenon. In the first case, little ambiguity is assumed to exist and therefore the encoding follows an automatic process.[63] In the second case, no immediate available schema exists, and a controlled categorization process is triggered to determine which schema is consistent with the dimensions of the accounting phenomenon. Both processes are suggested in the case of the encoding of information or performance appraisal:

Thus, both the automatic and controlled processes have the same end result: the assignment of a person to a category based on prototype-matching process. The difference is whether the stimulus person's behavior is sufficiently consistent with other cues to allow the categorization to proceed automatically or whether a controlled process must be used to determine which category is consistent with the individual's behavior. The actual category assignment is a function of contextual factors influencing the salience of particular categories and stimulus characteristics, as well as individual differences among perceivers that tender some categories and their prototypes more available than others and some stimulus features more salient than others.[64]

Basically, an accounting phenomenon may be categorized in a given schema, by virtue of its possession of obvious or salient attributes known to the perceiver.

When no salient category prototype or schema provides a natural framework, the automatic process is superseded by a controlled process or a consciously monitored process.[65]

The controlled process can be triggered by either a new accounting phenomenon or new features of a known phenomenon that are inconsistent with a previous categorization. In the latter case a recategorization is invoked until the inconsistency is resolved and a new schema is used to describe the accounting phenomenon, causing a reconstruction of memories about the phenomenon such that memories consistent with the new categorization are more available.

Schema Organization and Storage

After information about a given phenomenon is encoded to form a representation or schema, it is stored and maintained in long-term memory. E. Tulving distinguishes between episodic and semantic memory.[66] Basically, a person's episodic memories are personal while semantic memory is knowledge of words and symbols, their meanings and referent knowledge of the relations among words, and the rules or algorithms for manipulating words, symbols, and the relations among them. R. C. Atkinson and R. M. Shiffrin maintain that the basic structural features of episodic memory are three memory stores: the sensory register, the short-term store, and the long-term store.[67] Information enters the memory system through the various senses and goes first to the sensory register whose function is to preserve incoming information long enough for it to be selectively transmitted into the memory system. It is kept there less than a second and is lost through either decay or erasure by overwriting.

The information then goes to the short-term store, "working in memory" where conscious mental processes are performed. It is where consciousness exercises its function. Information can be kept indefinitely here provided it is given constant attention; if not, it is lost through decay in twenty to thirty seconds.

The information next goes to the long-term store through a conscious or unconscious process where it can be held indefinitely and often permanently (although it can be lost owing to decay or interference of various sorts). The long-term store is assumed to have unlimited capacity. In this multistore model information about the accounting phenomenon moves through different and separate memory systems, ending with a long-term store where semantic information is maintained along meaning-based codes or schemata. It is important to realize at this stage that if the person intends to remember the accounting phenomenon for all time, he/she must perform a different analysis on the input than when his/her intentions are temporary.[68] A person's intention determines whether the storage of the information on the accounting phenomenon is permanent or temporary. A different coding is used: a memory code for permanent storage and a perceptual role for temporary storage.

Different codes have different permanence. Codes of the sensory aspects of an input, such as appearance, are short lived. Hence, a person who looked at a word to decide whether it was printed in red or green would not remember the word's name very long because his coding would have emphasized color, not meaning. In contrast, a person who looked at a word to decide whether it was a synonym for some other word would form a semantic code, and he/she would remember the name of the examined word for quite a while.[69]

Stimulus and Attention and Recognition Processes

Upon observation of a triggering event or stimulus, the schema in the accounting phenomenon is activated. The activation, as a process of detection, search, and attention, can be either a controlled or an automatic processing.[70]

Basically, automatic detection, triggered by the recognition of a stimulus, operates independently of the person's control. Automatic processing is the apprehension of stimuli by the use of previously learned routines that are in the long-term storage.

Automatic processing as learned in long-term store, is triggered by appropriate inputs, and then operates independently of the subject's control. An automatic sequence can contain components that control information flow, attract attention, or govern overt responses. Automatic sequences do not require attention, though they may attract it if training is appropriate, and they do not use up short-term capacity. They are learned following the earlier use of controlled processing that links the same nodes in sequence. In search, detection, and attention tasks, automatic detection develops when stimuli are consistently mapped to responses; then the targets develop the ability to attract attention and initiate responses automatically, immediately, and regardless of other inputs or memory load.[71]

In these automatic processes, no conscious effort is involved in the search as well as in demanding attention owing to the learned sequence of the elements composing the schemata. On the other hand, controlled processes involve a temporary activation of novel sequences of processing steps that require attention, use short-term memory, and involve a conscious effort.

It is important to realize that in both processes, the use of schemata for encoding or retrieving information depends on accessibility in memory, where the accessibility of schemata is the probability that they can be activated, either for use in storage of incoming information or for retrieval of previously stored information.[72,73]

Accessibility of a schema depends upon such factors as the strength of the stored information, the extent of the overlap or match between input and schema, and the recency and frequency of previous activations. Each time a schema is activated for use, it becomes more accessible for successive activations. The instrumental effect of an activation on the accessibility of a schema is presumably a decreasing function of its prior strength. That is, a weak schema benefits more from an activation than a strong one.[74]

Empirical evidence on the increased accessibility of information with the frequency of activation is available.[75,76]

Retrieval of Stored Information Needed for Judgment/Decision

Either the automatic or controlled search processes activate the appropriate schema for the accounting phenomenon and allow the retrieval of information on the phenomenon. It is, however, the schema, a representation of the phenomenon, that is recalled rather than the actual phenomenon.[77–79] The effect becomes stronger as the time between observation and recall increases.[80]

The potential for different types of biases exists at this stage. For example, people may be more likely to recall information consistent with a schema confirming an expectation,[81] or may recall schema-consistent information that they never saw.[82] A good deal of evidence also suggests that schema-inconsistent information is more likely to be recalled[83] because of its novelty, saliency, and difficulty of incorporation into a schema.[84]

What is more likely to be recalled when faced with an accounting phenomenon, what types of biases affect the recall of schemata of accounting phenomena, and what can be done to reduce or eliminate the distortions in recall are some of the important questions in need of investigation. This model will assume that familiarity with the accounting phenomenon through constant record keeping and other forms of monitoring may result in less biased recall. The solution, in fact, is more complex and depends on the type of relationship between memory and judgment. Reid Hastie and Bernadette Park investigated these relationships and distinguished between two types of judgment tasks, memory-based and on-line. They also identified five information-processing models that relate memory for evidence to judgment based on the evidence: (1) independent processing, (2) availability, (3) biased retrieval, (4) biased encoding, and (5) incongruity-biased encoding.[85]

With regard to the five information-processing models, the distinction is threefold: (1) cases where there is no relationship between judgment and memory processes, which include the independent processing model; (2) cases where memory availability causes judgment, which include the availability-based information-processing model and the automatic search process described earlier; and (3) cases where judgment causes memory, which include the biased retrieval, the biased encoding, and incongruity-biased encoding models. The biased retrieval model is selective in the sense that traces that "fit" the judgment are more likely to be found at the memory decision stage. Such biases have been termed *selective recall, confirmatory memory*, and *access-biased memory*.[86–89]

The biased encoding model assumes that biasing takes place at the time of the encoding of evidence information and memory search will locate a biased sample of information reflecting the initial encoding bias.

The incongruity-based encoding model assumes that after the initial encoding, incoming information that is incongruent or contradictory is given special processing to enhance its memorability by being placed in "special tags" that strongly attach to memory. In memory search, the subject is more likely to find the incongruent information.[90, 91]

This model assumes that where the accounting phenomenon calls for an online task, the availability or automatic search model will characterize the retrieval of stored information needed for judgment decision. Selection of a processing model will depend on the individual objectives of the subject and the perceived consequences of his/her judgments on his/her economic and psychological welfare.

Reconsideration and Integration of Retrieved Information with Other Available Information

At this stage the process involves integration of the information retrieved from memory and other available information into a single evaluation of the accounting phenomenon.

Where familiarity with the phenomenon is present and previously learned routines are retrieved, active integration will not take place. An earlier integration is recalled from past stored output on the phenomenon. "What was once accomplished by slow, conscious, deductive reasoning is now arrived at by fast, unconscious perceptual processing."[92]

Where the phenomenon presents challenging and novel dimensions and where controlled processes were involved in attention and recognition, a cognitive integration of all the information is required to reach a single evaluation of the accounting phenomenon. G. Mandler describes the process of "response learning" as follows:

First, the organism makes a series of discrete responses, often interrupted by incorrect ones. However, once errors are dropped out and the sequence of behavior becomes relatively stable—as in running a maze, speaking a word, reproducing a visual pattern—the various components of the total behavior required in the situation are "integrated." Integration refers to the fact that previously discrete parts of a sequence come to behave functionally as a unit; the whole sequence is elicited as a unit and behaves as a single component response has in the past; any part of it elicits the whole sequence.[93]

Brunswick's lens model and Anderson's weighted average model provide support to the types of integration of information that take place.[94] The integration process is, however, also subject to various biases:

1. People may attach and give great weight to some type of information. For example, evidence in the employee appraisal literature shows that negative information has greater weight.[95, 96]

2. There is evidence in both psychology and accounting of an underutilization or underweighing of base rate or consensus information.[97]

3. There is ample evidence in psychology and accounting of the effect of various heuristics involved in decisions on and about accounting phenomena. They include (1) representativeness, (2) availability, (3) confirmation bias, (4) anchoring and adjustment, (5) conjunction fallacy, (6) hindsight bias, (7) illusory correlation and contingency judgments, (8) selective perception, (9) frequency, (10) concrete information, (11) data presentation, (12) inconsistency, (13) conservation, (14) nonlinear extrapolation, (15) law of small numbers, (16) habit/"rules of thumb," (17) "best-guess" strategy, (18) complexity in the decision environment, (19) social pressures in the decision environment, (20) consistency of information sources, (21) question format, (22) scale effects, (23) wishful thinking, (24) outcome-irrelevant learning structures, (25) misperceptions of chance fluctuations (gambler's fallacy), (26) success/failure attributions, and (27) logical fallacies in recall.[98]

The Judgment Process

The judgment process is the result of the integration process of information and the forming of a single evaluation of the accounting phenomenon if the attention, recognition, and integration processes are the result of controlled processes. The judgment made in this case requires a conscious access to all the mental processes implied in the model. If, however, the attention, retrieval recognition, and integration processes were the result of automatic processes, the judgment is not and will not be conscious. It does not require the conscious use of all the mental processes implied in this model.[99,100] It is a routine judgment.

Routine judgment involves the rapid matching of immediate perceptions to a template that provides, and executes, a specific response: "if total debts do not equal total credits, readd the total balance."

In the above example, there is no awareness of how the brain actually decides that the debits do not equal the credits. Even if awareness were possible, it is not normally necessary—a great many of our routine activities, such as keeping our eyes open or holding our pencils—are done without any particular conscious awareness, at least until something causes us to become aware.[101]

Decision/Action (Response)

The final step of the model is the decision or selection of a response to the accounting phenomenon. It is a conscious response preference resulting from the judgment process. It is an output of the judgment process and is clearly influenced by all the mental processes and biases described earlier. As a result, a new schema on the phenomenon will develop that will be part of the knowledge structure or the phenomenon stored in long-term memory.

The move from judgment to decision is a bridging process. It assumes that no obstacles stand in the way.

The decision/action has been investigated in various accounting environments and using various accounting phenomena. It has been found to differ from various normative decision models, including Bayerian-decision theory and expected value models.[102,103]

The bridging process, however, will be influenced by the cognitive steps described in this model as well as by other factors including the possible consequences of the decision on the accounting phenomenon. Gibbins, for instance, cites the following factors:

Personal attitudes may play a direct role, such as determining priorities within the search process. For example, some public accountants may use financial return as their first selection criterion; others may use moral propriety as their first. Personal attitudes can also play an indirect role, limiting past actions and thus limiting the experiences on which judgment guides are built. The applications of such attitudes to the judgment process need not be conscious—particularly for deeply ingrained beliefs.[104]

CONCLUSIONS

The essence of cognitive relativism in management accounting is the presence of a cognitive process that is assumed to guide the judgment/decision process. The model in this chapter shows that judgments and decisions made about accounting phenomena are the products of a set of social cognitive operations that include the observation of information on accounting phenomena and the formation of schemata that are stored in memory and later retrieved to allow the formation of judgments and/or decisions when needed.

NOTES

1. W.L. Felix, Jr. and W.R. Kinney, Jr., "Research in the Auditor's Opinion Formulation Process: State of the Art," *Accounting Review* (April 1988): 245–71.

2. F.C. Bartlett, *Remembering* (London: Cambridge University Press, 1932).

3. Ibid., 201.

4. Ibid., 197–98.

5. D.E. Rumelhart, "Schemata and the Cognitive System," in *Handbook of Social Cognition*, ed. R.S. Wyer, Jr., and T.K. Srull (Hillsdale, NJ: Erlbaum, 1984), 162.

6. Ibid.

7. Perry W. Thorndyke and B. Hayes-Roth, "The Use of Schemata in the Acquisition and Transfer of Knowledge," *Cognitive Psychology* 11 (1979): 83.

8. Jean Mandler, "Categorical and Schematic Organization in Memory," in R.C. Ruff, *Memory, Organization and Structure* (New York: Academic Press, 1979).

9. Robert S. Wyer, Jr. and S.E. Gordon, "The Cognitive Representation of Social Information," in *Handbook of Social Cognition*, vol. 2, eds. R.S. Wyer, Jr. and T.K. Srull (Hillsdale, NJ: Erlbaum, 1984), 82.

10. L. Ross, M.R. Lepper, and M. Hubbard, "Perseverance in Self-Perception and Social Perception: Biased Attribution Processes in the Debriefing Paradigm," *Journal of Personality and Social Psychology* 32 (1975): 880–92.

11. C.A. Anderson, "Inoculation and Counter-Explanation: Debasing Techniques in the Perseverance of Social Theories," *Social Cognition* 1 (1982): 126–35.

12. W.G. Chase and H.A. Simon, "The Mind's Eye in Chess," in *Visual Information Processing*, ed., W.G. Chase (New York: Academic Press, 1982).

13. M.T.H. Chi and R. Koeske, "Network Representations of a Child's Dinosaur Knowledge," *Developmental Psychology* 19 (1983): 29–35.

14. J.H. Larkin et al., "Models of Competence in Solving Physics Problems," *Science* 200 (1980): 1335–42.

15. K.B. McKeithen et al., "Knowledge Organization and Skill Differences in Computer Programmers," *Cognitive Psychology* 13 (1981): 307–25.

16. D.G. Bobrow and D.A. Norman, "Some Principles of Memory Schemata," in *Representations and Understanding: Studies in Cognitive Science*, ed. D.G. Bobrow and A.M. Collins (New York: Academic Press, 1975): 25–32.

17. D.E. Rumelhart, "Schemata and the Cognitive System," in *Handbook of Social Cognition*, vol. 1, ed. R.S. Wyer, Jr. and T.K. Srull (Hillsdale, N.J.: Erlbaum, 1984), 170.

18. W.F. Brewer and G.V. Nalsamura, "The Nature and Functions of Schemas," in *Handbook of Social Cognition*, vol. 1, ed. R.S. Wyer, Jr. and T.K. Srull (Hillsdale, NJ: Erlbaum, 1981), 141.

19. R.S. Woodswork and H. Schlosberg, *Experimental Psychology* (New York: Holt, 1954).

20. A.C. Graesser, S.E. Gordon, and J.D. Sawyer, "Memory for Typical and Atypical Actions in Scripted Activities: Test of a Script Pointer + Tag Hypothesis," *Journal of Verbal Learning and Behavior* 18 (1979): 503–15.

21. S.E. Taylor, and J. Crocker, "Schematic Bases of Social Information Processing," in *Social Cognition: The Ontario Symposium*. vol. 1, ed. E.T. Higgins, C.P. Herman, and M.P. Zanna (Hillsdale, NJ: Erlbaum, 1981).

22. H. Markus, "Self-Schemata and Processing Information about the Self," *Journal of Personality and Social Psychology* 38 (1980): 231–48.

23. H. Markus, and K.P. Sends, "The Self in Social Information Processing," in *Psychological Perspectives on the Self*, vol. 1, ed. J. Suls (Hillsdale, NJ: Erlbaum, 1982).

24. J.A. Bargh, "Attention and Automaticity in the Processing of Self-Relevant Information," *Journal of Personality and Social Psychology* 43 (1982): 425–36.

25. T.J. Ferguson, B.G. Rule, and D. Carlson, "Memory for Personally Relevant Information," *Journal of Personality and Social Psychology* 44 (1983): 251–61.

26. H. Rankus, "Self-Schema DNA Processing Information about the Self," *Journal of Personality and Social Psychology* 35 (1977): 63–78.

27. N.A. Kuiper, "Convergent Evidence for the Self as a Prototype," *Personality and Social Psychology Bulletin* 7 (1981): 438–43.

28. N. Canton and W. Mischel, "Prototypes in Person Perception," in *Advances in Experimental Psychology*, vol. 12, ed. L. Berkowitz (New York: Academic Press, 1979).

29. S.T. Fiske and S.E. Taylor, *Social Cognition* (New York: Random House, 1984), 154.

30. R.P. Abelson, "The Psychological Status of the Script Concept," *American Psychologist* 36 (1981): 715–25.

31. Fiske and Taylor, *Social Cognition*, 169.

32. R.S. Malpass, H. Lavingnern, and D.E. Weldon, "Verbal and Visual Training in Face Recognition," *Perception and Psychophysics* 14 (1973): 285–92.

33. P.W. Linville and E.E. Jones, "Polonized Appraisals of Outgroup Members," *Journal of Personality and Social Psychology* 42 (1982): 193–211.

34. S.E. Taylor et al., "Categorical Bases of Person Memory and Stereotyping," *Journal of Personality and Social Psychology* 36 (1978): 778–93.

35. R. Hastie, "Memory for Behavioral Information that Confirms or Contradicts a Personality Impression," in *Person Memory: The Cognitive Basis of Social Perception*, ed. R. Hastie et al. (Hillsdale, NJ: Erlbaum, 1981).

36. W.S. Waller and W.L. Felix, Jr., "The Auditor and Learning from Experience: Some Conjectures," *Accounting, Organizations and Society* (June 1984): 383–406.

37. Ibid., 390–406.

38. W.G. Chase and H.A. Simon, "Perception in Chess," *Cognitive Psychology* 4 (1973): 55–87.

39. H.L. Chiesi, G.J. Spilich, and J.F. Voss, "Acquisition of Domain-Related Information in Relation to High and Low Domain Knowledge," *Journal of Verbal Learning and Verbal Behavior* 18 (1979): 257–73.

40. A.R. Halpern and H.G. Bower, "Musical Expertise and Melodic Structure in Memory for Musical Notation," *American Journal of Psychology* 95 (1982): 31–50.

41. B. Schneiderman, "Exploratory Experiments in Programmer Behavior," *International Journal of Computer and Information Sciences* 5 (1976): 123–43.

42. McKeithen et al., "Knowledge Organization and Skill Differences in Computer Programmers," 307–25.

43. B. Adelson, "Problem Solving and the Developing of Abstract Categories in Programming Languages," *Memory and Cognition* 9 (1981): 422–33.

44. B. Adelson, "When Novices Surpass Experts: The Difficulty of a Task May Increase with Expertise," *Journal of Experimental Psychology: Learning, Memory and Cognition* 10 (1984): 483–95.

45. R. Weber, "Some Characteristics of the Free Recall of Computer Controls by EDP Auditors," *Journal of Accounting Research* (Spring 1980): 214–41.

46. D.M. Frederick and R. Libby, "Expertise and Auditors' Judgments of Conjunctive Events," *Journal of Accounting Research* (Fall 1986): 770–90.

47. Michael Gibbins, "Proposition about the Psychology of Professional Judgment in Public Accounting," *Journal of Accounting Research* (Spring 1984): 103–25.

48. Michael Gibbins, "Knowledge Structures and Experienced Auditor Judgment," in *Auditor Productivity in the Year 2000: 1987 Proceedings of the Arthur Young Professors' Roundtable*, ed. Andrew Bailey (Reston, VA: Arthur Young, 1988), 57.

49. Ibid., 51–73.

50. M. Gibbins and C. Emby, "Evidence on the Nature of Professional Judgment in Public Accounting," in *Auditing Research Symposium 1984*, ed. A.R. Abdel-Khalik and I. Solomon (Champaign: University of Illinois at Urbana/Champaign, 1985), 181–212.

51. C. Emby and M. Gibbins, "Good Judgment in Public Accounting: Quality and Justification," *Contemporary Accounting Research* (Spring 1988): 287–313.

52. Similar models have been proposed for the performance appraisal process. See, for example, A.S. De Nisi, T.P. Cafferty, and B.M. Meglino, "A Cognitive View of the Performance Appraisal Process: A Model and Research Proposition," *Organizational Behavior and Human Performance* 33 (1984): 360–96; J.M. Feldman, "Beyond Attribution Theory: Cognitive Processes in Performance Appraisal," *Journal of Applied Psychology* 66/2 (1981):127–48.

53. H.H. Kelly, "Attributions in Social Interactions," in *Attributions: Perceiving the*

Causes of Behavior, ed. E.E. Jones et al. (Norristown, NJ: General Learning Process, 1972).

54. B. Major, "Information Acquisition and Attribution Processes," *Journal of Personality and Social Psychology* 39 (1980): 1010–23.

55. De Nisi, Cafferty, and Meglino, "Performance Appraisal Process," 367–68.

56. H. Tajfel, "Social Perception," in *Handbook of Social Psychology*, vol. 1, ed. G. Lidzey and E. Aronson (Reading, MA: Addison-Wesley, 1969).

57. P. Slovic, B. Fischoff, and S. Lichtenstein, "Behavioral Decision Theory," *Annual Review of Psychology* 28 (1977): 119–39.

58. R.S. Wyer and T.K. Srull, "Category Accessibility: Some Theoretical and Empirical Issues Concerning the Processing of Social Stimulus Information," in *Social Cognition: The Ontario Symposium*, vol. 1, ed. E. Higgins, C. Herman, and M. Zanna (Hillsdale, NJ: Erlbaum, 1981).

59. M. Snyder and N. Cantor, "Treating Hypotheses about Other People: The Use of the Historical Knowledge," *Journal of Experimental Social Psychology* 15 (1979): 330–42.

60. M. Snyder, "Seek and Ye Shall Find: Testing Hypotheses about Other People," in *Social Cognition: The Ontario Symposium*, vol. 1, ed. M. Higgins, E.C. Herman, and M. Zarma (Hillsdale, NJ: Erlbaum, 1981), 33.

61. E.B. Ebbesen, "Cognitive Processes in Inferences about a Person's Personality," in *Social Cognition: The Ontario Symposium*, vol. 1, ed. M. Higgins, E.C. Herman, and M. Zarma (Hillsdale, NJ: Erlbaum, 1981), 55.

62. R.E. Nisbett and L. Ross, *Human Inference: Strategies and Shortcomings of Social Judgment* (Englewood Cliffs, NJ: Trent & Hall, 1980), 7.

63. Wyer and Srull, "Category Accessibility."

64. Feldman, "Beyond Attribution Theory," 129.

65. M. Snyder and S.W. Uranowity, "Reconstructing the Past: Some Cognitive Consequences of Person Perception," *Journal of Personality and Social Psychology* 37 (1979): 1660–72.

66. E. Tulving, "Episodic and Semantic Memory," in *Organization of Memory*, ed. E. Tulving and W. Donaldson (New York: Academic Press, 1972).

67. R.C. Atkinson and R.M. Shiffrin, "Human Memory: A Proposed System and Its Control Processes," in *Advances in the Psychology of Learning and Motivation Research and Theory*, vol. 2, ed. K.W. Spence and J.T. Spence (New York: Academic Press, 1968).

68. R.I. Craig, and R.S. Lockart, "Levels of Processing: A Framework for Memory Research," *Journal of Verbal Learning and Verbal Behavior* 11 (1972): 671–84.

69. R. Lachman, J.L. Lachman, and Earl C. Butterfield, *Cognitive Psychology and Information Processing: An Introduction* (Hillsdale, NJ: Erlbaum, 1979), 274.

70. Walter Schneider and Richard M Shiffrin, "Controlled and Automatic Human Information Processing: I. Detection, Search, and Attention," *Psychological Review* (January 1977): 1–53.

71. Ibid., 51.

72. E. Tulving and Z. Pearlstone, "Availability versus Accessibility of Information in Memory for Words," *Journal of Verbal Learning and Verbal Behavior* 5 (1966): 381–91.

73. B. Hayes-Roth, "Evolution of Cognitive Structures and Processes," *Psychological Review* 84 (1977): 260–78.

74. P.W. Thorndyke and B. Hayes-Roth, "The Use of Schemata in the Acquisition and Transfer of Knowledge," *Cognitive Psychology* 11 (1979): 86–87.

75. J. Perlmutter, P. Source, and J.L. Myers, "Retrieval Process in Recall," *Cognitive Psychology* 8 (1976): 32–63.

76. B. Hayes-Roth and F. Hayes-Roth, "Plasticity in Memorial Networks," *Journal of Verbal Learning and Verbal Behavior* (1979): 67–73.

77. Ibid.

78. A.G. Greenwald, "Cognitive Learning, Cognitive Response to Persuasion, and Attitude Change," in *Psychological Foundations of Attitudes*, ed. A. Greenwald, T. Brock, and T. Ostron (New York: Academic Press, 1960).

79. R. Schanke and R. Abelson, *Scripts, Plans, Goals, and Understanding* (Hillsdale, NJ: Erlbaum, 1977).

80. T.K. Srull and R.S. Wyer, "Category Accessibility and Social Perception: Some Implications for the Study, Memory and Interpersonal Judgments," *Journal of Personality and Social Psychology* 38 (1980): 841–56.

81. K.P. Sentis and E. Burnstein, "Remembering Schema Consistent Information: Effects of Balance Schema on Recognition Memory," *Journal of Personality and Social Psychology* 37 (1979): 2200–11.

82. C.E. Cohen, "Pearson Categories and Social Perception: Testing Some Boundaries of the Processing Effects of Prior Knowledge," *Journal of Personality and Social Psychology* 40 (1981): 441–52.

83. S.E. Taylor et al., "The Generalizability of Salience Effects," *Journal of Personality and Social Psychology* 37 (1979): 357–68.

84. R.I. Craig and E. Tulving, "Depth of Processing and the Retention of Words in Episodic Memory," *Journal of Verbal Learning and Verbal Behavior* 11 (1972): 671–84.

85. R. Hastie and Bernadette Park, "The Relationship between Memory and Judgment Depends on Whether the Judgment Task Is Memory-Based or On-Line," *Psychological Review* 93/3 (1986): 258–68.

86. E.J. Learner, A. Blank, and B. Chanowitz, "The Mindlessness of Ostensibly Thoughtful Action: The Role of Placebo Information in Interpersonal Interaction," *Journal of Personality and Social Psychology* 36 (1978): 635–42.

87. E.E. Learner, "False Models and Post-Data Model Construction," *Journal of the American Statistical Association* 69 (1974): 122–31.

88. E.E. Learner, "Explaining Your Results as Accent-Biased Memory," *Journal of the American Statistical Association* 70 (1975): 88–93.

89. M. Snyder and W. Uranowitz, "Reconstructing the Past: Some Cognitive Consequences of Person Perception," *Journal of Personality and Social Psychology* 36 (1978): 94–45.

90. A.C. Graesser and G.V. Nalsamura, "The Impact of Schema on Comprehension and Memory," *Psychology of Learning and Memory* 16 (1982): 60–102.

91. Graesser, Gordon, and Sawyer, "Memory for Typical and Atypical Actions in Scripted Activities," 319–32.

92. Chase and Simon, "Perception in Chess," 55–81.

93. G. Mandler, "From Association to Structure," *Psychological Review* 69 (1962): 415–27.

94. Ahmed Belkaoui, *Human Information Processing in Accounting* (Westport, CT: Quorum Books, 1989).

95. D.L. Hamilton and L.J. Huffman, "Generality of Impression Formation for Evaluative and Non-evaluative Judgments," *Journal of Personality and Social Psychology* 20 (1971): 200–7.

96. R.S. Wyer and H.L. Hinlele, "Information Factor Underlying Inferences about Hypothetical People," *Journal of Personality and Social Psychology* 34 (1976): 481–95.

97. Belkaoui, *Human Information Processing in Accounting*.

98. Ibid.

99. J. Jaynes, *The Origin of Consciousness in the Breakdown of the Bicameral Mind* (Toronto: University of Toronto Press, 1978).

100. R.E. Nisbett and T.D. Wilson, "Telling More Than We Can Know: Verbal Reports on Mental Processes," *Psychological Review* (May 1977): 231–59.

101. Gibbins, "Proposition about the Psychology of Professional Judgment in Public Accounting," 113.

102. Belkaoui, *Human Information Processing in Accounting*.

103. R.M. Hogarth, *Judgment and Choice: The Psychology of Decision* (Chichester: Wiley, 1980).

104. Gibbins, "Proposition about the Psychology of Professional Judgment in Public Accounting," 114.

SELECTED BIBLIOGRAPHY

Abelson, R.P. "The Psychological Status of the Script Concept." *American Psychologist* 36 (1981): 715–25.

Adelson, B. "When Novices Surpass Experts: The Difficulty of a Task May Increase with Expertise." *Journal of Experimental Psychology: Learning, Memory and Cognition* 10 (1984): 483–95.

———. "Problem Solving and the Development of Abstract Categories in Programming Languages." *Memory and Cognition* 9 (1981): 422–33.

Anderson, C.A. "Inoculation and Counter-Explanation: Debasing Techniques in the Perseverance of Social Theories." *Social Cognition* 1 (1982): 126–35.

Atkinson, R.C., and R.M. Shiffrin. "Human Memory: A Proposed System and Its Control Processes." In *Advances in the Psychology of Learning and Motivation Research and Theory*, vol. 2, ed. K.W. Spence and J.T. Spence. New York: Academic Press, 1968.

Bargh, J.A. "Attention and Automaticity in the Processing of Self-Relevant Information." *Journal of Personality and Social Psychology* 43 (1982): 425–36.

Bartlett, F.C. *Remembering*. London: Cambridge University Press, 1932.

Belkaoui, Ahmed. *Human Information Processing in Accounting*. Westport, CT: Quorum Books, 1989.

Bobrow, D.G., and D.A. Norman. "Some Principles of Memory Schemata." In *Representations and Understanding: Studies in Cognitive Science*, ed. D.G. Bobrow and A.M. Collins. New York: Academic Press, 1975.

Brewer, W.F., and G.V. Nalsamura. "The Nature and Functions of Schemas." In *Handbook of Social Cognition*, ed. R.S. Wyer, Jr., and T.K. Srull. Hillsdale, NJ: Erlbaum, 1984, 139–50.

Canton, N., and W. Mischel. "Prototypes in Person Perception." In *Advances in Experimental Psychology*, vol. 12, ed. L. Berkowitz. New York: Academic Press, 1979.

Chase, W.G., and H.A. Simon. "The Mind's Eye in Chess." In *Visual Information Processing*, ed. W.G. Chase. New York: Academic Press, 1982.

———. "Perception in Chess." *Cognitive Psychology* 4 (1973): 55–87.

Chi, M.T.H., and R. Koeske. "Network Representations of a Child's Dinosaur Knowledge." *Developmental Psychology* 19 (1983): 29–35.

Chiesi, H.L., G.J. Spilich, and J.F. Voss. "Acquisition of Domain-Related Information in Relation to High and Low Domain Knowledge." *Journal of Verbal Learning and Verbal Behavior* 18 (1979): 257–73.

Cohen, C.E. "Pearson Categories and Social Perception: Testing Some Boundaries of the Processing Effects of Prior Knowledge." *Journal of Personality and Social Psychology* 40 (1981): 441–52.

Craig, R.I., and R.S. Lockart. "Levels of Processing: A Framework for Memory Research." *Journal of Verbal Learning and Verbal Behavior* 11 (1972): 671–84.

Craig, R.I., and E. Tulving. "Depth of Processing and the Retention of Words in Episodic Memory." *Journal of Verbal Learning and Verbal Behavior* 11 (1972): 671–84.

De Nisi, A.S., T.P. Cafferty, and B.M. Meglino. "A Cognitive View of the Performance Appraisal Process: A Model and Research Proposition." *Organizational Behavior and Human Performance* 33 (1984): 360–96.

Ebbesen, E.B. "Cognitive Processes in Inferences about a Person's Personality." In *Social Cognition: The Ontario Symposium*, ed. M. Higgins, E.C. Herman, and M. Zarma. Hillsdale, NJ: Erlbaum, 1984, 52–59.

Emby, C., and M. Gibbins. "Good Judgment in Public Accounting: Quality and Justification." *Contemporary Accounting Research* (Spring 1988): 287–313.

Feldman, Jack M. "Beyond Attribution Theory: Cognitive Processes in Performance Appraisal." *Journal of Applied Psychology* 66/2 (1981): 127–48.

Felix, W.L., Jr., and W.R. Kinney, Jr. "Research in the Auditor's Opinion Formulation Process: State of the Art." *Accounting Review* (April 1988): 245–71.

Ferguson, T.J., B.G. Rule, and D. Carlson. "Memory for Personally Relevant Information." *Journal of Personality and Social Psychology* 44 (1983): 251–61.

Fiske, S.T., and S.E. Taylor. *Social Cognition*. New York: Random House, 1984, 154.

Frederick, D.M., and R. Libby. "Expertise and Auditors' Judgments of Conjunctive Events." *Journal of Accounting Research* (Fall 1986), 220–90.

Gibbins, Michael. "Knowledge Structures and Experienced Auditor Judgment." In *Auditor Productivity in the Year 2000: 1987 Proceedings of the Arthur Young Professors' Roundtable*, ed. Andrew Bailey. Reston, VA: Arthur Young, 1988, 57.

———. "Proposition about the Psychology of Professional Judgment in Public Accounting." *Journal of Accounting Research* (Spring 1984): 103–25.

Gibbins, M., and C. Emby. "Evidence on the Nature of Professional Judgment in Public Accounting." In *Auditing Research Symposium 1984*, ed. A.R. Abdel-Khalik and I. Solomon. Champaign: University of Illinois at Urbana/Champaign, 1985, 181–212.

Graesser, A.C., S.E. Gordon, and J.D. Sawyer. "Memory for Typical and Atypical Actions in Scripted Activities: Test of a Script Pointer + Tag Hypothesis." *Journal of Verbal Learning and Behavior* 18 (1979): 319–32, 503–15.

Graesser, A.C., and G.V. Nalsamura. "The Impact of Schema on Comprehension and Memory." *Psychology of Learning and Memory* 16 (1982):60–102.

Greenwald, A.G. "Cognitive Learning, Cognitive Response to Persuasion, and Attitude

Change." In *Psychological Foundations of Attitudes*, ed. A. Greenwald, T. Brock, and T. Ostron. New York: Academic Press, 1960.

Halpern, A.R., and H.G. Bower. "Musical Expertise and Melodic Structure in Memory for Musical Notation." *American Journal of Psychology* 95 (1982): 31–50.

Hamilton, D.L., and L.J. Huffman. "Generality of Impression Formation for Evaluative and Non-evaluative Judgments." *Journal of Personality and Social Psychology* 20 (1971): 200–7.

Hastie, R. "Memory for Behavioral Information that Confirms or Contradicts a Personality Impression." In *Person Memory: The Cognitive Basis of Social Perception*, ed. R. Hastie et al. Hillsdale, NJ: Erlbaum, 1981.

Hastie, R., and Bernadette Park. "The Relationship between Memory and Judgment Depends on Whether the Judgment Task Is Memory-Based or On-Line." *Psychological Review* 93/3 (1986):258–68.

Hayes-Roth, B. "Evolution of Cognitive Structures and Processes." *Psychological Review* 84 (1977), 260–78.

Hayes-Roth, B., and F. Hayes-Roth. "Plasticity in Memorial Networks." *Journal of Verbal Learning and Verbal Behavior* (1979): 61–73.

Hogarth, R.M. *Judgment and Choice: The Psychology of Decision*. Chichester: Wiley, 1980.

Jaynes, J. *The Origin of Consciousness in the Breakdown of the Bicameral Mind*. Toronto: University of Toronto Press, 1978.

Kelly, H.H. "Attributions in Social Interactions." In *Attributions: Perceiving the Causes of Behavior*, ed. E.E. Jones. Norristown, NJ: General Learning Process, 1972.

Kuiper, N.A. "Convergent Evidence for the Self as a Prototype." *Personality and Social Psychology Bulletin* 7 (1981): 438–43.

Lachman, R., J.L. Lachman, and Earl C. Butterfield. *Cognitive Psychology and Information Processing: An Introduction*. Hillsdale, NJ: Erlbaum, 1979.

Larkin, J.H. et al. "Models of Competence in Solving Physics Problems." *Science* 200 (1980): 1335–42.

Learner, E.E. "Explaining Your Results as Accent-Biased Memory." *Journal of the American Statistical Association* 70 (1975): 88–93.

———. "False Models and Post-Data Model Construction." *Journal of the American Statistical Association* 69 (1974): 122–31.

Learner, E.J., A. Blank, and B. Chanowitz. "The Mindlessness of Ostensibly Thoughtful Action: The Role of Placebo Information in Interpersonal Interaction." *Journal of Personality and Social Psychology* 36 (1978): 635–42.

Linville, P.W., and E.E. Jones. "Polonized Appraisals of Outgroup Members." *Journal of Personality and Social Psychology* 42 (1982): 193–211.

McKeithen, K.B., et al. "Knowledge Organization and Skill Differences in Computer Programmers." *Cognitive Psychology* 13 (1981): 307–25.

Major, B. "Information Acquisition and Attribution Processes." *Journal of Personality and Social Psychology* 39 (1980): 1010–23.

Malpass, R.S., H. Lavingnern, and D.E. Weldon. "Verbal and Visual Training in Face Recognition." *Perception and Psychophysics* 14 (1973):285–92.

Mandler, G. "From Association to Structure." *Psychological Review* 69 (1962):415–27.

Mandler, Jean. "Categorical and Schematic Organization in Memory." In *Memory, Organization and Structure*, ed. R.C. Ruff. New York: Academic Press, 1979.

Markus, H. "Self-Schemata and Processing Information about the Self." *Journal of Personality and Social Psychology* 38 (1980):231–48.

Markus, H., and K.P. Sentis. "The Self in Social Information Processing." In *Psychological Perspectives on the Self*, vol. I, ed. J. Suls. Hillsdale, NJ: Erlbaum, 1982.

Nisbett, R.E., and L. Ross. *Human Inference: Strategies and Shortcomings of Social Judgment*. Englewood Cliffs, NJ: Trent & Hall, 1980.

Nisbett, R.E., and T.D. Wilson. "Telling More Than We Can Know: Verbal Reports on Mental Processes." *Psychological Review* (May 1977):231–59.

Perlmutter, J., P. Source, and J.L. Myers. "Retrieval Process in Recall." *Cognitive Psychology* 8 (1976): 32–63.

Rankus, H. "Self-Schema DNA Processing Information about the Self." *Journal of Personality and Social Psychology* 35 (1977):63–78.

Ross, L., M.R. Lepper, and M. Hubbard. "Perseverance in Self-Perception and Social Perception: Biased Attribution Processes in the Debriefing Paradigm." *Journal of Personality and Social Psychology* 32 (1975):880–92.

Rumelhart, D.E. "Schemata and the Cognitive System." In *Handbook of Social Cognition*, vol. 1, ed. R.S. Wyer, Jr. and T.K. Srull. Hillsdale, NJ: Erlbaum, 1984.

Schanke, R., and R. Abelson. *Scripts, Plans, Goals, and Understanding*. Hillsdale, NJ: Erlbaum, 1977.

Schneider, Walter, and Richard M. Shiffrin. "Controlled and Automatic Human Information Processing: I. Detection, Search, and Attention." *Psychological Review* (January 1977):1–53.

Schneiderman, B. "Exploratory Experiments in Programmer Behavior." *International Journal of Computer and Information Sciences* 5 (1976):123–43.

Sentis, K.P., and E. Burnstein. "Remembering Schema Consistent Information: Effects of Balance Schema on Recognition Memory." *Journal of Personality and Social Psychology* 37 (1979):2200–11.

Slovic, P., B. Fischoff, and S. Lichtenstein. "Behavioral Decision Theory." *Annual Review of Psychology* 28 (1977):119–39.

Snyder, M., and N. Cantor. "Treating Hypotheses about Other People: The Use of the Historical Knowledge." *Journal of Experimental Social Psychology* 15 (1979): 330–42.

Snyder, M., and S.W. Uranowity. "Reconstructing the Past: Some Cognitive Consequences of Person Perception." *Journal of Personality and Social Psychology* 37 (1979):941–45, 1660–72.

Srull, T.K., and R.S. Wyer. "Category Accessibility and Social Perception: Some Implications for the Study of Person, Memory and Interpersonal Judgments." *Journal of Personality and Social Psychology* 38 (1980):841–56.

Tajfel, H. "Social Perception." In *Handbook of Social Psychology*, vol. 1, ed. G. Lidzey and E. Aronson. Reading, MA: Addison-Wesley, 1969.

Taylor, S.E., and J. Crocker. "Schematic Bases of Social Information Processing." In *Social Cognition: The Ontario Symposium*, vol. 1, ed. E.T. Higgins, C.P. Herman, and M.P. Zanna. Hillsdale, NJ: Erlbaum, 1981.

Taylor, S.E., J. Aoker, S.T. Fiske, M. Springer, and J. Winkler. "The Generalizability of Salience Effects." *Journal of Personality and Social Psychology* 37 (1979):357–68.

Taylor, S.E., S.T. Fiske, N.L. Etcoff, and A.J. Ruderman. "Categorical Bases of Person

Memory and Stereotyping." *Journal of Personality and Social Psychology* 36 (1978):778–93.

Thorndyke, P.W., and B. Hayes-Roth. "The Use of Schemata in the Acquisition and Transfer of Knowledge." *Cognitive Psychology* 11 (1979): 86–87.

Tulving, E. "Episodic and Semantic Memory." In *Organization of Memory*, ed. E. Tulving and W. Donaldson. New York: Academic Press, 1972.

Tulving, E., and Z. Pearlstone. "Availability versus Accessibility of Information in Memory for Words." *Journal of Verbal Learning and Verbal Behavior* 5 (1966):381–91.

Waller, W.S., and W.L. Felix, Jr. "The Auditor and Learning from Experience: Some Conjectures." *Accounting, Organizations and Society* (June 1984):383–406.

Weber, R. "Some Characteristics of the Free Recall of Computer Controls by EDP Auditors." *Journal of Accounting Research* (Spring 1980):214–41.

Woodswork, R.S., and H. Schlosberg. *Experimental Psychology.* New York: Holt, 1954.

Wyer, R.S., Jr., and S.E. Gordon. "The Cognitive Representation of Social Information." In *Handbook of Social Cognition*, vol. 2, ed. R.S. Wyer, Jr. and T.K. Srull. Hillsdale, NJ:Erlbaum, 1984.

Wyer, R.S., and H.L. Hinlele. "Informational Factor Underlying Inferences about Hypothetical People." *Journal of Personality and Social Psychology* 34 (1976):481–95.

Wyer, R.S., and T.K. Srull. "Category Accessibility: Some Theoretical and Empirical Issues Concerning the Processing of Social Stimulus Information." In *Social Cognition: The Ontario Symposium*, vol. 1, ed. E. Higgins, C. Herman, and M. Zanna. Hillsdale, NJ: Erlbaum, 1981.

6

Contingency Approaches to the Design of Accounting Systems

INTRODUCTION

A perfect match between specific contingencies and the various characteristics of accounting systems is the objective of the method of theoretical and empirical research generally known as the contingency approach to the design of accounting systems. Research of this type dismisses the notion that universality in the design of accounting systems can be reached to accommodate all situations through a search for the factors that can best ensure the effectiveness of the accounting systems. The purposes of this chapter are to explain the contingency approach and to elaborate on the various theoretical and empirical studies that have adopted it.

CONTINGENCY THEORY

The contingency theory approach to the design of accounting systems assumes that a general strategy applicable to all organizations does not exist. On the contrary, it assumes that the design of various components of accounting systems depends on specific contingencies that can create a perfect match. It is then the perfect link or match between the design of accounting systems and the specific contingencies that is the scope of contingency theory. To date, the contingency formulations have considered the effects of technology, organizational structure and theory, and the environment in attempting to explain how accounting systems differ in various situations. All of these formulations point to the accepted thesis that there is no universal, "best design" for a management accounting information system, and that "it all depends upon situational factors."[1]

These formulations adopt a general framework that links (1) some contingent variables (that is, variables that cannot be influenced by the organization) to (2) any components of an organizational control package (consisting of accounting information design, other management information design, organizational design, or organizational control arrangements), and then through (3) some intervening variables provide a link to (4) a measure of organizational effectiveness.[2] The formulations are either empirical or theoretical. In what follows, both types are discussed.

THEORETICAL FORMULATIONS

Five theoretical formulations have been proposed in the literature. They are as follows:

(A) Efficient design of a management accounting system and a choice of control mechanisms that depend on the structure and context of an organization.[3] The contextual variables that shape the organizational structure are assumed to be technology and environment. Technology is conceptualized as variable, from routine to nonroutine, based on the nature of raw materials and search processes. Environment is mapped on a continuum from highly predictable to highly unpredictable. The properties of the organizational structure that are shaped by technology and environment are the distribution of authority and power, the question of centralization versus decentralization, and the issue of procedure specification. In other words, the distribution of organizational authority and the extent to which procedures can be specified depend on technology and environment. The type of organizational structure, in turn, is assumed to affect management accounting processes such as planning, resource allocation, and measures of performance.

(B) Gordon and Miller proposed a contingency framework for the design of accounting information systems that takes into account the environment, organizational attributes, and managerial decision-making styles.[4] The environment is characterized by three key dimensions: dynamism, heterogeneity, and hostility. The organizational attributes include decentralization, differentiation, integration, bureaucratization, and resources. Finally, the decision-making style of executives is characterized by the following six dimensions: analysis of decisions, decision time horizons, multiplexity of decision making, adaptiveness, proactivity, and consciousness of strategies. These contextual factors and their key dimensions are assumed to have an impact on such prerequisites of the accounting information system as information load, centralization of reporting, cost allocation methods, frequency of reporting, method of reporting, time element of information, performance evaluation, measurement of events, and valuation methods. While the number of permutations of these variables may suggest an unmanageable number of situations, Gordon and Miller suggested, in fact, that "it seems that environmental, organizational, and decision style traits are not distributed randomly but actually cluster together to form commonly accruing configurations."[5] Three archetypes—the adaptive firm, the firm running blind, and the stagnant bureaucracy—are presented as evidence of the need for a contingency approach in the design of an accounting information system.

(C) Macintosh and Daft investigated the relationship between one characteristic of the organization and the control system design.[6] By interdependence they meant the extent to which departments depend on each other and exchange information and resources to accomplish a task. It is also a variable relevant to control systems. Interdependence can be (1) *pooled* when the departments are relatively autonomous and little work flows between them, (2) *sequential* when the departments are linked in a serial fashion, with the output of one department used as the input of the next department, and (3) *reciprocal* when the departments work jointly on a project and work flows back and forth between them.[7] The management control system is viewed in terms of three control subsystems: operating budgets, statistical reports, and standard operating procedures and policies. The hypothesized relationships and the use of management control systems are as follows:

1. In the case of pooled departmental interdependency, the preferred means of control is standardization and a greater reliance on standard operating procedures than on either operating budgets or statistical reports.

2. In the case of sequential departmental interdependency, the preferred means of control are planning and measurement, with more reliance on operating budgets and statistical reports than on standard operating procedures.

3. In the case of reciprocal departmental interdependency, the preferred means of control is mutual adjustment; less reliance is put on operating budgets, statistical reports, and standard operating procedures.

The results of Macintosh and Daft's field study showed that when interdependence is low, control is focused on the use of standard operating procedures; when it is moderate, control rests on budgets and statistical reports; and when it is high, the role of the three control systems diminishes.

(D) Macintosh proposed a contextual model of information systems that embraces both a macroorganizational concept—technology and a human information processing system construct—and personal decision style.[8] Basically, the model combines personal decision style, technology type, and organizational structure to derive an information system style. These variables are defined as follows:

1. Driver and Mock's decision-style model is used to define the decision-style variables.[9] The model assumes two dimensions of information processing: amount of information used (from minimum to maximum) and degree of focus in the use of data (from one solution to multiple solutions). These two dimensions are combined to derive four distinctive styles: decisive, flexible, hierarchic, and integrative.

The *decisive* style assumes the use of a minimum amount of data to generate different meanings at different times. Decisive individuals look for efficiency, speed, and consistency in the information to be used. They prefer brief communications and summary reports focusing on one solution, results, and action. They like to be in hierarchic organizations with a short, clear span of control and clear rules.

The *flexible* style assumes the use of a minimum amount of data to generate different meanings at different times. Flexible individuals look for speed, adaptability, and intuition rather than developing and operating in accordance to a plan. They prefer brief communications that focus on a variety of solutions. They favor loose and fluid organizational patterns.

The *hierarchic* style assumes the use of masses of data to generate one firm opinion. Hierarchic individuals look for thoroughness, precision, and perfectionism. They prefer long, formal, thorough reports that present problems, methods, and data and generate one best solution. They like to be in a classic organization with a broad span and control as well as elaborate procedures.

The *integrative* style assumes the use of masses of data to generate a multitude of possible solutions. Integrative individuals look for the creative use of information in experiments, simulations, and games. They prefer complex and fluid communication that emphasizes discussion rather than reports. They like to work in nonautocratic teams and in nonhierarchic organizations of the matrix type.[10]

2. Perrow's categories of technology are used to define the technology variable.[11] The model assumes two dimensions of technology: task knowledge (from analyzable to unanalyzable) and task variety (from low to high). These two dimensions derive from distinctive categories of knowledge: (a) craft technology (analyzable task knowledge and low craft technology task variety); (b) routine technology (analyzable task knowledge and low task variety); (c) research technology (unanalyzable task knowledge and high task variety); and (d) technical-professional technology (analyzable task knowledge and high task variety). Each of these categories of knowledge is assumed to be best served by a distinctive organizational structure that fits the special needs of the task.

3. Finally, four information styles are differentiated in terms of two dimensions: amount and ambiguity. Macintosh defined them in the following manner:

The concise information system. Small to moderate amounts of information that are precise and unambiguous, and are used in a quick and decisive way.

The elaborate information system. Large amounts of information, frequently in the form of databases or simulation models, which tend to be detailed and precise; recipients normally use such information in a slow and deliberate manner.

The cursory information system. Small amounts of information, neither precise nor detailed and frequently superficial, that are used in a causal yet decisive way.

The diffuse information system. Moderate to large amounts of information, covering a wide range of material, frequently ill-defined and imprecise, that typically are used in a slow, deliberate manner.[12]

(E) Ewusi-Mensah investigated the impact of the external organizational environment on management information systems.[13] The organizational environment was classified as either static or dynamic, and as controllable, partially controllable, or uncontrollable. Variations in organizational environments are assumed to require different decision processes and, consequently, different information characteristics, including information quality, information availability, information value, impact on decision making, organizational interaction, organizational search, response time, time horizon, information source, and information type.

EMPIRICAL STUDIES IN CONTINGENCY THEORY

Use of Capital Budgeting Techniques

The use of discounted cash-flow techniques has been touted in the corporate finance literature as superior to nondiscounting techniques as tools for the selection of capital investments. Several empirical studies have attempted to confirm the thesis that a firm should not perform better if it uses naive techniques.[14] Their results, however, have been mixed. To correct for a variety of theoretical and methodological limitations, Haka, Gordon, and Pincher used a theoretical model, derived from financial economic theory, which showed that improved firm performance (a measurement of stock market data) was not significantly associated with discounted cash-flow techniques.[15] The relationship between the use of capital budgeting techniques and firm performance is obviously mitigated by contingent, firm-specific characteristics. Using such a perspective, Haka developed and tested a contingency theory that could predict which firms were most likely to benefit from using sophisticated capital budgeting techniques.[16] The external characteristics used in the model were (1) the strategy of the firm (defender or prospector), (2) environmental predictability (stable or dynamic), and (3) environmental diversity (homogeneous or heterogeneous). The internal characteristics were (1) the information system (supportive or nonsupportive), (2) the reward structure, and (3) the degree of decentralization. The results of the survey study provided evidence of a positive relationship between the effectiveness of the sophisticated capital budgeting techniques and a predictable environment, the use of long-term reward systems, and the degree of decentralization.

Business Strategy and Control Systems

Business strategy is another source of contingency in the design of organizations and control systems.[17] Govindarajan and Gupta examined the linkages between strategy, incentive bonus systems, and effectiveness at the strategic business unit level within diversified firms.[18] A survey of general managers of strategic business units (SBUs) in diversified firms yielded the following results:

(1) greater reliance on long-run criteria as well as greater reliance on subjective (non-formula) approaches for determining the SBU general managers' bonus contributes to effectiveness in the case of built SBUs but hampers it in the case of harvest SBUs, and (2) the relationship between the extent of bonus system's reliance on short-run criteria and SBU effectiveness is virtually independent of SBU strategy.[19]

The first result stands to reason, given the expectation that built units will face greater environmental uncertainty than will harvest units. Built strategies take place in the growth stage of the product life cycle, whereas harvest strategies take place in the mature and decline stages of the product life cycle. This explains the greater changes and unpredictability in factors such as technology, product design, process design, market demand, number of completions, and competitive structure in the growth stage of the product life cycle.[20] Subjective bonus determinations may alleviate the burden of the dependencies that face the build manager.

The relationship between business strategy and accounting-based control system attributes was also examined by Simons.[21] This study was motivated, first, by the inconclusive attempts to test Burns and Stalker's findings that unstructured, organic organizations with minimal formal controls were best suited to a strategy of innovation, and, second, by Miller and Friesen's conclusion that controlling for the strategy of the firm is critical to understanding the relationship between control and innovation.[22] Using interviews and a derived questionnaire, Simons expressed the attributes of control systems in terms of tightness of budget goals, use of control, frequency of reporting, and intensity of the monitoring of performance results. Using Miles and Snow's typology, strategies were classified with reference to defenders, prospectors, and analyzers.[23] These types were defined as follows: Defenders operate in relatively stable product areas, offer more limited products than competitors, and compete through cost leadership, quality, and service. They engage in little product/market developments. Prospectors, on the other hand, compete through new products and market development. Product lines change over time and this type of firm is constantly seeking new market opportunities. Analyzers are an intermediate hybrid, combining both defender and prospector strategies.[24] The results of the study verified the proposition that firms that rely on different strategies use accounting control systems in different ways.

Perceived Importance and Use of Budget Control

The empirical literature in contingency theory attempted to explain variations in the perceived importance and/or use of budget control on various contingency variables. Khandwalla reported that managers' perceived use of flexible budget control is a positive function of the competition that confronts their organization.[25] He concluded in the following manner:

This implies that as competition intensifies, the expected benefits from the application of these controls tend to outweigh their costs. Thus, for those entrusted with the planning of control systems, it is important to know the degree of competition faced by the firm. Other things being equal, an elaborate control system for a firm not facing serious competition may also do more harm than good.[26]

Burns and Waterhouse found that the importance and use of budget control is higher in larger, decentralized, more technologically sophisticated organizations in which there are formal and standard operating procedures.[27] They observed that those in highly structured organizations tend to perceive themselves as having more influence, they participate more in budget planning, and they appear to be satisfied with budget-related activities. Managers in organizations where authority is concentrated are generally held accountable for fewer financial variables, they experience superior-initiated pressure, they see budgets as being less useful and limiting their flexibility, but they appear to be satisfied with the use of budgets by their superiors.[28]

Merchant found, furthermore, that the use and importance of budget control is higher in larger, more differentiated, decentralized organizations that have automated technology.[29] Smaller firms were found to rely more on social controls, that is to say, vigorous personnel selection policies, hazing, direct supervision, oral communication, personal interaction, and professional membership.

Finally, Rockness and Shields analyzed differences in the perceived importance of expenditure budget control in research and development work groups that were due to the organizational context (organizational size, expenditure budget size, source of funds) and the management control system (importance of social control, steps in the control process).[30] The results were significant and supportive of previous research, in that they provided additional evidence of a contingency relationship between budget control and organizational context.

Choice of Control Actions and Systems

The effectiveness of organizations depends to a large extent on the achievement of organizational control and the maintenance of overall organizational integrity. The ability of the organization's members to design and maintain control systems appropriate with the overall structure may also be contingent on other various factors. Das, for example, using a simulated setting, found that persons working in organic organizations are more likely to choose intrinsically motivating control strategies, and that those who work in mechanistic organizations are more likely to choose extrinsically motivating control strategies.[31] Das concluded:

Based on the current research evidence, it would appear that major changes in managerial styles (especially in the context of the control process) cannot be expected to emerge until some important changes in the perceptions of organizational characteristics and climate have occurred. Thus, a mere introduction of sophisticated training programs in leadership practices may not bring about the desired effects in the control behaviors of managers if they do not perceive the organizational characteristics and climate to be consistent with these new practices. In this sense, organizational socialization and prevailing organizational norms about appropriate managerial behavior may have greater effects on control behaviors of managers than has hitherto been suspected.[32]

Belkaoui also investigated the relationship between self-disclosure and attitudes to responsibility accounting.[33] Because a responsibility accounting system requires making public one's performance and implies an implicit trust between those controlled and their managers, reported self-disclosure can be related to the attitudes to responsibility accounting system. A field study involving fifty-five purchasing managers from the Department of Supply and Services in the Canadian government and based on the use of a self-disclosure instrument showed that the attitudes to responsibility accounting were positively related to the amount and control depth factors of self-disclosure and negatively related to the positive-negative, honesty-accuracy, and intended disclosures. Belkaoui concluded as follows:

The first result implies that those subjects willing to talk openly about themselves are more likely to accept one of the conditions of a responsibility accounting system which is responsibility over the controllable costs. The second result implies that the same subjects will be less willing to accept the above condition of a responsibility accounting system if the intended disclosure is to reveal negative versus positive things about themselves, or to assess the sincerity of their statements. Both results may be interpreted to imply the creation of both an open atmosphere and a trust between those controlled toward the acceptance of responsibility within a responsibility accounting system.[34]

Contingency Approach to Performance Assessment

A contingency approach to performance assessment was demonstrated by Hayes' study.[35] His results indicated that (1) internal factors are the major explanations for the performance of production departments, and (2) environmental as well as interdependency variables provide approximately equal contributions to the explanation of performance by marketing departments. Govinadarajan examined the contingency relationship between environmental uncertainty and performance evaluation style.[36] Performance evaluation style was defined as "the degree of reliance superiors place on formula vs. subject (nonformula) approaches towards the evaluation of the subordinate's performance and in deciding the subordinate's rewards (such as incentive bonus)."[37] The results supported the following propositions: (1) superiors of business units that face higher environmental uncertainty will use a more subjective performance appraisal approach; and (2) a stronger fit between environmental uncertainty and performance evaluation style is associated with higher business unit performance. These results were used to reconcile Hopwood's[38] dysfunctional effects of the budget constraint style with Otley's opposite findings by arguing that Otley studied units that might have operated in relatively stable environmental conditions while Hopwood may have examined units that might have operated in relatively uncertain environmental conditions.

Determinants of Accounting Information Systems

A. Technology was examined as a major explanatory variable of an effective accounting information system by Daft and Macintosh[39] Their study based on questionnaires sent to 253 individuals in twenty-four different work units produced high correlations between four types of technology and four categories of information systems.

B. Perceived environmental uncertainty and organizational structures were also examined as to how they related to the information system by Gordon and Narayanan.[40] Their study indicated that the characteristics of information perceived to be important by decision makers are related to perceived environmental uncertainty, but that their relationships to organizational structure are a result of both sets of variables (that is, characteristics of information and structure) being related to perceived environmental uncertainty.

C. Pijer[41] found that the financial control structure of an organization depends on the complexity of the task it faces (as defined by, for example, the range of products sold, the diversity of the range, seasonal variations, and variations in type of outlet). He also learned that task complexity depends on the financial control structure by way of the intervening variable of organizational structure, products sold, the diversity of the range, seasonal variations, and variations in type of outlet. He also learned that task complexity depends on the financial control structure by way of the intervening variable of organizational structure.

D. The determinants of change in management accounting systems were investigated by Libby and Waterhouse.[42] Their results indicate that the components that support decision making and control changed more frequently than components that support planning or directing, or are concerned with product costing. In addition, the changes in management accounting systems were best predicted by organizational capacity.

  The role and effect of automation on the link between reliance on budgetary control and production subunit performance was examined and verified by Dunk.[43] Basically, firms may benefit from the reliance on budgetary control in the evaluation of production subunit performance as manufacturing processes become more automated. This is in line with the thesis of the importance of contextual variables in the implementation of an effective budgetary control system.[44] One powerful argument is that they showed a matching between budgetary control and the activities of the subunits. A similar result supporting the use of budgetary control systems in present-day manufacturing is presented in the research conducted Lyall et al.[45]

E. The effects of manufacturing controls on performance efficiency and effectiveness were examined by Young et al.[46] Three manufacturing controls were examined, namely, inventory and production (pull vs. push), incentives (fixed vs. contingent), and quality control (process vs. output). The results show that both incentives and quality control systems had an effect on performance efficiency while incentives had an effect on performance effectiveness. The implication of these results is that firms may be able to improve manufacturing performance by matching production/inventory control systems and control systems, along with the use of performance-contingent incentive controls.[47] This is very much in line with evidence on manufacturing firms making controls more congruent with their changing environments.[48]

F. The managers' motivation to implement new management accounting techniques like just-in-time was examined by Griffin and Harrell.[49] Expectancy theory was used to provide appropriate conceptual models for understanding the motivational issues. The results of the study were understandably supportive of both the valence and force models, with the valence model predicting the valence (attractiveness) of implementing just-in-time procedures to middle managers and supervisors, and the force model predicting the motivation of middle managers and supervisors to implement the use of just-in-time procedures.

G. An empirical analysis of the association between the use of executive support systems (ESS) and perceived organizational competitiveness was conducted by Vanderbosch.[50] Two major findings emerged: "First, ESS information uses can be clustered into four types: (1) score keeping, (2) improving individual understanding, (3) focusing organizational attention and learning, and (4) legitimizing decisions. Second, all four hypotheses relating types of information use and usefulness of the ESS for enabling competitiveness were supported."[51]

H. The influence of self-interest and ethical considerations on managers' evaluation judgments was examined by Rutledge and Karim.[52] A conflict resides in that agency theory predicts self-interest as the role basis for economic decisions while cognitive moral development (CMD) theory suggests that decision makers will allow ethical/moral considerations to constrain their economic behavior.[53] Both moral reasoning level and adverse-selection conditions (self-interest) are found to leave a significant effect on managers' project evaluation decisions. The interesting and major implication of the study is stated as follows: "In particular, the contention from agency theory that individuals make economic decisions based solely on their self-interest is not supported in this study. Rather managerial self-interest may be constrained by ethical considerations, which casts doubt on the agency theory assumption that behavior is motivated solely by self-interest."[54]

I. The main argument of contingency theory is that the effective performance of organizations depends on adequate matching of structures and control systems with contextual variables. This "fit" hypothesis was tested, for example, by Abernethy and Stoelwinder.[55] The main argument of the study is that the extent to which individuals will behave in an "administratively" rational manner and wittingly or unwittingly match the use of control strategies to organizational contextual variables rests on whether they identify with the organization as a system.[56] A testing of the interaction between task uncertainty, budget use, and system goal orientation verified the fit hypothesis.

Basically, the fit between budgeting, task uncertainty and system goal orientation leads to a performance improvement. The practical implications are stated as follows: "Second, it suggests that the implementation of effective formal management control systems such as budgeting in these organizations requires a recognition that professionals in managerial positions may not have the necessary orientation toward these systems. The implementation of these systems may require, therefore, changes in the socialization and education of professionals, and/or the implementation of control strategies which match the professional model of control."[57]

Dysfunctional Behavior and Management Control

Dysfunctional behavior involves the attempts by a subordinate to manipulate elements of an established control system for his/her own purposes. These attempts at strategically manufacturing information flows and falsifying information have been noted in the organizational behavior and behavioral accounting literature.[58,59] In gaming a performance indication, the subordinate chooses an action that will be beneficial to him/her regardless of what is expected by the superior. This can be accomplished by rigid bureaucratic behavior, in cases where the subordinate strives to maximize a performance indicator that is not consistent with the firm's goal.[60] An example would be the case of sales representatives focusing on increasing sales volume on which they are evaluated, even though it may lead to lower profitability or a deterioration of long-term customer relations.[61]

Jaworski and Young[62] developed and tested a model that posits that three contextual variables (goal congruence, perceived peer dysfunctional behavior, and information asymmetry between superior and subordinates) affect the extent of role conflict and job tension experienced by the subordinate. The results were as predicted with the result that role conflict increases job tension and job tension increases the extent of dysfunctional behavior.

The Effects of Incentive Contracts

It is generally assumed in management accounting in general and management accounting in particular that incentive contracts can be used to motivate individuals to exert effort and use feedback to improve performance. Witness the following quote:

Monetary rewards, which are contingent on achieving goals experienced in terms of accounting numbers, are used to direct and control individual actions. Bonus systems and budgets, for example, represent mechanisms intended to induce employees to exert additional effort and attain higher levels of performance.[63]

A. Some of the early research examined the impact of monetary incentive on various measures of judgment performance. Positive effects of incentives in performance were formed in subjective probability tasks[64] and in the reduction of subjects' reliance on the anchoring heuristic in complex and cognitively demanding tasks.[65] There was, however, a need to investigate the impact of moderating variables. Awasthi and Pratt,[66] investigating the impact of perceptual differentiation, which is the individual's ability to perceptually abstract from a complex setting certain familiar concepts or relationships, provided such a study. Their results indicate that while monetary incentives increase effort, their effect on performance depends on the decision maker's perceptual differentiation, suggesting that cognitive characteristics should be considered in the development of performance evaluation and incentive systems.

B. Other research examined how incentive-based compensation contracts compare to flat-wage compensation contracts in motivating individual learning and performance in multiperiod tasks that encourage learning from feedback. Most of the studies showed that in contrast to economic theory, performance-based contracts do not improve, and sometimes even degrade, learning and performance relative to flat-wage contracts.[67-69] However, in a multiperiod cognitive task where the accounting system generates information that has both a contracting role and a belief-revision role, incentives were found to enhance performance and the rate of improvement in performance by increasing both: (1) the amount of time participants devoted to the task, and (2) participants' analysis and use of information.[70] The implications of this experiment are stated as follows:

First, the results suggest that incentives can increase the rate of improvement in performance and accelerate the learning curve. The finding is of particular interest given firms' recent emphasis on continuous improvement and enhancing productivity. Second, the results indicate that incentives improve performance by motivating individuals to increase both the duration and intensity of their efforts. Thus, incentives not only motivate individuals to work longer on a task, but the evidence also suggests that incentives enhance the quality of attention individuals devote to the task. This in turn enables individuals to develop better strategies that help them make decisions more consistent with profit maximization.[71]

The Judgment Effects of Common and Unique Performance Measures

Firms rely on a strategic formulation and matching of their capability and investment opportunities that may help them in the realization of their goals. Industry analysis is an important step in the strategic process. It generally focuses on five variables: (a) competitors, (b) potential entrants in the market, (c) equivalent products, (d) bargaining power of customers, and (e) bargaining power of import supplies.[72] A strategy, including a consideration of the above five forces, can best be implemented by a balanced scorecard. Developed by Kaplan and Norton,[73] the balanced scorecard expresses a firm's mission and strategy into a combination of traditional financial measures and other performance measures, to be used for the implementation of its strategy. These measures generally span financial performance, customer relations, internal business processes, and the firm's learning and growth activities and, as a result, capture the firm's total planned business strategy. For example, the objectives and measures of a balanced scorecard can be as follows:

1. For the financial perspective, the objective may be:
   - To increase shareholder value shareholder value to be measured by a) operating income from productivity gains, b) operating income from growth and c) revenue growth.
2. For the customer perspective, the objectives may be:
   - To increase market share to be measured by market share in communication networks segment and new customers.
   - To increase customer satisfaction to be measured by customer satisfaction survey.
3. For the internal business process perspective, the objectives may be:
   - To improve manufacturing capability to be measured by a) percentage of processes with advanced controls.
   - To improve manufacturing quality and productivity to be measured by a) yield.
   - To reduce delivery time to customers to be measured by a) order delivery time.
   - To meet specified delivery dates to be measured by a) on-time delivery.
4. For the learning and growth perspective, the objectives may be:
   - To develop process skill to be measured by the percentage of employees trained in process and quality management.
   - To empower workforce to be measured by the percentage of frontline workers empowered to manage processes.
   - To align employee and organizational goals to be measured by employees satisfaction survey.
   - To enhance information systems capabilities to be measured by percentage of manufacturing processes with real-time feedback.
   - To improve manufacturing processes to be measured by number of major improvements in process controls.[74]

One result of the balanced-scorecard system is that the system will include some measures common to multiple units and other measures that are unique to a particular unit. Therefore, at regular intervals, multiple subordinate units (and their managers) are based on both common and unique measures. This raises questions about the judgmental effects of the scorecard—specifically, how balanced scorecards that include some measures unique to a particular unit affect superiors' evaluations of that unit's performance.[75] The question is of importance, given that in a classic judgment and decision-making study, Slovic and MacPhillamy[76] found that participants weighed the common measures more heavily than unique measures for both the judgment and the choice, even after taking into account monetary incentives and feedback. The common information had a greater impact because it was easier to use in making comparisons. Unlike this classic judgment and decision-making study, Lipe and Salterio[77] argued instead that performance evaluation using the balance scorecard will be affected by both unique measures and common measures. MBA subjects acted as senior executives (superior) making a performance evaluation judgment of the managers of their units based on two factors: (a) a particular pattern of performance and (b) a particular pattern of performance based on their unique measures. The results showed that the subjects succumbed to the simplifying strategy of using only common measures in evaluating multiple managers.

Their results have major implications for the unit manager's ex ante decision-making strategy. In effect, Holmstrom and Milgrom[78] show analytically that (a) agents' decisions are affected by items that are included in their performance evaluation and compensation, and (b) items not included in evaluation and compensation of an agent will have little effect on the agent's decisions.

Given these results suggesting that common measures that drive the unit managers' evaluations will have more effect on unit managers' decisions than will the unique measures that are not used in the evaluation, more research is needed to replicate the findings under different contexts.

1. A first context may involve subjects who are effectively high-level managers instead of MBA students and who have participated in the development of the unique measures. In other words, the ego involvement that may result from participating in the construction of unique measures may make them more salient in the performance evaluation process.[79]

2. A second context is to change the order of presentation of common and unique measures to see whether they may be some primary effects or they may be some primary or recency effects.[80]

3. A third context is to investigate whether personality traits, like intolerance of ambiguity, may have an effect on the choice of common versus unique measures.[81]

Theories of Distributive Justice and Intrafirm Resource Allocation

For intrafirm resource allocation, as well as for all cases involving asymmetrical information between parties to a contract, agency theory predicts unconstrained opportunistic behavior. It ignores, however, various social and psychological factors, which may reduce misrepresentations in firms, for example corporate culture and personal morals. The opportunistic behaviors are in accord with the self-regarding utilitarian theory of fairness, where resources are perceived as rights by one of the parties to a contract. However, where other theories, of distributive justice are instituted, a more egalitarian behavior is expected. Accordingly, Riahi-Belkaoui[82] reported an experiment examining the effects of entitlements, rights, and fairness on unit manager behavior in intrafirm resource allocation. Experimental institutions were used to trigger a particular concept of justice, indicating which distribution or set of distributions is fair within the experiment. The experimental setting was adapted from Hoffman and

Spitzer.[83,84] The decentralized firm consisted of two related units. A common resource given to a first unit can also be used by the other unit. The first unit is entitled by central management to distribute the common resource between himself/herself and the unit manager of the second unit. The distribution could be unilateral or involve bargains struck between the two unit managers who have opposing payoff functions and full information of one another's payoffs. The experiment focuses on the amount in excess of an equal split received by the first manager, called a "greed index," under experimental institutions triggering these concepts of fairness in distribution: (1) utilitarian theory of distributive justice, (2) egalitarian theory of distributive justice, and (3) Lockean theory of distributive justice. As predicted, utilitarian subjects behaved in a greedy fashion whereas egalitarian subjects were less greedy than utilitarian subjects and not as egalitarian as egalitarian subjects. Basically, the opportunistic behaviors, in accord with the self-regarding utility theory of fairness where resources are perceived as rights by one of the parties to a contract, change to a more egalitarian behavior when other theories of justice or a Lockean theory of earned desert is instituted. While some subjects, left on their own, appeared unreservedly opportunistic, others did constrain their own behavior out of compliance to an instituted ethical code. As suggested by Noreen,[85] the simple fact of instruction is successful in reducing agency costs by moderating certain self-seeking behavior. This is not surprising given the experimental evidence that people who understand the benefits of cooperation are more likely to cooperate, and, apparently some sermonizing even may help.[86]

NOTES

1. D.T. Otley, "The Contingency Theory of Management Accounting: Achievement and Prognosis," *Accounting, Organizations and Society* (December 1980): 413–28.

2. Ibid., pp. 420–21.

3. J.H. Waterhouse and P. Tiessen, "A Contingency Framework for Management Accounting Systems Research," *Accounting, Organizations and Society* (August 1978): 65–76.

4. L.A. Gordon and D. Miller, "Design of Accounting Information Systems," *Accounting, Organizations and Society* (June 1976): 59–69.

5. Ibid., 65.

6. N.B. Macintosh and R.L. Daft, "Management Control Systems and Departmental Interdependencies: An Empirical Study," *Accounting, Organizations and Society* (January 1987): 49–61.

7. J.D. Thompson, *Organizations in Action* (New York: McGraw-Hill, 1967).

8. N.B. Macintosh, "A Contextual Model of Information Systems," *Accounting, Organizations and Society* (February 1981): 39–52.

9. M.J. Driver and T.J. Mock, "Human Information Processing: Decision Style Theory and Accounting Information System," *The Accounting Review* (July 1975): 497.

10. In spite of more critical doubts cast on the empirical support for the decision-style model, Driver and Mock argued for a relationship between decision style and the amount

of information used. For a criticism of their results, see P.A. Tiessen and D.M. Baker, "Human Information Processing, Decision Style Theory, and Accounting Information Systems: A Comment," *The Accounting Review* (October 1977): 984–87.

11. C. Perrow, *Organizational Analysis: A Sociological Review* (Belmont, CA: Wadsworth Publishing, 1970).

12. Macintosh, "A Contextual Model," 47.

13. K. Ewusi-Mensah, "The External Environment and Its Impact on Management Information Systems," *Accounting, Organizations and Society* (December 1981): 301–16.

14. G.A. Christy, *Capital Budgeting—Current Practices and Their Efficiency* (Eugene: University of Oregon, Bureau of Business and Economic Research, 1966); T.P. Klammer, "The Association of Capital Budgeting Techniques with Firm Performance," *The Accounting Review* (April 1973): 353–64; G.L. Sundem, "Evaluating Simplified Capital Budgeting Models Using a Time-State Performance Matrix," *The Accounting Review* (April 1974): 306–20; G.L. Sundem, "Evaluating Capital Budgeting Models in Simulated Environments," *Journal of Finance* (September 1975): 977–92; S.H. Kim, "An Empirical Study on the Relationship between Capital Budgeting Practices and Earnings Performance," *Engineering Economist* (Spring 1982): 185–96.

15. S.F. Haka, L.A. Gordon, and G.E. Pincher, "Sophisticated Capital Budgeting Selection Techniques and Firm Performance," *The Accounting Review* (October 1985): 651–69.

16. S.F. Haka, "Capital Budgeting Techniques and Firm Specific Contingencies: A Conditional Analysis," *Accounting, Organizations and Society* (January 1987): 31–48.

17. A.K. Gupta and V. Govindarajan, "Business Unit Strategy, Management Characteristics and Business Unit Effectiveness at Strategy Implementation," *Academy of Management Journal* (March 1984): 221–33.

18. V. Govindarajan and A.K. Gupta, "Linking Control Systems to Business Unit Strategy: Impact on Performance," *Accounting, Organizations and Society* (January 1985): 51–66.

19. Ibid.

20. C.W. Hofer and D.E. Schendel, *Strategy Formulation: Analytical Concepts* (St. Paul, MN: West Publishing, 1978); D.C. Hambrick, I.C. MacMillan, and D.I. Day, "Strategic Attributes and Performance in the Four Cells of the BCG-matrix: A PIMS-Based Analysis of Industrial-Product Business," *Academy of Management Journal* (January 1982): 510–31.

21. R. Simons, "Accounting Control Systems and Business Strategy: An Empirical Analysis," *Accounting, Organizations and Society* (July 1987): 357–74.

22. T. Burns and G.F. Stalker, *The Management of Innovation* (London: Tavistock, 1961); D. Miller and P.H. Friesen, "Innovation in Conservation and Entrepreneurial Firms," *Strategic Management Journal* (February 1982): 1–27.

23. R.E. Miles and C.C. Snow, *Organizational Strategy, Structure, and Process* (New York: McGraw-Hill, 1978).

24. Simons, "Accounting Control Systems," 359.

25. P.N. Khandwalla, "The Effects of Different Types of Competition in the Use of Management Controls," *Journal of Accounting Research* (Autumn 1982): 275–285.

26. Ibid., 282.

27. W.J. Burns and J.H. Waterhouse, "Budgetary Control and Organizational Structure," *Journal of Accounting Research* (Autumn 1975): 177–203.

28. Ibid., 179.

29. Kenneth A. Merchant, "The Design of the Corporate Budgeting System: Influences on Managerial Behavior and Performance," *The Accounting Review* (October 1981): 813–29; idem, "Influences on Departmental Budgeting: An Empirical Examination of a Contingency Model," *Accounting, Organizations and Society* (June 1984): 291–307.

30. H.O. Rockness and M.D. Shields, "An Empirical Analysis of the Expenditure Budget in Research and Development," *Contemporary Accounting Research* (Spring 1988): 568–81.

31. H. Das, "Organizational and Decision Characteristics and Personality as Determinants of Control Actions: A Laboratory Experiment," *Accounting, Organizations and Society* (May 1986): 215–31.

32. Ibid., 226.

33. A. Belkaoui, "The Relationship between Self-Disclosure Style and Attitudes to Responsibility Accounting," *Accounting, Organizations and Society* 6, no. 4 (1981): 281–90.

34. Ibid., 287.

35. D.C. Hayes, "The Contingency Theory of Management Accounting," *The Accounting Review* (January 1977): 22–39.

36. V. Govindarajan, "Appropriateness of Accounting Data in Performance Evaluation: An Empirical Examination of Environmental Uncertainty as an Intervening Variable," *Accounting, Organizations and Society* (February 1984): 125–35.

37. Ibid., 130.

38. A.G. Hopwood, "An Empirical Study of the Role of Accounting Data in Performance Evaluation," supplement to *Journal of Accounting Research* (1972): 156–82; David T. Otley, "Budget Use and Managerial Performance," *Journal of Accounting Research* (Spring 1978): 122–49.

39. R.L. Daft and N.B. Macintosh, "A New Approach to Design and Use of Management Information," *California Management Review* (Fall 1978): 82–92.

40. L.A. Gordon and V.K. Narayanan, "Management Accounting Systems, Perceived Environmental Uncertainty and Organizational Structures: An Empirical Investigation," *Accounting, Organizations and Society* (December 1983): 33–47.

41. J. Pijer, "Determinants of Financial Control Systems for Multiple Retailers—Some Case Study Evidence," unpublished paper, University of Loughborough, 1978.

42. Theresa Libby and John H. Waterhouse, "Predicting Change in Management Accounting Systems," *Journal of Management Accounting Research* 8 (1996): 137–50.

43. A.S. Dunk, "Reliance on Budgetary Control, Manufacturing Process Automation and Production Subunit Performance: A Research Note," *Accounting, Organizations and Society* 17 (1992): 195–203.

44. D.T. Otley, "The Contingency Theory of Management Accounting: Achievement and Prognosis," *Accounting, Organizations and Society* 15 (1980): 413–428.

45. D. Lyall, K. Okoh, and A. Puscty, "Cost Control in the 1990s," *Management Accounting* 10 (February 1990): 44–45.

46. S. Mark Young, Michael D. Shields, and Gerrit Wolf, "Manufacturing Controls and Performance: An Experiment," *Accounting, Organizations and Society* 13, no. 6 (1988): 607–18.

47. Ibid., 617.

48. R.J. Schonberger, *World Class Manufacturing* (New York: Free Press, 1986).

49. Lynn Griffin and Adrian Harrell, "An Empirical Examination of Managers' Mo-

tivation to Implement Just-in-Time Procedures," *Accounting, Organizations and Society* 3 (1991): 36–44.

50. Betty Vanderbosch, "An Empirical Analysis of the Association between the Use of Executive Support Systems and Perceived Organizational Competitiveness," *Accounting, Organizations and Society* 26 (1999): 77–92.

51. Ibid., 87.

52. Robert W. Rutledge and Khoudkar E. Karim, "The Influence of Self-Interest and Ethical Considerations in Managers' Evaluation Judgments," *Accounting, Organizations and Society* 24 (1999): 173–84.

53. Ibid., 173.

54. Ibid., 181–82.

55. Margaret A. Abernethy and Johannes U. Stoelwinder, "Budget Use, Task Uncertainty, System Goal Orientation and Subunit Performance: A Test of the 'Fat' Hypothesis in Not-for-Profit Hospitals," *Accounting, Organizations and Society* 16 (1991): 105–20.

56. Ibid., 105.

57. Ibid., 115.

58. E.E. Lawler and J.G. Rhode, *Information and Control in Organizations* (Pacific Palisades, CA: Goodyear, 1976).

59. J.G. Birnberg, L. Turopolec, and S.M. Young, "The Organizational Content of Accounting," *Accounting, Organizations and Society* 15 (1983): 111–29.

60. S. Kerr, "On the Folly of Rewarding A while Hoping for B," *Academy of Management Journal* 13 (1975): 769–83.

61. B. Weitz, "Effectiveness and Sales Interaction: A Contingency Framework," *Journal of Marketing* 5 (1981): 85–103.

62. Bernard J. Jaworski and S. Marls Young, "Dysfunctional Behavior and Management Control: An Empirical Study of Marketing Managers," *Accounting, Organizations and Society* 17, no. 1 (1992): 17–35.

63. Vidya Awasthi and Jamie Pratt, "The Effects of Monetary Incentives on Effort and Decision Performance: The Role of Cognitive Characteristics," *The Accounting Review* (October 1990): 797–811.

64. W.F. Wright and M.E. Ahoul-Ezz, "Effects of Extrinsic Incentives on the Quality of Frequency Assessments," *Organizational Behavior and Human Decision Performance* 41 (April 1988): 143–52.

65. W.F. Wiger and U. Anderson, "The Effects of Situational Familiarity and Financial Incentives on the Use of the Anchoring and Adjustment Heuristic for the Probability Assessment," *Organizational Behavior and Human Decision Performance* 66 (February 1989): 68–82.

66. Awasthi and Pratt, "Role of Monetary Incentives on Effort and Decision Performance."

67. H.R. Arkes, R.M. Dawes, and C. Christensen, "Factors Influencing the Use of a Decision Rule in a Probabilistic Task," *Organizational Behavior and Human Decision Process* (February 1986): 93–110.

68. R.H. Ashton, "Pressure and Performance in Effects of Incentives, Feedback and Justification," *Journal of Accounting Research* 28, Supplement (1990): 148–80.

69. R.M. Hogarth, B.J. Gibbs, C.R. McKenzie, and M.A. Marquis, "Learning from Feedback: Exactingness and Incentives," *Journal of Experimental Psychology: Learning, Memory and Cognition* 17 (July 1991): 734–52.

70. Geoffrey B., Sprinkle, "The Effect of Incentive Contracts on Learning and Performance," *The Accounting Review* (July 2000): 299–326.

71. Ibid., 301.

72. M. Porter, *Competitive Strategy* (New York: Free Press, 1980).

73. R. Kaplan and D. Norton, *The Balanced Scorecard* (Boston: Harvard Business School Press, 1996).

74. C.T. Horngen, G. Foster, and S.M. Datar, *Cost Accounting: A Managerial Emphasis*, 10th ed. (Upper Saddle River, NJ: Prentice-Hall, 2000), 467.

75. Marlys Gasclio Lipe and Steven E. Salterio, "The Balanced Scorecard: Judgmental Effects of Common and Unique Performance Measures," *The Accounting Review* (July 2000): 285–98.

76. P. Slovic and D. MacPhillamy, "Dimensional Commensurability and Cue Utilization in Comparative Judgement," *Organizational Behavior and Human Performance* 10 (1991): 33–64.

77. Lipe and Salterio, "Balanced Scorecard: Judgmental Effects of Common and Unique Performance Measures."

78. B. Holstrom and P. Milgrom, "Multitask Principal-Agent Analyses: Incentive Contracts, Asset Ownership, and Job Design," *Journal of Law, Economics, and Organization* 7 (1991): 24–52.

79. A. Belkaoui, "Learning Order and Acceptance of Accounting Techniques," *The Accounting Review* (October 1975): 897–99.

80. A. Belkaoui, "Primary-Recency, Ego-Involvement and the Acceptance of Accounting Techniques," *The Accounting Review* (January 1977): 252–56.

81. A. Belkaoui, "How Receptive Are Accountants to Innovation? Personality Can Hinder Progress," *The Chartered Accountant Magazine* (May 1982): 46–49.

82. Ahmed Riahi-Belkaoui, "An Experimental Study of Entitlements, Rights, Fairness and Intrafirm Resource Allocation," *Accounting and Business Review* (July 1996): 201–14.

83. E. Hoffman and M.L. Spitzer, "Entitlements, Rights and Fairness: An Experimental Examination of Subjects' Concepts of Distinctive Justice," *Journal of Legal Studies* 14 (1985): 59–97.

84. E. Hoffman and M.L. Spitzer, "The Coase Theorem: Some Experimental Tests," *Journal of Law and Economics* 25 (1892): 73–98.

85. E. Noreen, "The Economics of Ethics: A New Perspective on Agency Theory," *Accounting, Organizations and Society* (June 1988): 359–70.

86. R.M. Dawes, "Social Dilemmas," *Annual Review of Psychology* 2 (1980): 169–93.

SELECTED BIBLIOGRAPHY

Belkaoui, A. "The Relationship between Self-Disclosure Style and Attitudes to Responsibility Accounting." *Accounting, Organizations and Society*, 6, no. 4 (1981): 281–85.

Burns, T., and G.H. Stalker. *The Management of Innovation*. London: Tavistock, 1961.

Burns, W.J., and J.H. Waterhouse. "Budgetary Control and Organizational Structure." *Journal of Accounting Research* (Autumn 1975): 177–203.

Christy, G.A. *Capital Budgeting—Current Practices and Their Efficiency*. Eugene: University of Oregon, Bureau of Business and Economic Research, 1966.

Daft, R.L., and N.B. Macintosh. "A New Approach to Design and Use of Management Information." *California Management Review* (Fall 1978): 82–92.

Das, H. "Organizational and Decision Characteristics and Personality as Determinants of Control Actions: A Laboratory Experiment." *Accounting, Organizations and Society* (May 1986): 215–21.

Driver, M.J., and T.J. Mock. "Human Information Processing: Decision Style Theory and Accounting Information System." *The Accounting Review* (July 1975): 497.

Ewusi-Mensah, K. "The External Environment and Its Impact on Management Information Systems." *Accounting, Organizations and Society* (December 1981): 301–16.

Gordon, L.A., and D. Miller. "Design of Accounting Information Systems." *Accounting, Organizations and Society* (June 1976): 59–69.

Gordon, L.A., and V.K. Narayanan. "Management Accounting Systems, Perceived Environmental Uncertainty and Organizational Structures: An Empirical Investigation." *Accounting, Organizations and Society* (December 1983): 33–47.

Govindarajan, V. "Appropriateness of Accounting Data in Performance Evaluation: An Empirical Examination of Environmental Uncertainty as an Intervening Variable." *Accounting, Organizations and Society* (February 1984): 125–35.

Govindarajan, V., and A.K. Gupta. "Linking Control Systems to Business Unit Strategy: Impact on Performance." *Accounting, Organizations and Society* (January 1985): 51–66.

Gupta, A.K., and V. Govindarajan. "Business Unit Strategy, Management Characteristics and Business Unit Effectiveness at Strategy Implementation." *Academy of Management Journal* (March 1984): 221–33.

Haka, S.F. "Capital Budgeting Techniques and Firm Specific Contingencies: A Conditional Analysis." *Accounting, Organizations and Society* (January 1987): 31–48.

Haka, S.F., L.A. Gordon, and G.E. Pincher. "Sophisticated Capital Budgeting Selection Techniques and Firm Performance." *Accounting Review* (October 1985): 651–69.

Hambrick, D.C., I.C. MacMillan, and D.I. Day. "Strategic Attributes and Performance in the Four Cells of the BCG-matrix: A PIMS-Based Analysis of Industrial-Product Business." *Academy of Management Journal* (January 1982): 510–31.

Hayes, D.C. "The Contingency Theory of Management Accounting." *The Accounting Review* (January 1977): 22–39.

Hofer, C.W., and D.E. Schendel. *Strategy Formulation: Analytical Concepts*. St. Paul, MN: West Publishing, 1978.

Hopwood, A.C. "An Empirical Study of the Role of Accounting Data in Performance Evaluation." Supplement to *Journal of Accounting Research* (1972): 156–82.

Khandwalla, P.N. "The Effects of Different Types of Competition in the Use of Management Controls." *Journal of Accounting Research* (Autumn 1982): 275–85.

Kim, S.H. "An Empirical Study on the Relationship between Capital Budgeting Practices and Earnings Performance." *Engineering Economist* (Spring 1982): 185–96.

Klammer, T.P. "The Association of Capital Budgeting Techniques with Firm Performance." *The Accounting Review* (April 1973): 353–64.

Macintosh, N.B. "A Contextual Model of Information Systems." *Accounting, Organizations and Society* (February 1981): 39–52.

Macintosh, N.B., and R.L. Deft. "Management Control Systems and Departmental Interdependencies: An Empirical Study." *Accounting, Organizations and Society* (January 1987): 49–61.

Merchant, Kenneth A. "The Design of the Corporate Budgeting System: Influences on Managerial Behavior and Performance." *The Accounting Review* (October 1981): 813–29.

———. "Influences on Departmental Budgeting: An Empirical Examination of a Contingency Model." *Accounting, Organizations and Society* (June 1984): 291–307.

Miles, R.E., and C.C. Snow. *Organizational Strategy, Structure, and Process.* New York: McGraw-Hill, 1978.

Miller, D., and P.H. Friesen. "Innovation in Conservation and Entrepreneurial Firms." *Strategic Management Journal* (February 1982): 1–27.

Otley, David T. "Budget Use and Managerial Performance." *Journal of Accounting Research* (Spring 1978): 122–49.

———. "The Contingency Theory of Management Accounting: Achievement and Prognosis." *Accounting, Organizations and Society* (December 1980): 413–28.

Perrow, C. *Organizational Analysis: A Sociological Review.* Belmont, CA: Wadsworth Publishing, 1970.

Pijer, J. "Determinants of Financial Control Systems for Multiple Retailers—Some Case Study Evidence." Unpublished paper, University of Loughborough, 1978.

Rockness, H.O., and M.D. Shields. "An Empirical Analysis of the Expenditure Budget in Research and Development." *Contemporary Accounting Research* (Spring 1988): 568–81.

Simons, R. "Accounting Control Systems and Business Strategy: An Empirical Analysis." *Accounting, Organizations and Society* (July 1987): 357–74.

Sundem, G.L. "Evaluating Capital Budgeting Models in Simulated Environments." *Journal of Finance* (September 1975): 977–92.

———. "Evaluating Simplified Capital Budgeting Models Using a Time-State Performance Matrix." *The Accounting Review* (April 1974): 306–20.

Thompson, J.D. *Organizations in Action.* New York: McGraw-Hill, 1967.

Tiessen, P.A., and D.M. Baker. "Human Information Processing, Decision Style Theory, and Accounting Information Systems: A Comment." *The Accounting Review* (October 1977): 984–87.

Waterhouse, J.H., and P. Tiessen. "A Contingency Framework for Management Accounting Systems Research." *Accounting, Organizations and Society* (August 1978): 65–76.

Functional and Data Fixation

INTRODUCTION

Functional fixation, as it is used in accounting, suggests that under certain circumstances a decision maker might be unable to adjust his or her decision process to a change in the accounting process that supplied him or her with input data. Borrowed from the literature of psychology, the phenomenon has been used in a slightly different way by accounting researchers. The purposes of this chapter are, first, to differentiate between the functional-fixation phenomenon as it is understood in psychology and the data-fixation phenomenon as it is used in accounting; second, to examine the results of the various experimental studies in the area; and third, to provide possible theoretical explanations of the phenomenon and to suggest better methodologies for studying the phenomenon in management accounting.

NATURE OF FUNCTIONAL FIXATION

Functional Fixation in Psychology

Functional fixation originated as a concept in psychology, arising from an investigation of the impact of past experience on human behavior. In his examination of the relation between stimulus equivalence and reasoning, Maier identified several ways in which past experience can affect the problem-solving process.[1] He viewed past experience as a salient factor in problem solving, in that problem solving can be facilitated by equivalences that exist in immediate problem situations and in past experiences. In addition, the background of past learning is an essential repertoire of behavior that is available for restructuring when it is needed for new situations. Not all psychologists, however, have viewed past experience as a positive factor. Some have seen it as an obstacle that prevents productive thinking. Duncker introduced the concept of functional fixation to illustrate the negative role of past experiences.[2] He investigated the hypothesis that an individual's prior use of an object in a function dissimilar to that required in a present problem would serve to inhibit the discovery of an appropriate, novel use for the object. His results supported the functional-fixation hypothesis with regard to several common objects, for example, boxes, pliers, weights, and paper clips. Birch and Rabinowitz criticized Duncker's experiments, showing that an individual can also learn about an object's versatility and therefore display a relatively low degree of fixation even if learning about one function of an object restricts the number of ways in which it is used.[3] A series of experiments by Flavell, Cooper, and Loisell supported this conclusion.[4]

Others who have refined Duncker's experiments nevertheless have supported the functional-fixation hypothesis. Adamson, in his box experiment, gave subjects the task of attaching three small candles to a screen, at a height of about five feet, using to accomplish the task any of a large number of objects that were lying on the table, namely three pasteboard boxes, five matches, and five thumbtacks.[5] The solution consisted of putting one candle on each box by melting wax on the box, sticking the candle to the box, and then tacking the boxes to the screen. The idea was to have the box be used as a platform on which to attach the candle, a novel function for boxes. Two groups were used. The experimental one was presented with the objects inside the box; the control group had the objects on the table. "Hence, the boxes had their initial function, that of containing, whereas in their solution function, they had to be used as supports or platforms."[6] The results showed that the control group outperformed the experimental group in terms of both the number of solutions and the time required to reach the solutions. This suggested that the subjects in the experimental group were functionally fixated on using boxes as containers rather than as platforms.

In the two-string experiments, Adamson and Taylor asked their subjects to tie together the free ends of strings hanging from the ceiling.[7] Because the strings were placed so far apart, the problem could be solved only by tying a weight to one string, swinging it like a pendulum, and catching it while holding the other string. The task then could be completed by tying the two strings together. Of the various objects provided to the subjects, only two—an electrical switch and an electrical relay—were sufficiently heavy to serve as weights. Half of the subjects were trained before the experiment to use the switch to complete an electrical circuit, while the other half were trained to use a relay for the same task. The results of the experiment supported the functional-fixation hypothesis for the reason that the subjects trained to use the switch to complete the circuit used the relay to solve the two-string task, while those who had been trained to use the relay to complete the circuit used the switch as a pendulum weight. This fixation phenomenon was reported in a series of other experiments.[8] The degree of fixity also was found to depend on some mediating factors, such as the span of time since the object was previously used,[9] the necessity of using the object in a novel way to solve the problem,[10] hints,[11] and intelligence.[12]

Data Fixation in Accounting

Ijiri, Jaedicke, and Knight viewed the decision process as being characterized by three factors: decision inputs, decision outputs, and decision rules. They then introduced the conditions under which a decision maker cannot adjust his or her decision process to a change in the accounting process. For example, changes in depreciation methods or inventory techniques lead to different profit figures. Ijiri, Jaedicke, and Knight attributed the inability to adjust, if it existed, to the psychological factor of functional fixation.[13] They stated:

Psychologists have found that there appears to be functional fixation in most human behavior in which the person attaches a meaning to a title or object (e.g., manufacturing cost) and is unable to see alternative meanings or uses. People intuitively associate a value with an item through past experience, and often do not recognize that the value of the item depends, in fact, upon the particular moment in time and may be significantly different from what it was in the past. Therefore, when a person is placed in a new situation, he views the object or term as used previously.[14]

To link the psychological concept of functional fixation to accounting, they merely stated the following:

If the outputs from different accounting methods are called by the same name, such as profit, costs, etc., people who do understand accounting well tend to neglect the fact that alternative methods may have been used to prepare the outputs. In such cases, a change in the accounting process clearly influences the decisions.[15]

This extrapolation of a psychological concept to accounting is welcome if it is interpreted correctly. The literature now recognizes the point that the focus in psychology is on functions, whereas Ijiri, Jaedicke, and Knight focused on outputs. If we go back to the example of a change in inventory techniques, functional fixation in psychology implies that the decision makers are accustomed to using the data for one function (such as price decisions) and now fail to see its potential use for another function (for example, production decisions). As introduced by Ijiri, Jaedicke, and Knight, functional fixation implies that decision makers are fixated on the accounting output (for example, the profit output) and are unable to adjust to see that the change in output is due to the change in inventory techniques. Thus, while psychologists are interested in functional fixation involving functions or objects, accounting research, influenced by Ijiri, Jaedicke, and Knight's extrapolation, is interested in functional fixation involving data. One might assume correctly that most of the interest in psychology has been on functional fixation. The exceptions to this assumption are a psychological data-fixation study by Knight and a mixed data-fixation/ functional-fixation study in accounting by Barnes and Webb.[16] Ashton also has recognized the difference between the two views of functional fixation in accounting and psychology.[17] He came to a peculiar conclusion, however, when he stated:

We should recognize that the functional fixation hypothesis in accounting is a modified form (or forms) of the hypothesis in psychology. The modified functional hypothesis should be subjected to research in accounting contexts, rather than relying entirely on the original functional fixation research as Ijiri, Jaedicke, Knight, and subsequent researchers appear to have done.[18]

The approach should consider two forms of the functional-fixation hypothesis, one focusing on function and one focusing on output or data. There lies the main difference: in the case of functional fixation, psychologists used objects such as medallions, string, and boxes to solve relatively simple tasks, whereas the data-fixation experiments all used data to solve unstructured problems.

DATA-FIXATION RESEARCH IN ACCOUNTING

Data-Fixation Research Based on the Ijiri-Jaedicke-Knight Paradigm

Functional-fixation research in accounting generally has followed Ijiri, Jaedicke, and Knight's prescriptions, focusing on data rather than function, and has led to a series of data-fixation experiments. Ashton used M.B.A. students to assess the extent to which individual decision makers alter their decision processes after the occurrence of an accounting change, from full-cost to variable-cost data, as evidenced by the effect of this cognitive change on subsequent decisions.[19] Ashton not only discussed the accounting change with the subjects but also mentioned whether it reflected more or less important informational content, and consequently may have dictated a change in the decision behavior of the subjects. This result suggests that a large proportion of subjects in the experimental groups failed to adjust significantly their decision process in response to the accounting change, thereby providing evidence of the existence of functional fixation in accounting. The study was not met with complete approval. First, Libby criticized it for an experimental design that might have become confounded with the effects of the accounting change.[20] He concluded that

serious questions concerning the way in which the conceptual network was operationalized, coupled with methodology deficiencies, question whether any conclusions can change the subjects, the manipulation of the moderating variables information and importance, and the method of measuring the change in the subject's decision process.[21]

Second, Pearson, a practitioner, simply rejected the study's objectives and results as irrelevant to accounting.[22] These criticisms, as might be expected, motivated further empirical research.

Swieringa, Dyckman, and Hoskin looked into Libby's criticisms and found that subjects tended to adjust their information processing as a result of the accounting change even though the significance of these adjustments differed depending on how they were measured.[23] The amount of information provided was found to influence the subjects' adjustments of their information processing. Swieringa, Dyckman, and Hoskin had made two modifications in Ashton's experimental design. One modification was to isolate the effects of the amount and form of the information about the accounting change. The second modification was to have the data received by the control groups be equivalent to the data received by the experimental groups.

A second study by Dyckman, Hoskin, and Swieringa merely replicated the earlier study by Swieringa, Dyckman, and Hoskin with subjects who, on average, were older and had more exposure to accounting and business matters.[24] The students used in the first study were enrolled in an introductory accounting course in a college of agriculture and life sciences and did not know what direct costing meant. In addition, the second study relied on a cross-sectional approach instead of a time-series approach to analyze the effects of the experimental conditions and demographic variables on the prices set by the subjects for each product. The results of the second study were found to be similar to those of the first one.

In their experiment, Chang and Birnberg provided M.B.A. students with a cost variance report and a cost standard.[25] The subjects were required to indicate (1) whether they would investigate the production process, and (2) how large a variance would be necessary to justify an investigation. Their results pointed to the existence of a "weak form" of data fixity when a change in the variance amount was introduced. The "weak form" label was used to characterize a slight change in behavior; no change in behavior was evidence of the "strong form" of fixity. Two significant findings were noted by the authors:

First, fixity is not a phenomenon that is unavoidable. Research indicates that once we are aware of its presence, we can take steps to cope with it. The real question becomes one of finding the manner in which it can be reduced and efficient ways of doing so. Second, unfortunately, once alerted to the problem, there is reason to believe that the subject's behavior will continue to reflect elements of past behavior—behavior which should have been forgotten along with the superseded data set. This then suggests two topics for future research. One is how past experience affects the subject's behavior. The other is how to extinguish the older, now unnecessary patterns of behavior.[26]

Abdel-Khalik and Keller used bank investment offices and security analysts in their investigation of functional fixation.[27] They articulated their research problems as follows:

If investors are functionally fixated on the use of reported accounting earnings, then they will tend to ignore other accounting information which is not consistent with accounting numbers. The accounting signal which we chose to be inconsistent with reported earnings is the decision of management to switch the method of inventory valuation from First-in, First-out (FIFO) or from average cost to Last-in, First-out (LIFO) for both accounting and tax purposes.[28]

Because of the higher cash flows that result from change to LIFO in a period of rising prices, the investor using a cash-flow discounted model would value the firm higher, while another relying and fixated on earnings would value it lower. The results of the experiment showed evidence of functional fixation, as the subjects relied on the adjusted net income rather than cash flows in evaluating the securities. One problem with Abdel-Khalik and Keller's study is the fact that the firms that switched to LIFO received qualified audit opinions, while those on FIFO obtained unqualified opinions. This could explain why the LIFO firms generally were viewed as having lower expected returns.

Bloom, Elgers, and Murray extended the Ashton study by examining both individual and group decisions in response to a fully disclosed, cosmetic change in depreciation method.[29] The results of the study showed a moderate shift in the decision behavior of individuals, a phenomenon similar to what Chang and Birnberg called the weak form of fixation. In addition, they found that groups exhibited a higher degree of fixation than did individuals. Among the reasons given for this difference were the following: "One explanation is that the group process inhibited the collective or individual intellectual functioning of its members; yet another is that the groups incurred a higher cost in developing a new decision rule in response to the accounting change than did the individuals."[30]

Another explanation was that the difference could be a reflection of the nature of the task, which consisted of the need both to reach a decision within the group on a decision rule and to make a decision on the task.[31]

Another accounting study provided evidence of functional fixation without being based on Ashton's and Ijiri, Jaedicke, and Knight's paradigms. A National Association of Accountants (NAA) research study on the effects of software accounting policies on bank lending decisions and stock prices showed clear evidence of fixation by loan officers making a decision on a loan to two fictional firms: the Campbell Corporation, which capitalized software expenditures; and the Edwards Corporation, which expensed all software costs.[32] Without mentioning data fixation per se, the results were indicative of the presence of the phenomenon. Witness the following:

Campbell was favored over Edwards by 62.2% of the respondents; Edwards was favored by 11.1%; 13.3% would treat the companies equally, but did not give any reason for the equal treatment; and 13.3% would treat the companies equally because a company's software policy would not influence the lending decision. Only 27.3% of the bankers would grant a $3 million, five year unsecured loan to Edwards; compare with 61.4% for Campbell. Of those respondents that gave an interest rate for both companies, 55% would charge Campbell a lower rate, 5% would charge Edwards a lower rate, and 40% would charge the same rate to both companies.[33]

A similar finding was made in another study. Belkaoui conducted an experiment in which bank loan officers evaluated a loan application that was accompanied by financial statements based on either accrual or modified cash accounting.[34] The loan officers in the experiment believed that the loan applicant presenting accrual accounting financial statements (1) was more likely to repay the loan, (2) was more likely to be granted the loan, (3) was given a different interest rate premium, and (4) had statements that were more reliable and freer of clerical errors.

Other Data-Fixation Research

Other accounting research studies have used the Ijiri-Jaedicke-Knight paradigm to explain their own results. This strategy has taken place both in the research of investor decisions and in capital market research.

In the research of investor decisions, a cross-sectional orientation was given to functional fixation as it was applied to alternative accounting methods rather than to changes in accounting methods over time. Jensen examined the impact of alternative depreciation and inventory costing methods on investor decisions.[35] To explain his findings that alternative accounting techniques affected decision making, he suggested that his subjects might be functionally fixated on net earnings. Livingstone examined the effects of alternative, interperiod tax-allocation methods on regulatory rate-of-return decisions affecting the electric utility industry.[36] In light of his findings that some rate-making books focus on "raw" rates of return and ignore the effects of alternative tax-allocation methods, he offered the explanation that some predictions might be functionally fixated on net operating revenue. Livingstone stated the following:

It is therefore hypothesized that the reason that original-cost jurisdictions have been so much slower to adjust for alternative treatments of deferred taxes is that they are functionally fixated with respect to financial statement data. Since normalizing changes the amount but not the name of net operating revenue, it is intended that original-cost jurisdictions tend to view net operating revenue under normalizing as being the same as without it.[37]

Livingstone also suggested that users of accounting information could have formed a learning set after having experience with a significant number of different problems, all of which can be solved in the same manner. One solution went as follows: "If the hypothesis of a learning set with respect to alternative accounting methods is valid, multi-informational accounting statements would tend to stimulate learning and reduce functional fixation by providing users with information on accounting alternatives."[38] Mlynarczyk examined the effect of alternative tax-accounting methods on common-stock prices of electric utility companies and related functional fixation to his work.[39]

In capital market research, the functional-fixation hypothesis has been used to explain the lack of efficiency in the capital market. Beaver argued, however, that the market is not functionally fixated.[40] He stated the following:

In essence, the implication of the functional fixation hypothesis is that two firms (securities) could be alike in all "real" economic respects and yet sell for different prices, simply because of the way the accountant reported the results of operations. The implication is that the market ignores the fact that observed signals are generated from different information systems. Hence, it does not distinguish between numbers generated by different accounting methods either over time or across firms. Needless to say, this implies market inefficiency. . . . The functional fixation hypothesis as described above is a rather extreme form of the market inefficiency argument, in that it implies that disequilibrium could exist indefinitely and presumably permanently.[41]

DATA FIXATION AND FUNCTIONAL FIXATION IN ACCOUNTING AND PSYCHOLOGY

As stated earlier, most accounting research has focused on data fixation, while psychological research has focused on functional fixation. The exceptions to this are a data-fixation study in psychology by Knight and a mixed data-fixation functional-fixation study in accounting by Barnes and Webb.[42]

Knight conducted an experiment to investigate the impact of the successful solving of n water jug problems on the problem-solving techniques used in trial $n + 1$. The results showed that a series of successes caused the subject to persist in his early behavior, making it difficult for him to see the alternative (correct) approach. Furthermore, the subject would give complex, correct solutions to even trivial problems in cases where the complex solutions had led to successful results in the previous n trials.

Barnes and Webb were interested in the investigation of both the data-fixation and the functional-fixation hypothesis in accounting. Actual managers were asked to make price decisions based on real-life case studies that differed in their method of inventory valuation (full costing versus direct costing). The data-fixation hypothesis was confirmed in that the subjects were fixated by the total costs figure, altering their projected price in response to the changes in reported costs caused by the measurement change. However, the functional-fixation hypothesis was not confirmed because the subjects did not try to recover overhead costs, even though they were instructed that this was necessary, simply because they were not used to doing so. The lack of evidence for the functional-fixity hypothesis, a phenomenon widely observed in psychology, was attributed to the use of highly experienced and intelligent scientists. This is not surprising since intelligence has been found to mitigate fixity.[43]

DETERMINANTS OF FUNCTIONAL FIXATION IN ACCOUNTING

The Conditioning Hypothesis

The impact of accounting data on users and their behavior has always been a subject of interest for social scientists. One extreme concern, expressed by Schumpeter, goes as follows:

Capitalist practice turns the unit of money into a tool of rational cost-profit calculations, of which the towering monument is double-entry bookkeeping. . . . Primarily a product of the evolution of economic rationality, the cost-profit calculus in turn reacts upon that rationality; by crystallizing and defining numerically, it powerfully propels the logic of enterprise. . . . This type of logic or attitude or method then starts upon its conqueror's career subjugating—rationalizing—man's tools and philosophies, his medical practice, his picture of the cosmos, his outlook on life, everything in fact including his concepts of beauty and justice and his spiritual ambitions.[44]

Accounting researchers have not reached the point of Schumpeter's consensus, but they also have stressed the notion that the socialization of accountants, with its emphasis on particular cost and income considerations, can lead to a form of conditioning and might explain some of the empirically observed decision processes. The argument is that users, individually or in aggregate, react because they have been conditioned to react to accounting data rather than because the data have any informational content. For example, Sterling contends that

if the response of receivers to accounting stimuli is to be taken as evidence that certain kinds of accounting practices are justified, then we must not overlook the possibility that those responses were conditioned. Accounting reports have been issued for a long time, and their issuance has been accompanied by a rather impressive ceremony performed by the managers and accountants who issue them. The receivers are likely to have gained the impression that they ought to react and have noted that others react, and thereby have become conditioned to react.[45]

It may also be argued that the recipients of accounting information react when they should not react or should not react the way they do. The conditioning hypothesis has also been advanced by Revsine as follows:

The process by which users may be conditioned to the data they receive could occur in at least two ways. First, as students in business training curricula, the prospective students are introduced to generally accepted accounting principles and the financial statements that result from the applications of these principles and their derivative procedures. Furthermore, they are taught manipulative operations and techniques such as ratio and funds flow analysis that utilize accounting data as a means of evaluating enterprise performance and prospects. In short, users are generally indoctrinated concerning the relevance and utility of traditionally disseminated information. Second, this formal conditioning is continually reinforced by each external report that users receive.[46]

One explanation of the data-fixation findings may be that subjects of the experiments, mostly accounting students, have been conditioned to react to some form of accounting outputs (for instance, cost or income income outputs), and have failed to adjust their decision processes in response to a "well-disclosed" accounting change. The conditioning phenomenon inhibits the subjects from adopting the correct behavior, which is to adjust to the accounting change, and has led them to act as they have been conditioned to act in their previous behaviors or socialization sessions. Thus, the phenomenon is a form of functional fixation, as the subjects no longer are able to discriminate.

Prospect Theory and the Framing Hypothesis

Kahneman and Tversky's prospect theory states that potential gains and losses are evaluated by an S-shaped value, function, one that is convex (indicating a risk-averse orientation) for losses.[47] Four effects are observable in the process of choosing among bets:

1. *Certainty effect*: "People overweigh outcomes that are considered certain relative to outcomes which are merely probable."[48]
2. *Reflection effect*: "The selection of prospects around 0 reverses the preference order."[49]
3. *Aversion to probabilistic insurance*: Subjects do not like the idea of probabilistic insurance because it pays off with a probability of less-than-one but diminishes the premium.
4. *Isolation effect*: "In order to simplify the choice between alternatives, people often disregard components that distinguish them."[50]

The concept of framing options adds the key idea that the frame of the decision is simply the decision maker's concept of the decision problem or its structure. The frame is defined as follows: "The decision-maker's conception of the acts, outcomes and contingencies [is] associated with a particular choice. The frame that a decision-maker adopts is controlled partly by the formulation of the problem and partly by the norms, habits and personal characteristics of the decision-maker."[51]

Framing occurs because the wording of a question has the potential to alter a subject's response. Functional fixation may be viewed as a result of the particular choice of framing options made by the subjects in the experiments. The formulation of the decision tasks as well as the norms, habits, and personal characteristics of the subjects affect the framing of the decision and lead to the functional- or data-fixation results.

Interference Theory: Stimulus Encoding versus Retroactive Intuition

The learning theory holds that prior knowledge can either interfere with or facilitate effective decision making. The interference theory emerged from the two possible outcomes of the transfer-of-training hypothesis. According to the latter hypothesis, the transfer of training may have either facilitating or inhibitory effects. When a subject learns two tasks, task 1 and task 2, then is asked to perform task 1, the effects of the transfer of training are as follows: "Transfer may facilitate the learning of the second task, or conceivably have an inhibitory effect and interfere with the second learning and the mastery of the second task may help or hinder the subsequent performance of the first task"[52] What results, then, are two possible effects:

1. A negative transfer is labeled retroactive inhibition or retroactive interference.[53] In such a case the learning of task 2 affects the performance of the first task. The design used for the study of retroactive interference is as follows:[54]

Experimental group: Learn Task 1 Learn Task 2 Test Task 1
Control group: Learn Task 1 Test Task 1

Functional fixity has been viewed as "a classic case of negative transfer."

2. A positive or facilitator effect is labeled *retroactive facilitation*. This positive transfer motivates the stimulus-encoding hypothesis, whereby a distinction is made between the nominal stimulus provided by the experiments and the functional stimulus perceived by the subject. No functional fixity would result from the stimulus-encoding process.[55]

Haka, Friedman, and Jones used the above interference theory to test the hypothesis that exposure to cost and income measures causes fixated responses in a decision-making setting where market value is the appropriate response."[56] If subjects are presented with two stimulus-response pairs for market price (*A-B*) and one for cost or income (*C-D*), with separate stimulus and responses for each, and if *C* is confused with *A*, resulting in an *A-B, C-B* paradigm, then response *B* becomes the fixated response because of retroactive interference. In other words:

The hypothesis posited that prevalence of cost and profit information interferes with (that is, causes fixation) or facilitates appropriate market-based decision models. In particular, if stimulus encoding is dominant, then subjects with more cost and profit exposure should be more likely to use the market price data than those with less exposure. If retroactive inhibition dominates, then the opposite effect should be discerned.[57]

The results of the study did not support the proposition that exposure to accounting concepts in accounting courses interferes with decision processes. In addition, only some moderate support was found for the theory that stimulus encoding causes some retroactive facilitation.

Primacy versus Recency and Ego Involvement

The findings on data fixation in accounting for the most part have been obtained by having students placed in a stressful situation make a given choice (for example, a price decision) before and after an accounting change. The students know the nature of the accounting change (such as from full costing to variable costing) from their courses and the learning process preceding the experiment. A relevant research question would be the impact of this learning order on the acceptance of accounting techniques and on the results observed in data-fixation research. The impact should be more obvious if the students are placed under stress. This is related to a general hypothesis in psychology that specifies that under stress an organism will respond with the behavior appropriate to the situation that was learned first.[58] Consequently, Belkaoui tested the specific hypothesis that if a student learns two alternative responses to an accounting problem or stimulus and is placed under stress unrelated to the behavior being observed, he or she will respond to the stimulus with the first-learned method.[59] The results supported the hypothesis. Few implications of importance to the data-fixation hypothesis were made:

1. The appraisal of the usefulness of accounting technique cannot be ascertained when subjects are exposed to a stressful situation.
2. Given that stressful situations are likely to be present in both classroom and professional situations, there will be a predisposition to the use of the first learned accounting method.
3. Finally, the theoretical justifications pertaining to the choice of the appropriate accounting procedure by the firms can be reinforced by the learning order and the learning techniques to which the accountants have been exposed in their schools.[60]

The communication literature has addressed extensively the problem of the effects of order of presentation.[61] Known as the primacy-recency question, it is expressed by the following question: When both sides of a problem are presented successively, does the first-presented side (primacy) or the last-presented side (recency) have the advantage?

Different studies have supported the principle of primacy,[62] while other studies have created a controversy by reporting primacy effects under some conditions[63] and recency effects under others.[64] Consequently, Hovland, Jarvis, and Kelly recommended conducting research on the factors leading to the inconsistent effects of primacy and recency in the various experiments.[65] Examples of these factors include reinforcement, strength, involvement, and commitment.

Ego involvement is also believed to be a variable that affects primacy and recency. Morteson noted:

Despite an absence of research, there is reason to believe that ego involvement may work against either primacy or recency, and often in a brutal way. Stated as a hypothesis, we may say that the more highly involved one is on a belief-discrepant topic, the less is the chance for either a primacy or recency effect.[66]

Belkaoui investigated the impact of the primacy and recency effects of ego involvement or commitment to one's stand on an accounting topic.[67] He reasoned that under conditions of ego involvement, the forces for reinforcement were likely to be particularly active and the impact of primacy or recency to be particularly passive. Subjects coming in contact with a stressful situation, in the form of resolving an accounting problem, would revert to the technique or the side of the message that was more clear or basic to them. The results of his experiments, which used accounting students, showed that the students under stress responded with the "accounting behavior" that was more clear or basic to them. In other words, in matters of ego involvement with an accounting technique just learned, subjects will give importance to what is perceived as relevant, significant, or meaningful. This could explain some of the data-fixation findings where the subjects have reverted either to the use of the first-learned method (primacy) or the second-learned method (recency), or to the method more clear or basic to their ego involvement.

PROBLEMS IN DATA-FIXATION RESEARCH

Several problems exist in the present state of data-fixation research.

1. Most studies have not distinguished between data fixation, with its focus on output, and functional fixation, with its focus on function. Research is needed on both concepts, as they provide insight into and represent different aspects of the behavior of decision makers.

2. Extrapolations made by accounting researchers could contain serious flaws if the simple fact of ignorance is confused with the psychological phenomenon of functional fixation, especially since most of the subjects used have been students rather than actual decision makers. This was Pearson's main criticism of Ashton's study; Pearson claimed that the inability of the subjects to adjust their decision process was due entirely to ignorance.[68] This fact was explicitly recognized by Barnes and Webb when they stated: "It is our view that functional fixity and ignorance are separate phenomena and that in order to identify the former empirically, the absence of the latter needs to be insured."[69]

3. Fundamental evidence points to the fact that intelligence mitigates fixity. The point has been recognized both in the psychological[70] and the accounting experiments.[71] Again, Barnes and Webb have stated:

It would appear that those who were not fixated were less concerned with financial matters than their colleagues, as they were more concerned with providing an intellectual stimulus for their staff. Two groups appear therefore: those who can see around "trivial" financial matters and are concerned with "high matters" and those who are not. The implication again is that intelligence mitigates fixity.[72]

4. There are two methodologies in the functional-fixation research: (a) The *"one-object" approach*, where subjects are given an experimental task to perform and a novel or new way can be used in the solution. Fixity occurs when only a small number of solutions emerge from the group of subjects, for whom the usual function of an object is accentuated. (b) The *"two-objects" approach*, where subjects are given two objects and a control group is given the use of one of the objects. Functional fixation results from the tendency of the subjects to use that object in the critical problem whose function has not been accentuated. All the accounting studies have used the one-object approach, and therein lies a problem, which has been expressed by Flavell, Cooper, and Loisell:

While functional fixedness in the first case is a matter of solution vs. non-solution . . . , it is, in the second case a matter of choice of objects or means for the solution of a comparatively simple problem. It is to be expected that the last method is the one that gives the purest measure of functional fixedness. In the first method a difficult problem is used and the non-solution of this problem may very well be attributed to other factors than functional fixation.[73]

Thus, there is a need for evidence from accounting research that uses the two-object approach.

5. Most accounting research on data fixation has been concerned with whether fixity exists rather than why it exists. With the exception of the study by Haka, Friedman, and Jones, none of the accounting experiments has offered explanations about why fixity exists or has provided ways to remove it. In contrast, the psychological literature began to focus on its causes immediately after discovering the phenomenon. Removing fixation became the objective as experiments investigated factors such as time and the number of "other functions" shown for the fixated objects that affect the degree of fixity.[74] Later studies focused on the various ways of providing hints and cues to overcome fixation.[75] Needless to say, accounting research should now deal with the question of why fixity exists and how it can be mitigated. Wilner and Birnberg have stated the following to that effect:

Despite the popularity among accounting researchers of the question of whether decision makers are fixated, the critical question would appear to be why at least a portion of decision makers exhibit fixation. Given that we know from various non-accounting studies that certain factors do inhibit creative problem analysis and solving, the role of accounting research should be to ascertain which of these inhibiting factors operate in the domain of accounting and to ascertain how we can reduce their detrimental effect.[76]

6. Wilner and Birnberg have pointed to the following problems in the design of existing studies on fixation:

1. The studies used an input-output methodology and the divergence between the inputs and the expected outputs were attributed to functional fixation while in fact there may be other reasons why a subject fails to alter his information processing after an accounting change.

2. While random assignment of subjects to tasks is used to lessen the effects of individual differences, it still remains that it cannot overcome the systematic characteristics that prevent all subjects from understanding the task.

3. Most of the subjects used in these experiments are not sophisticated enough for the risks, which suggests that they were not fixated but rather naive or ignorant.

4. Unlike the psychological experiments, which provided feedback to subjects, the accounting experiments not only did not provide any feedback, but used experimental tasks that were judgmental rather than optimal (right or wrong), which suggests that the subjects in the accounting experiments never knew if their behavior was appropriate.

5. Some knowledgeable subjects may have resisted changing their decision (model) following the accounting change for reasons other than fixation if (a) they viewed the change as irrelevant, (b) they viewed changing his decision process as not worthwhile in that it leads to a different action than that already performed, (c) they viewed the benefits of "better decisions" as not outweighing the costs of learning how to process the change, (d) they thought it beneficial to act in a fixated manner because of their double role as information senders as well as information users, and (e) possibly they formed a set that they could not overcome.[77]

ALTERNATIVE METHODOLOGY FOR DATA-FIXATION RESEARCH

Most of the empirical studies in data-fixation research have been based on laboratory or field experiments, with the exception of one single case based on a survey. In addition, with few exceptions, these experiments have used students as subjects, thereby raising problems of external validity. The tasks have not been realistic or motivating and have required judgmental rather than optimal behavior. What stands out upon review of the accountancy and psychological literature on the phenomenon is the urgent need for a better methodology, one that will allow direct observation of the process by which a decision is made. An appropriate methodology would be some form of protocol analysis, in which the subjects are asked to think aloud while solving the requirements of an experimental task. Such an approach would answer some very important questions.

1. Did the subject note the change?
2. Did the subject give any indication of appreciating its relevance?

3. Was the change understood?

4. Was the change ignored on grounds of its materiality, etc.?[78]

Better insights on the phenomenon of functional fixation may be possible through the use of protocol analysis, as the experiments use richer tasks, smaller pools of subjects, and better debriefing.

CONCLUSION

Functional fixation as observed in psychology and data fixation as observed in accounting need to be better examined and explained. Future research should provide theoretical as well as empirical explanations of the reasons why subjects in accounting experiments persist in failing to adjust their decision process in response to accounting changes. In addition, richer and more realistic experimental tasks, sophisticated subjects, as well as protocol analysis ought to be used to provide better explanations of the phenomenon if it exists.

NOTES

1. N.R.F. Maier, "Reasoning in Humans: The Mechanisms of Equivalent Stimuli and Reasoning," *Journal of Experimental Psychology* (April 1945): 349–60.

2. K. Duncker, "On Problem Solving," *Psychological Monographs* 58, no. 5 (1945).

3. H.G. Birch and H.S. Rabinowitz, "The Negative Effect of Previous Experience on Productive Thinking," *Journal of Experimental Psychology* (February 1951): 121–25.

4. J.H. Flavell, A. Cooper, and R.H. Loisell, "Effect of the Number of Pre-utilization Functions on Functional Fixedness in Problem Solving," *Psychological Reports* (June 1958): 343–50.

5. R.E. Adamson, "Functional Fixedness as Related to Problem Solving: A Repetition of Three Experiments," *Journal of Experimental Psychology* (October 1952): 288–91.

6. Ibid., 288.

7. R.E. Adamson and D.W. Taylor, "Functional Fixedness as Related to Elapsed Time and to Set," *Journal of Experimental Psychology* (February 1954): 122–26.

8. S. Glucksberg and J.H. Danks, "Functional Fixedness: Stimulus Equivalence Mediated by Semantic-Acoustic Similarity," *Journal of Experimental Psychology* (July 1967): 400–405; J. Jensen, "On Functional Fixedness: Some Critical Remarks," *Scandinavian Journal of Psychology* (Winter 1960): 157–62.

9. Adamson and Taylor, "Functional Fixedness."

10. Duncker, "On Problem Solving."

11. P. Saugstad and K. Raaheim, "Problem Solving, Past Experience and Availability of Functions," *British Journal of Psychology* (May 1960): 97–104.

12. A.S. Luchins and E.H. Luchins, "New Experimental Attempts at Presenting Mechanization in Problem Solving," in *Thinking and Reasoning: Selected Readings*, ed. P.C. Watson and P.N. Johnson Laird (Hammondsworth, Eng.: Penguin, 1968), 42–44.

13. Y. Ijiri, R.K. Jaedicke, and K.E. Knight, "The Effects of Accounting Alternatives on Management Decisions," in *Research in Accounting Measurement*, ed. R.K. Jaedicke,

Y. Ijiri, and O. Nielsen (Sarasota, FL: American Accounting Association, 1966), 186–99.

14. Ibid., 194.

15. Ibid., 194.

16. K.E. Knight, "Effect of Effort on Behavioral Rigidity in Luchins' Water Jar Task," *Journal of Abnormal and Social Psychology* (1960): 192–94; Paul Barnes and John Webb, "Management Information Changes and Functional Fixation: Some Experimental Evidence from the Public Sector," *Accounting, Organizations and Society* (February 1986): 1–18.

17. R.H. Ashton, "Cognitive Changes Induced by Accounting Changes: Experimental Evidence on the Functional Fixation Hypothesis," supplement to *Journal of Accounting Research* (1976): 1–17.

18. Ibid., 5.

19. Ibid., 1–7.

20. Robert Libby, "Discussion of Cognitive Changes Induced by Accounting Changes—Experimental Evidence on the Functional Fixation Hypothesis," supplement to *Journal of Accounting Research* (1976): 18–24.

21. Ibid., 23.

22. David B. Pearson, "Discussion of Cognitive Changes Induced by Accounting Changes: Experimental Evidence on the Functional Fixation Hypothesis," supplement to *Journal of Accounting Research* (1976): 25–28.

23. R.J. Swieringa, T.R. Dyckman, and R.E. Hoskin, "Empirical Evidence about the Effects of an Accounting Change on Information Processing," in *Behavioral Experiments in Accounting II*, ed. T.J. Burns (Columbus: Ohio State University Press, 1979), 225–59.

24. T.R. Dyckman, R.E. Hoskin, and R.J. Swieringa, "An Accounting Change and Information Processing Changes," *Accounting, Organizations and Society* (February 1982): 1–11.

25. D.L. Chang and J.G. Birnberg, "Functional Fixity in Accounting Research: Perspective and New Data," *Journal of Accounting Research* (Autumn 1977): 300–312.

26. Ibid., 311.

27. R.A. Abdel-Khalik and T.F. Keller, "Earnings or Cash Flows: An Experiment on Functional Fixation and the Valuation of the Firm," *Studies in Accounting Research* 16 (Sarasota, FL: American Accounting Association, 1979).

28. Ibid., 17.

29. Robert Bloom, Pieter T. Elgers, and Dennis Murray, "Functional Fixation in Product Pricing: A Comparison of Individuals and Groups," *Accounting, Organizations and Society* 9, no. 1 (1984): 1–11.

30. Ibid., 8.

31. Neil Wilner and Jacob Birnberg, "Methodological Problems in Functional Fixation Research: Criticism and Suggestions," *Accounting, Organizations and Society* (February 1986): 74.

32. Robert W. McGee, "Software Accounting, Bank Lending Decisions, and Stock Prices," *Management Accounting* (July 1984): 20–23.

33. Ibid., 20.

34. Ahmed Belkaoui, "Accrual Accounting, Modified Cash Basis of Accounting and the Loan Decision: An Experiment in Functional Fixation," unpublished manuscript, University of Illinois at Chicago, 1988.

35. Robert E. Jensen, "An Experimental Design for the Study of Effects of Accounting Variations in Decision Making," *Journal of Accounting Research* (Autumn 1966): 224–38.

36. J.L. Livingstone, "A Behavioral Study of Tax Allocation in Electric Utility Regulation," *The Accounting Review* (July 1967): 544–52.

37. Ibid., 550–51.

38. Ibid., 552.

39. F.A. Mlynarczyk, Jr., "An Empirical Study of Accounting Methods and Stock Prices," supplement to *Journal of Accounting Research* (1969): 63–81.

40. W.H. Beaver, "The Behavior of Security Prices and Its Implications for Accounting Research Methods," supplement to *The Accounting Review* (1972): 407–37.

41. Ibid., 420–21.

42. Knight, "Effect of Effort on Behavioral Rigidity"; Barnes and Webb, "Management Information Changes and Functional Fixation."

43. Luchins and Luchins, "New Experimental Attempts."

44. J.A. Schumpeter, *Capitalism. Socialism and Democracy*, 3d ed. (New York: Harper & Row, 1950), 123–24.

45. Robert R. Sterling, "On Theory Construction and Verification," *The Accounting Review* (July 1970): 433.

46. L. Revsine, *Replacement Cost Accounting* (Englewood Cliffs, NJ: Prentice-Hall 1973), 50–51.

47. D. Kahneman and A. Tversky, "Prospect Theory: An Analysis of Decision under Risk," *Econometrika* (March 1979): 263–91.

48. Ibid., 265.

49. Ibid., 268.

50. Ibid., 271.

51. R.S. Woodworth and H. Schosberg, *Experimental Psychology* (New York: Henry Holt, 1954), 733.

52. Ibid.

53. G.E. Muller and F. Schumann, "Experimentelle Beitrage Zur Untersuchung de Gedachtnisses," *Zeitschrift für Psychologie* (1894): 81–190, 257–339.

54. A.C. Catania, *Learning* (Englewood Cliffs, NJ: Prentice-Hall, 1979).

55. J. Kagan and E. Havemann, *Psychology: An Introduction*, 3d ed. (New York: Harcourt Brace Jovanovich, 1976), 149.

56. Susan Haka, Lauren Friedman, and Virginia Jones, "Functional Fixation and Theoretical and Empirical Investigation," *The Accounting Review* (July 1986): 455–74.

57. Ibid., 460.

58. R.P. Barthol and Nari D. Ku, "Specific Regression under a Nonrelated Stress Situation," *American Psychologist* (February 1963): 482.

59. Ahmed Belkaoui, "Learning Order and the Acceptance of Accounting Techniques, *The Accounting Review* (October 1975): 897–99.

60. Ibid., 898–99.

61. C. Hovland, I. Jarvis, and H. Kelly, *Communication and Persuasion* (New Haven, CT: Yale University Press, 1953).

62. F.H. Lund, "The Psychology of Belief: IV. The Law of Primacy in Persuasion," *Journal of Abnormal and Social Psychology* (1925): 236–49; F.H. Kroner, "Experimental Studies of Changes in Attitudes: II. A Study of the Effect of Printed Arguments on Changes in Attitudes," *Social Psychology* (1936): 522–32.

63. R. Lana, "Controversy on the Topic and the Order of Presentation in Persuasive Communications," *Psychological Reports* (April 1963): 163–70.

64. C.A. Insko, "Primacy versus Recency in Persuasion as a Function of the Timing of Arguments and Measurement," *Journal of Abnormal and Social Psychology* (1964): 381–91.

65. Hovland, Jarvis, and Kelly, *Communication and Persuasion.*

66. David C. Morteson, *Communication: The Study of Human Interaction* (New York: McGraw-Hill, 1972).

67. Ahmed Belkaoui, "The Primacy-Recency Effect, Ego Involvement and the Acceptance of Accounting Techniques," *The Accounting Review* (January 1977): 252–56.

68. Pearson, "Discussion of Cognitive Changes Induced by Accounting Changes."

69. Barnes and Webb, "Management Information Changes and Functional Fixation."

70. Luchins and Luchins, "New Experimental Attempts."

71. Barnes and Webb, "Management Information Changes and Functional Fixation."

72. Ibid., 12.

73. Flavell, Cooper, and Loisell, "Effect of the Number of Pre-utilization Functions."

74. Adamson and Taylor, "Functional Fixedness"; Flavell, Cooper, and Loisell, "Effect of the Number of Pre-utilization Functions."

75. N.A. Wilner and J.G. Birnberg, "A Comparison of the Accounting and Psychological Literature on Functional Fixation," unpublished working paper, University of Pittsburgh, 1984.

76. N.A. Wilner and J.G. Birnberg, "Methodological Problems in Functional Fixation Research: Criticisms and Suggestions," *Accounting, Organizations and Society* (February 1986): 75.

77. Ibid., 75–78.

78. Ibid., 78–79.

SELECTED BIBLIOGRAPHY

Adamson, R.E. "Functional Fixation as Related to Problem Solving: A Repetition of Three Experiments." *Journal of Experimental Psychology* (October 1952): 288–91.

Adamson, R.E., and D.W. Taylor. "Functional Fixedness as Related to Elapsed Time and to Set." *Journal of Experimental Psychology* (February 1954): 122–26.

Ausubel, D., L.C. Robbins, and E. Blake. "Retroactive Inhibition and Facilitation in the Learning of School Materials." *Journal of Educational Psychology* (October 1957): 334–43.

Ausubel, D., M. Stager, and A.J.H. Gaite. "Retroactive Facilitation in Meaningful Verbal Learning." *Journal of Educational Psychology* (August 1968): 159–78.

Belkaoui, Ahmed. "Accrual Accounting, Modified Cash Basis of Accounting and the Loan Decision: An Experiment in Functional Fixation." Unpublished manuscript, University of Illinois at Chicago, 1988.

———. "Learning Order and the Acceptance of Accounting Techniques." *The Accounting Review* (October 1975): 897–99.

———. "The Primacy-Recency Effect, Ego Involvement and the Acceptance of Accounting Techniques." *Accounting Review* (January 1977): 252–56.

Birch, H.G., and H.S. Rabinowitz. "The Negative Effect of Previous Experience on Productive Thinking." *Journal of Experimental Psychology* (February 1951): 121–25.

Catania, A.C. *Learning*. Englewood Cliffs, NJ: Prentice-Hall, 1979.

Duncker, K. "On Problem Solving." *Psychological Monographs* 58, no. 5 (1945).

Dyckman, T.R., M. Gibbins, and R.J. Swieringa. "Experimental and Survey Research in Financial Accounting: A Review and Evaluation." In *The Impact of Accounting Research on Practice and Disclosure*, ed. A.R. Abdel-Khalik and T.F. Relier. Durham, NC: Duke University Press, 1978, 48–105.

Flavell, J.H., A. Cooper, and R.H. Loisell. "Effect of the Number of Pre-utilization Functions on Functional Fixedness in Problem Solving." *Psychological Reports* (June 1958): 343–50.

Glucksberg, S., and J.H. Danks. "Functional Fixedness: Stimulus Equivalence Mediated by Semantic-Acoustic Similarity." *Journal of Experimental Psychology* (July 1967): 400–405.

Hoch, S.J. "Availability and Interference in Predictive Judgements." Working paper, Center for Decision Research, Graduate School of Business, University of Chicago, March 1984.

Hovland, C., I. Jarvis, and H. Kelly. *Communication and Persuasion*. New Haven, CT: Yale University Press, 1953.

Insko, C.A. "Primacy versus Recency in Persuasion as a Function of the Timing of Argument and Measurement." *Journal of Abnormal and Social Psychology* (1964): 381–91.

Jensen, J. "On Functional Fixedness: Some Critical Remarks." *Scandinavian Journal of Psychology* (Winter 1960): 157–62.

Kagan, J., and E. Havemann. *Psychology: An Introduction*, 3d ed. New York: Harcourt Brace Jovanovich, 1976.

Kahneman, D., and A. Tversky. "Prospect Theory: An Analysis of Decision under Risk." *Econometrika* (March 1979): 263–91.

Knight, K.E. "Effect of Effort on Behavioral Rigidity in Luchins' Water Jar Task." *Journal of Abnormal and Social Psychology* (1960): 192–94.

Krowner, F.H. "Experimental Studies of Changes in Attitudes: II. A Study of the Effect of Printed Arguments on Changes in Attitudes." *Social Psychology* (1936): 522–32.

Lana, R. "Controversy on the Topic and the Order of Presentation in Persuasive Communications." *Psychological Reports* (April 1963): 163–70.

Larcker, D.F., and V.P. Lessig. "Perceived Usefulness of Information : A Psychometric Examination." *Decision Sciences* (January 1980): 121–34.

Luchins, A.S., and E.H. Luchins. "New Experimental Attempts at Presenting Mechanization in Problem Solving." In *Thinking and Reasoning: Selected Readings*, ed. P.C. Watson and P.N. Johnson Laird. Hammondsworth, Eng.: Penguin, 1968, 42–44.

Lund, F.H. "The Psychology of Belief: IV. The Law of Primacy in Persuasion." *Journal of Abnormal and Social Psychology* (1925): 236–49.

Martin, E. "Verbal Learning Theory and Independent Retrieval Phenomena." *Psychological Review* (July 1971): 314–32.

Mehle, T., C.F. Gettys, C. Manning, S. Baca, and S. Fisher. "The Availability Explanation Plausibility Assessment." *Acta Psychologica* (November 1981): 127–40.

Morteson, David C. *Communication: The Study of Human Interaction.* New York: McGraw-Hill, 1972.

Muller, G.E., and F. Schumann. "Experimentelle Bertrage Zur Untersuchung de Gedachtnisses." *Zeitschrift für Psychologie* (1894): 81–190, 257–339.

Roediger, H.L. "Recall as a Self-Limiting Process." *Memory and Cognition* (January 1978): 54–63.

Saugstad, P, and K. Raaheim. "Problem Solving, Past Experience and Availability of Functions." *British Journal of Psychology* (May 1960): 97–104.

Sherif, C.W., and M. Sherif. *Attitude, Ego Involvement, and Change.* New York: Wiley, 1967.

Sherif, M., and C.I. Hovland. *Social Judgement: Assimilation and Contrast Effects and Attitude Change.* New Haven, CT: Yale University Press, 1961.

Sterling, Robert R. "Accounting Research, Education and Practice." *Journal of Accountancy* (September 1973): 44–52.

———. "A Case of Valuation and Learned Cognitive Dissonance." *The Accounting Review* (April 1967): 376–78.

———. *Theory of Measurement of Enterprise Income.* Lawrence, TX: Scholars Book Co., 1970.

Tversky, A. "Features of Similarity." *Psychological Review* (July 1977): 327–52.

Tversky, A., and D. Kahneman. "The Framing of Decisions and the Psychology of Choice." *Science* (January 1981): 453–58.

Wong, M. "Retroactive Inhibition in Meaningful Verbal Learning." *Journal of Educational Psychology* (October 1970): 410–15.

Woodworth, R.S., and H. Schosberg. *Experimental Psychology*, rev. ed. New York: Henry Holt, 1954.

8 _____

Goal Setting, Participative Budgeting, and Performance

INTRODUCTION

Both the psychological and the behavioral accounting literature have focused on the effects of goal setting, or standard setting, on performance. In addition, while the conventional accounting literature has assumed participation in goal setting to be a means for affecting motivation, behavior, and task performance, the behavioral accounting literature has examined the effects of participative budgeting attitudes and performance. This chapter will elaborate on the results of research into the effects of goal setting in general and participative budgeting in particular on task and/or attitude outcomes.

GOAL SETTING AND TASK PERFORMANCE

Evidence in Psychology

A goal can be defined as "what an individual is trying to accomplish . . . the object or aim of an action."[1] Its equivalent in accounting is the performance standard. Goal setting, or standard setting, is assumed to affect motivation, behavior, and task performance.

Among the attributes of goals are (1) *goal specify*, which refers to the extent performance level to be accomplished is explicit as to its content and clarity;[2] (2) *goal difficulty*, which is the probability of accomplishment. A survey of empirical studies has shown that most studies support the hypothesis that setting specific, hard goals produces better performance than medium, easy, do-your-best, or no goals.[3] Mechanisms, psychological processes, and cognitive activities that influence the effects of goal setting include: (1) *direction*, which refers to what needs to be done in the work setting; (2) *effort* mobilized to accomplish the goal; (3) *persistence* of the individual at the task; and (4) *strategy development*, which refers to the development of strategies, or action plans, for attaining goals. In addition, feedback on progress toward a goal, rewards given for goal attainment, and participation in the setting of goals have been found to mediate the positive effects of goal setting *on* performance. Of the individual differences, only need for achievement and self-esteem appear promising as moderating variables of the relationship between goal setting and task performance.

Evidence in Accounting

Several studies have examined the effects of setting budget goals on performance.[4] Rockness tested the effect of goal-setting difficulty, alternative reward structures, and performance feedback on both performance measures and satisfaction.[5] The results of the experiment verified parts of a budgetary model that predicted that (1) subjects in the high-budget condition differed from those in the medium-budget condition, (2) absolute performance increased with more direct reward structure, and (3) differences in planned performance existed between subjects receiving formal feedback and those receiving nonformal feedback.

A study by Chow explored the linkages between job-standard tightness, type of compensation scheme, and performance.[6] In addition to conducting the conventional investigation of the relation between goal setting (in this case job-standard tightness) and performance, Chow built on the agency research and adverse selection studies to suggest that goal setting and type of compensation scheme affect not only workers' effort but also their self-selection among employment contracts and, through these, job performance.[7] The results of the experiment indicated that (1) for subjects with assigned treatments, job-standard tightness and type of compensation scheme had significant independent but insignificant interactive effects on performance; (2) when permitted a choice of compensation schemes (given an assigned job standard), subjects self-selected among them by skill; and (3) the selection of one's own compensation scheme enhanced performance.

These results add to the large body of evidence showing that setting specific, difficult goals generates higher performance than specific moderate goals, specific easy goals, or general (i.e., do-your-best) goals.[8] Various studies have also shown that goals promote performance by increasing motivation (i.e., the direction and level of effort) as well as stimulating the search for, and consistent use of, relatively effective task strategies.[9] The motivational effects of goals on the level of performance depend, however, on the levels of moderating variables. For example, task uncertainty and task complexity have been found to moderate the relation between goals and performance, whereby as task complexity increases, goals are less effective in promoting performance.[10] Hirst and Yelton[11] confirmed the beneficial effect of budget goals on promoting performance levels but found that task interdependence does not moderate the relationships.

Toward a Theoretical Framework: The Role of Task Uncertainty

As these results suggest, accounting studies concur with the psychological literature in the finding that setting specific difficult budget goals leads to higher task performance than setting either specific moderate goals, specific easy goals, or general goals. Naylor and Ilgen have suggested, however, that research should expand to search for the moderating variables that mediate the relationship between goal setting and performance.[12] Hirst gave the following two reasons to make such a search:

First, it has the potential to delineate situations in which goal setting does *not* have a positive effect on performance. This is significant because it suggests a need to control for moderator variables in future studies that empirically investigate both the direct effects of goal setting on performance, and the way goal setting combines with other factors (e.g., participation) to affect performance. Second, knowledge about moderator variables can have practical implications. In particular, the designers of goal setting programs can use such knowledge to anticipate the effects of their programs, and to introduce goal setting interventions in one of those situations where they are expected to have a positive effect on performance.[13]

In fact, Hirst proposed a theoretical framework that traced the effect of a potential moderating variable, task uncertainty, on the relationship between goal setting and performance. The relationship between goal setting and performance is linked by a hypothesized sequence of activities in line with models of task performance provided by Locke et al. and Porter, Lawler, and Hackman. The model includes four conditional mechanisms along the path linking goal setting to task outcomes. These are: (1) goal setting, in terms of difficulty and specificity; (2) a set of cognitive activities interpretation, strategy search, and selection of valid strategies; (3) intentions, in terms of direction, level, and duration of effort; and (4) action, in terms of the task performance. Hirst argued that difficulties can arise in performing the cognitive activities where task uncertainty is high. It postulates the negative effects of task uncertainty on the completeness of task knowledge and the positive effects of goal setting based on complete task knowledge. As a result, Hirst proposed a hypothesis of task uncertainty as a moderating variable:

H_1: There is an interaction between goal setting and task uncertainty affecting task performance.[14]

Exhibit 8.1
The Effects of Task Uncertainty on the Relationship between Goal Setting and Task Outcomes

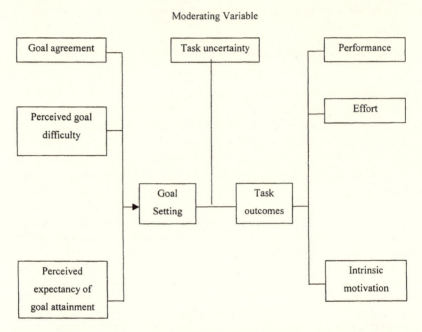

While the focus has been on task uncertainty, future theoretical and empirical attempts will focus on identifying other moderating variables and integrating the findings to provide a sound basis for the design of budgetary control systems.[15,16]

Hirst's model indicates that goal-setting effects are conditioned on the completeness of task knowledge, which is in turn dependent on task uncertainty, and goal setting is where task uncertainty will moderate the relationship between goal setting and performance. Basically, when the interaction between goal setting and task uncertainty is low, goal setting will cause either a smaller increase or a reduction in performance. The model depicted in Exhibit 8.1 expands Hirst's model on two counts: (1) by showing the nature of task outcomes, and (2) by presenting limiting restrictions on the nature of goal setting. Both additions are now explained:

1. Limiting restrictions on goal setting are presented as the conditions necessary for the subject's acceptance of the level of difficulties of the goals assigned to him or her. These are a verbal agreement by the subject accepting the goal,[17] perceived goal difficulty, and perceived expectancy of goal attainment by the subjects.[18] These conditions must be satisfied before the relationship between goal setting and performance is examined, as failure to accept a misrepresentation of the level of difficulty of the goal creates a new strain on three cognitive factors (i.e., goal interpretation, strategy

search, and selection) that must be performed if goal setting is to have a positive effect on task performance.

2. The task outcomes include measures of performance, motivation, and task satisfaction. Two measures of performance are (a) a measure of successful completion of the task and (b) a measure of effort.[19] One measure of intrinsic motivation was included as a task outcome following research findings that indicate that goal setting may influence variables associated with intrinsic motivation.[20]

The conclusion from this model was formally stated in the following hypothesis:

H_2: Given that goal setting has been found acceptable in terms of goal agreement, perceived goal difficulty, and perceived expectancy of goal attainment, there is an interaction between goal setting and task uncertainty affecting task outcomes and performance, effort and intrinsic motivation.[21]

The results of an experiment by Belkaoui[22] suggest that both goal difficulty and task uncertainty affect task outcomes. The goal difficulty results verify earlier findings in both accounting and psychology that show that setting specific difficult goals leads to higher task performance than setting either specific moderate goals or general goals. The task uncertainty results verify the thesis that the level of task uncertainty will affect both performance and effort. Basically, the more certain the task, the higher the performance and effort put in a job.

The interaction effects results suggest that given that goal setting has been found acceptable in terms of goal agreement, perceived goal difficulty, and perceived expectancy of goal attainment, there is an interaction between goal setting and task uncertainty affecting task outcomes of performance, effort, and intrinsic motivation. Basically, as tasks increased, both performance and effort were found to decrease. Task interest, however, was found to increase as the task became more uncertain and then decrease as the task uncertainty continued to increase. The results, coupled with earlier results of goal setting on performance, imply that (a) given the choice between presenting an individual with an easy goal or a difficult goal, the more useful course in terms of performance, effort, and task interest seems to be the latter, and (b) given the choice between presenting the individual with a certain task or an uncertain task, the more useful course in terms of performance and effort seems to be the former. To motivate task interest some degree of task uncertainty seems to be beneficial.

Future research may need to investigate the same research issue under different conditions. Gender differences, which were not taken into account in the present work, sometimes induce different cognitive patterns and these are not necessarily eliminated by random assignments to groups. Another neglected condition is related to the self-selection and effort effects of different employee contracts. Task uncertainty differences may affect not only workers' efforts, but also their self-selection among employment contracts and, through these, job performance.

PARTICIPATIVE BUDGETING AND PERFORMANCE

Participation in budgeting entails the involvement of subordinates in the setting of standards that affect their operations and rewards. The implied benefit of participative budgeting is that it will improve attitudes, productivity, and/or performance. The results, however, have been mixed. Some studies have supported the argument that budgetary participation leads to higher job satisfaction,[23] higher motivation to achieve the budget,[24] and higher performance.[25] Other studies, however, found either a weak association between participation and performance[26] or a negative association between the two variables.[27]

While findings on the relationship between participative budgeting and performance have been mixed, participation in decision making has been broadly defined as the "organizational process whereby individuals are involved in, and have influence on, decisions that have direct effects on those individuals."[28] Brownell reviewed participation in decision making and found evidence of positive effects of *antecedent moderators* on participation and positive effects of participation on outcomes conditioned by *consequence moderators*. The antecedent moderators included: (1) the cultural variables of nationality,[29] legislative systems,[30] race,[31] and religion; and (2) the organizational variables of environmental stability,[32] technology,[33] task uncertainty,[34] and organizational structure.[35] The consequence moderators included: (1) the interpersonal variables of task stress,[36] group size,[37] intrinsic satisfaction of task,[38] and congruence between task and individual,[39] and (2) the individual level variables of locus of control,[40] authoritarianism,[41] external reference points,[42] and perceived emphasis placed on accounting information.[43] A comprehensive review of participation in decision making (hereafter PDM) was attempted by Locke and Schweiger.[44]

They reached the following interesting conclusions:

(1) The use of PDM is a practical rather than a moral issue; (2) the concept of participation refers to shared or joint decision making, and therefore excludes delegation; (3) there are numerous mechanisms both cognitive and motivational through which PDM may produce high morale and performance; (4) research findings yield equivocal support for the thesis that PDM necessarily leads to increased satisfaction and productivity, although the evidence for the former outcome is stronger than the evidence for the latter; (5) the evidence indicates that the effectiveness Of PDM depends upon numerous contextual factors; and (6) PDM is the only way to motivate employees.[45]

Moderating Factors in the Link between Participative Budgeting and Performance

The view that the relationship between participation and performance holds under all conditions is known as the universalistic perspective. As we have seen, support for this view is mixed. Another view, that the relationship between participation and performance is moderated by organizational, task-related, structural, attitudinal, and personality variables, is known as the contingency perspective. This perspective accounts for the moderating effects of motivation, leadership style, task uncertainty, role ambiguity, reward structure, cognitive dissonance, authoritarianism, locus of control, and the Pelz effect. Findings on the impact of these moderating variables demonstrate the superiority of the contingency perspective in the analysis of the relationship between participative budgeting and performance. Before reviewing these findings, it is appropriate to note that the literature on participation in decision making has also identified more intervening mechanisms that mediate the effects of participation in decision making.

Motivation, Participative Budgeting, and Performance

Participative budgeting has long been assumed to enhance managerial performance by positively affecting motivation.[46] Cost accounting textbooks have made such claims in advocating the use of participative budgeting.[47] The accuracy of this assertion rests on establishing positive connections between participation and performance, participation and motivation, and motivation and performance, as well as an intervening linkage between participation and performance through motivation.

First, as was seen earlier in this chapter, the relationship between participation and performance is unsure at best, suggesting the need to examine the impact of moderating variables.

Second, with regard to the connection between participative budgeting and motivation, the evidence has been supportive.[48] To measure motivation, these studies relied upon: (1) Vroom's expectancy model; (2) subordinates' ratings of their superiors' budget-related behaviors to assess the superiors' motivation; and (3) the three-item instruments developed by either Hackman and Lawler or Hackman and Porter.[49]

Third, with regard to the relationship between motivation and performance, both the accounting and the organizational behavior literature give strong evidence of a positive relationship.[50]

Fourth, Brownell and McInnes provided results that failed to confirm the hypothesis that motivation mediates the effect of participation on performance although participation and performance were found to be positively related.[51] Basically, the path between participation and performance through motivation was not evident. The expectancy model developed by House and introduced in the accounting literature by Ronen and Livingstone was used to measure motivation.[52] The model is as follows:

$$M = IV_b + P_1 \left[IV_a + \sum_{i=1}^{n} (P_{2i}EV_i) \right], i = 1, \cdots, n$$

where

M = motivation,
IV_a = intrinsic valence associated with work-goal accomplishment,
IV_b = intrinsic valence associated with goal-directed behavior,
EV_i = extrinsic valence associated with the ith extrinsic reward
    contingent on work-goal accomplishment,
P_l = the expectancy that goal-directed behavior will lead
    to work-goal accomplishment, and
P_{2i} = the expectancy that work-goal accomplishment
    will lead to the ith extrinsic reward.

In the Brownell and McInnes study, the expectancies were positively related to participative budgeting, while the intrinsic values were negatively related to participative budgeting. The following interpretation was proposed: "Hence, a possible interpretation of the study's findings is that managers negotiate slack budgets in response to participation's reinforcements of the expectation of formal rewards being based on attaining budget, in essence trading off expectations of intrinsic for extrinsic rewards."[53]

Fifth, Mia[54] adopted a contingency approach in the evaluation of the effectiveness (in terms of managerial performance) of budget participation where the contingent variables included managerial attitudes (toward their job and company) and motivation (to work). The result supported the moderating effects of both contingent variables. More precisely the participation in the budgeting process by managers who reported a more favorable attitude or motivation was associated with improved performance, whereas participation by managers who exhibited a less favorable attitude and/or motivation was linked to a hampered performance.

Leadership Style, Organizational Performance, Job Tension, and Participative Budgeting

Studies of the relationship between managerial leadership styles and measures of organizational effectiveness, such as performance of subordinates, have produced various results. Early findings were that the effectiveness of budgetary systems is associated with supervisory leadership style.[55] Then Hopwood investigated the impact of three styles of evaluation that make distinctly different uses of data: budget-constrained style, profit-conscious style, and nonaccounting style. He suggested that one significant dimension of budget use is the relative importance attached to the budget in evaluating managerial performance.[56] The leadership style characterized by a heavy emphasis on budget-related performance was found to be significantly associated with job-related tension. Noting Hopwood's primary emphasis on the effect of budget use on managers' beliefs and feelings, Otley extended the hypothesis to include the overall effectiveness of operation.[57] He stated the hypothesis as follows:

When a manager perceives that he is evaluated primarily on his ability to meet his budget (rather than on the basis of a more flexible use of budgetary information), he is more likely to (a) experience job-related and budget-related tension; (b) distrust his superior; (c) be clear about how his performance is evaluated; (d) consider his evaluation to be unfair. His response to such feelings will be such that he is more likely to (e) bias his budget estimates by building in "slack" so that the budget becomes easier to attain; (f) have a short-term view of his job in that his performance measure is short-term; (g) perform poorly, particularly on those aspects of performance which yield only long-term benefits.[58]

Otley's results suggested that superior performance levels are associated with a budget-focus leadership, the reverse of Hopwood's finding. To reconcile the conflicting results, Brownell confirmed the hypothesis that directly observable associations between leadership evaluative style and performance should not be expected, because the relationship will be moderated by budgetary participation.[59] The foundations for the hypothesis were based on the operant conditioning[60] and balance[61] theoretical paradigms.[62,63,64]

Brownell's findings were that when budgetary participation is high (low) a high (low) budget emphasis is associated with enhanced managerial performance. To reconcile Hopwood's and Otley's results, Hirst[65] suggested that when budget emphasis is high (low) and task uncertainty is low (high), job-related tension is minimized. Similarly, Brownell and Hirst[66] were unable to find support for the hypothesis that the alignment of budget participation and budget emphasis in evaluation would hold only when task uncertainty was low. However, after incorporating variations in measurement and sampling, Brownell and Dunk[67] found results providing strong support for Brownell and Hirst's hypothesis.

The same type of literature examined the individual and conceptual variables that impact on managerial job-related tension. Kahn et al.[68] found a positive relation between job-related tension and role conflict. The association of a budget-conscious style with job-related tension was supported by Hopwood[69] and refuted by Otley.[70] This discrepancy between Hopwood and Otley led to various attempts at reconciling both results. First, Kenis[71] found that job-related tension was significantly and positively related to the use of budgets employed in a primitive fashion in performance evaluation, and negatively associated with budget goal clarity. Second, Hirst[72] maintained that in cases of high task uncertainty, job-related tension was high for those subordinates evaluated by a reliance on accounting performance measures. Third, Brownell and Hirst[73] found that only in cases of low task uncertainty would a budget emphasis in performance evaluation interact with budgetary participation. Fourth, by systematically varying both the measurement of managerial performance and the use of random sampling, Dunk[74] reported results that (a) suggest that the association between job-related tension and performance is significant and negative, and (b) do not support the moderating role of participation in the relation between job-related tension and performance.

Task Uncertainty and Participative Budgeting

Galbraith and later Tushman and Nadler have argued that the effectiveness of participation in decision making depends on task uncertainty.[75] As the task environment of a subunit becomes more uncertain, the need for information and greater information-processing capacity at the subunit level increases. As uncertainty increases, the organization develops strategies to deal with the need to process information. One strategy, of a decentralizing nature, consists of creating lateral relations, which is equivalent to moving the level of decision making down to where the information exists instead of bringing the information upward in the hierarchy. Lawrence and Lorsch provided some empirical evidence in their finding that, faced with higher environmental uncertainty, successful firms resort to a design of organizational structure that facilitates the flow of information both horizontally and vertically, allowing for higher participation in decision making.[76] While Lawrence and Lorsch focused on the relationship between uncertainty and participation in decision making, Govindarajan extended the analysis to participative budgeting, arguing that the greater the environmental uncertainty the greater the positive impact of participation on managerial performance or attitudes.[77] Data from responsibility-center managers verified the assertion. Task uncertainty was also used to explain the dysfunctional behavior of subordinates associated with different uses of accounting information. Hirst developed the hypothesis that a medium to high (medium to low) reliance on such measures minimizes the incidence of dysfunctional behavior in situations of low (high) task uncertainty.[78] Furthermore, the results of a field study by Brownell and Hirst supported the hypothesis that compatible combinations of participation and budget emphasis (high/high and low/low) are more effective in reducing job-related tension in low, as opposed to high, task uncertainty activities.[79]

Role Ambiguity and Participative Budgeting

Role ambiguity has been viewed as the extent to which clear information is missing with regard to expectations associated with a role, methods for fulfilling role expectations, and/or the consequences of role performance.[80] Role ambiguity was found to be negatively related to job satisfaction,[81] performance,[82] effort,[83] and productivity.[84] It has also been found to be negatively related to participative budgeting.[85] Given these findings on role ambiguity, Chenhall and Brownell proposed that an understanding of participative budgeting's effects on job satisfaction and performance could best be reached by considering the intervening effect that role ambiguity has in these relationships.[86] They hypothesized that the relationship between participative budgeting and job satisfaction or subordinated performance could be explained by an *indirect* effect, in which participation reduces role ambiguity and thereby enhances job satisfaction and subordinate performance. Empirical results based on a survey of thirty-six middle-level managers and a path analysis confirmed the hypothesis that participative budgeting is most helpful in decreasing managers' role ambiguity, which in turn improves job satisfaction and performance.

Reward Structure and Participative Budgeting

Cherrington and Cherrington[87] argued that it is not budgets per se that affect people, but rather the positive and negative reinforcing consequences and the reward contingencies associated with budgets. They contended that the principles of operant conditioning, as introduced by Skinner, can be applied to the budgeting process to predict or control attitudes and behavior.[88] Cherrington and Cherrington predicted that (1) task performance is a function of the reward contingencies—high performance is expected in conditions where appropriate reinforcements are made contingent upon high performance; and (2) there is a direct relationship between the occurrence of appropriate reinforcement and measures of satisfaction. Their findings provided significant evidence of the strong intervening effect of reward on the relationship between participative budgeting and performance.

Cognitive Dissonance and Participative Budgeting

Cognitive dissonance has been defined as "a negative drive state which occurs whenever an individual simultaneously holds two cognitions (ideas, beliefs, opinions) which are psychologically inconsistent. Stated differently, two cognitions are dominant if, considering these two cognitions alone, the opposite of one follows from the other. Since the occurrence of dissonance is presumed to be unpleasant, individuals strive to reduce it."[89]

Individuals choose among alternatives but find that they themselves experience dissonance as a result of the choice. They try to reduce the dissonance by seeking information or adopting attitudes that emphasize the positive aspects of the choice and deemphasize the negative aspects. Similarly, when asked to participate in the setting of performance standards, individuals need to reduce the dissonance that results from their choice by connecting themselves to the chosen standard. Foran and DeCoster advanced the theory that feedback about the acceptability of a choice allows dissonance reduction to begin through the commitment to the chosen alternative.[90] They tested the validity of this model by investigating the effect on the dependent variables of cognitive dissonance and postdecisional modes of dissonance reduction of the following independent variables: (1) channeled and nonchanneled communication networks, (2) the personality of authoritarianism, and (3) feedback about performance standards. The findings of their study show that favorable feedback results in significantly more commitment to standards than does unfavorable feedback. They concluded as follows:

This finding allows speculation about the policy implications for accountants. Participation in the process of establishing standards is not adequate to insure workers' commitment to performance standards. The workers must participate and then be given feedback about their selections. Thus, based on this study, accountants must consider the development of performance standards as a multistep process including participation, involvement, free choice, and feedback (favorable if possible) about the results of planning. Only then will there be commitment to the performance standards.[91]

Tiller tested a dissonance model of participative budgeting that specified three conditions under which participative budgeting would lead to increased commitment to budget achievement and increased performance on the part of the subjects: conditions of low pay (insufficient justification), a high budget (aversive consequence), and participation (perceived decision freedom).[92] The experiment demonstrated that when the budgeting context allows individuals to perceive themselves as having exercised freedom of decision in the setting of difficult-to-achieve budgets, participative budgeting yields both increased commitment to award budget achievement and increased performance, even in the absence of a performance-contingent reward structure.

Personality Factors and Participative Budgeting

The search for moderating variables in the relationship between participative budgeting and measures of managerial performance has included several personality variables.

Authoritarianism

Authoritarianism has been examined as one moderating variable of the effectiveness of participation in budgeting. It has been known to have a potential for affecting individuals' work attitudes.[93] As a moderating variable of the impact of participation, its effect has been mixed, with some evidence showing participation to be most effective among low authoritarians[94] and other evidence finding it to be of no effect.[95] These studies, however, only examined the authoritarianism of one individual, usually the subordinate, which could explain their mixed results. Accordingly, Chenhall hypothesized and confirmed that the effects of participative budgeting on subordinates' satisfaction with their jobs and budgets are moderated by the configuration of authoritarianism between the subordinate and the superior.[96] More specifically, participative budgeting results in strong positive attitudes in homogeneous dyads, that is, in pairings of superiors and subordinates who have the same level of authoritarianism, be it high or low. Similar findings in psychology have related homogeneous dyads to co-operative personal exchanges[97] and low-authoritarian dyads to trusting behavior.[98]

Locus of Control

Another personality variable, locus of control, has been examined as a moderating variable, or "conditional factor," in the relationship between budgetary participation and performance. As a construct, locus of control denotes the distribution of individuals according to the degree to which they accept personal responsibility for what happens to them.[99] As a general principle:

Internal control refers to the perception of positive and/or negative events as being a consequence of one's own actions and thereby under personal control; external control refers to the perception of positive and/or negative events as being unrelated to one's own behaviors in certain situations and therefore beyond personal control.[100]

Following the basic psychological tenet that task performance is a function of personality/situation congruence, Brownell suggested the potential for significant interaction between budgetary participation and locus of control that would affect performance.[101] Basically, he stated:

Characterizing high budgetary participation as an internally controlled situation, this will be congruent only for individuals who are internals on the locus of control dimension and they are hypothesized to perform better in this situation. Conversely, low participation will be congruent only for externals, and they are hypothesized to perform better under low than under high participation conditions.[102]

The result of a laboratory experiment showed a statistically significant interaction between participation and locus of control that affected performance. A field study by the same author confirmed the moderating effect of locus of control.

The Pelz Effect

Researchers of superior-subordinate communication have studied the effect of leadership style and a superior's upward influence on his or her relationship with subordinates. The evidence, known as the Pelz effect, shows a positive association between a superior's upward hierarchical influence and the subordinate's satisfaction with the performance of the superior, provided the superior also exhibits a "supportive" leadership style in interactions with the employee. As Pelz noted: "If the superior has *little* power or influence, then neither his helpful behavior nor his restraining behavior will have much concrete effect on the employees."[103] Several studies have supported the Pelz effect.[104]

In accordance with the findings on the Pelz effect, it could be argued that dyadic configurations of leadership style and a superior's upward influence create situations where budget participation affects subordinate satisfaction with

Exhibit 8.2
Dyadic Configuration Resulting from Dimensions of Superior's Leadership Style and Upward Influence

		Supervisor's Leadership Support Style	
		High	Low
Supervisor's	High	(1) +	(2) −
Upward			
Influence	Low	− (2)	+ (1)

(1) Homogeneous group implying a positive relationship between budget participation and subordinate satisfaction.

(2) Heterogeneous group implying a negative relationship between budget participation and subordinate satisfaction.

work and budget. As Exhibit 8.2 shows, there are four possible combinations of dyads defined in terms of leadership style and superior's upward influence. Two are homogeneous in the sense that both variables are high or both variables are low. Two are heterogeneous in the sense that one variable is high while the other is low.

It is hypothesized that in the homogeneous dyads, participative budgeting will have a positive effect on attitudes toward the job and the budget. In the case where both leadership support style and upward influence are high, the superior's reliance on support and high status in the firm create a predisposition toward budget participation and subordinate satisfaction. In the case where both leadership support style and upward influence are low, it is hypothesized that subordinate satisfaction with budget and job will still exist. Subordinate attitudes will be at their most negative in this instance where superiors are perceived to be low in upward influence as well as nonsupportive.

It is also hypothesized that in the heterogeneous dyads, mixed subordinate attitudes toward the job and the budget will be associated with participative budgeting. If the leader is supportive but has an organizationally marginal status, studies supporting the Pelz effect suggest there will be an impact on budget participation. People will be less inclined to participate under those conditions. Similarly, if the leader is nonsupportive but has an organizationally high status, the Pelz effect will also lead to low budget participation and low satisfaction with the budget.

Therefore, Belkaoui has proposed the following hypothesis: "For subordinates who perceive their superiors as supportive and their level of hierarchical influence high, budget participation affects positively subordinate job satisfaction and their satisfaction with the budget."[105] A field study presented evidence that a superior's leadership style and upward influence in work-related decisions mediate the effect of participation in job and budget satisfaction.

Another study by Murray[106] also showed that participative budgeting may prove successful in complex managerial tasks where the subordinate is provided feedback and the superior acts in a supportive and considerate manner.

Antecedents of Participative Budgeting

Most of the studies investigating the link between participative budgeting (the independent variable) and individual or organizational performance (the dependent variable) have assumed three scenarios: (a) a direct, linear or nonlinear, link between the dependent and independent variable, (b) an independent variable causing an intervening (or moderating) variable that is itself a cause of the dependent variable, and (c) a moderating variable that affects the relationship between an independent and a dependent variable but is not a cause of the dependent variable as is an independent variable. Fewer studies have examined the potential of antecedent variables to participative budgeting.[107–110]

A specific study of the antecedents of participative budgeting was provided by Shields and Shields,[111] who reported the results of a survey identifying reasons why managers participate in setting their budgets and how these reasons are associated with four theoretical antecedents—environmental and task uncertainty, task interdependence, and superior-subordinate information asymmetry. The findings show that participative budgeting is most important for planning and control, especially vertical information sharing and coordinating interdependence, and that specific reasons for participative budgeting are correlated with three of the antecedents.[112]

Budget Adequacy, Organizational Commitment, and Budget Participation

Budget adequacy is the degree to which an individual perceives that budgeted resources are adequate to fulfill requirements.[113] It is more likely to happen in an atmosphere and culture of budget participation. Similarly, organizational commitment is the bond that links the individual to an organization.[114] As Hanson[115] argues: "by becoming involved in the creation of the budget (through participative budgeting), members of the organization associate themselves more closely with and become better acquainted with budget goals." Accordingly, Nomi and Parker[116] proposed that budget participation affects job performance by means of these two intervening variables: budget adequacy and organizational commitment. The results of a faith analysis supported the above thesis.

CONCLUSION

What appears from the literature covered in this chapter is the need for an investigation of additional moderating variables that can mediate the link between goal setting in general, participative budgeting in particular, and task performance. Development of a theoretical framework that incorporates moderating variables as a link between goal setting and participative budgeting on the one hand and performance on the other should be a first step before empirical investigation. The practical results of investigating the moderating variables will be the help they provide to designers of goal-setting programs not only to anticipate the impact of their programs, but also to give a role to moderating variables in those situations where they are expected to have an impact.

NOTES

1. E.A. Locke, K.N. Shaw, L.M. Saari, and G.P. Latham, "Goal Setting and Task Performance: 1969–1980," *Psychological Bulletin* (1981): 126.

2. Ibid., 131.

3. Ibid.

4. A. Stedry and E. Kay, "The Effects of Goal Difficulty on Performance: A Field Experiment," *Behavioral Science* (November 1966): 459–70; G.H. Hofstede, *The Game of Budget Control* (London: Tavistock, 1968); H.O. Rockness, "Expectancy Theory in a Budgetary Setting: An Empirical Examination," *The Accounting Review* (October 1977): 893–903; C. W. Chow, "The Effects of Job Standard Tightness and Compensation Scheme on Performance: An Exploration of Linkages," *The Accounting Review* (October 1983): 667–85.

5. Rockness, "Expectancy Theory in a Budgetary Setting."

6. Chow, "Effects of Job Standard Tightness and Compensation Scheme on Performance."

7. J.S. Demski and G.A. Feltham, "Economic Incentives in Budgetary Control Systems," *The Accounting Review* (April 1978): 336–59.

8. M.K. Hirst and S.M. Iowy, "The Linear, Additive and Interactive Effects of Budget Goal Difficulty and Feedback Performance," *Accounting, Organizations and Society* 11 (1990): 425–36.

9. E. Locke and G. Latham, *Goal Setting: A Motivational Technique that Works* (Englewood Cliffs, NJ: Prentice-Hall, 1990).

10. P.C. Earley, T. Connolly, and G. Elsegren, "Goals, Strategy Development and Task Performance: Some Limits on the Efficiency of Goal Setting," *Journal of Applied Psychology* 74 (1989): 24–33.

11. Mark K. Hirst and Philip W. Yelton, "The Effects of Budget Goals and Task Interdependence on the Level and Variance in Performance: A Research Note," *Accounting Organizations and Society* 24 (1999): 205–16.

12. J.C. Naylor and D.R. Ilgen, "Goal Setting: A Theoretical Analysis of a Moti-

vational Technology," in *Research in Organizational Behavior*, vol. 6, ed. B. M. Staw and L.L. Cummings (Greenwich, CT: JAI Press, 1984), 95–140.

13. Mark K. Hirst, "The Effects of Setting Budget Goals and Task Uncertainty on Performance: A Theoretical Analysis," *The Accounting Review* (October 1987): 774–84.

14. Ibid., 775.

15. Locke et al., "Goal Setting and Task Performance"; L.W. Porter, E.E. Lawler III, and J.R. Hackman, *Behavior in Organizations* (New York: McGraw-Hill, 1975).

16. Hirst, "Effects of Setting Budget Goals and Task Uncertainty on Performance," 780.

17. R.D. Pritchard and M. I. Curts, "The Influence of Goal Setting and Financial Incentives on Task Performance," *Organizational Behavior and Human Performance* 10 (1973): 893–903.

18. G.A. Yubal and G.P. Latham, "Interrelationships among Employee Participation, Individual Differences, Goal Difficulty, Goal Acceptance, Goal Instrumentality and Performance," *Personnel Psychology* 31 (1978): 305–23.

19. U.J. Campbell and D.R. Ilgen, "Additive Effects of Task Difficulty and Goal Setting on Subsequent Task Performance," *Journal of Applied Psychology* 3 (1976): 319–24.

20. S.J. Carol and H.L. Tosi, "The Goal Characteristic and Personality Factors in a Management by Objectives . . . ," *Administrative Science Quarterly* 15 (1970): 295–305.

21. Ahmed Belkaoui, "The Effects of Goal Setting and Task Uncertainty on Task Outcomes," *Management Accounting Research* 1 (1990): 92.

22. Ibid., 91–60.

23. R.J. Swieringa and R.H. Moncur, *Some Effects of Participative Budgeting on Managerial Behavior* (New York: National Association of Accountants, 1974).

24. Hofstede, *The Game of Budget Control*; D. Searfoss and R. Monczka, "Perceived Participation in the Budget Process and Motivation to Achieve the Budget." *Academy of Management Journal* (December 1973): 541–54.

25. I. Kenis, "Effects of Budgetary Goal Characteristics on Managerial Attitudes and Performance," *The Accounting Review* (October 1979): 707–21.

26. K.W. Milani, "The Relationship of Participation in Budget-Setting to Industrial Supervisor Performance and Attitudes: A Field Study," *The Accounting Review* (April 1975): 274–85.

27. A.C. Stedry, *Budget Control and Cost Behavior* (Englewood Cliffs, NJ.: Prentice-Hall, 1960); J.F. Bryan and E.A. Locke, "Goal Setting as a Means of Increasing Motivation," *Journal of Applied Psychology* 10 (1967): 274–77.

28. P. Brownell, "Participation in the Budgeting Process: When It Works and When It Doesn't," *Journal of Accounting Literature* (Spring 1982): 124–53.

29. Industrial Democracy in Europe International Research Group, "Participation: Formal Rules, Influence and Involvement," *Industrial Relations* (Fall 1979): 273–94; L. Coch and J.R.P. French, Jr., "Overcoming Resistance to Change," *Human Relations* (August 1948): 512–32; J.R.P. French, Jr., J. Israel, and D. Ho, "An Experiment on Participation in a Norwegian Factory: Interpersonal Discussions of Decision-Making," *Human Relations* (February 1960): 3–19.

30. C.D. King and M. van de Vail, *Models of Industrial Democracy* (New York: Moulton, 1978).

31. S. Melman, "Managerial vs. Cooperation Decision in Israel," *Studies in Comparative International Development* 6 (1970–1971): 15–26.

32. P.R. Lawrence and J. W. Lorsch, *Organization and Environment* (Cambridge, MA: Harvard University Graduate School of Business Administration, 1967).

33. J.D. Thompson, *Organizations in Action* (New York: McGraw-Hill, 1967).

34. Jay Galbraith, *Designing Complex Organizations* (Reading, MA: Addison-Wesley, 1973).

35. W.J. Burns, Jr. and J.H. Waterhouse, "Budgetary Control and Organizational Structure," *Journal of Accounting Research* (Autumn 1975): 177–203.

36. A.W. Halpin, "The Leadership Behavior and Combat Performance of Airplane Commanders," *Journal of Abnormal and Social Psychology* 10 (1954): 19–22.

37. H.H. Meyer, "The Effective Superior: Some Surprising Findings," in *The Failure of Success*, ed. A.J. Marrow (New York: Amacom, 1972).

38. R.J. House, A.C. Filley, and S. Kerr, "Relation of Leader Consideration and Initiating Structure to R.D. Subordinates' Satisfaction," *Administrative Science Quarterly* (March 1971): 19–30.

39. R.W. Griffin, "Relationships among Individual, Taste Design, and Leader Behavioral Variables," *Academy of Management Journal* (December 1980): 665–83.

40. P. Brownell, "Participation in Budgeting, Locus of Control and Organizational Effectiveness," *The Accounting Review* (October 1981): 844–60.

41. V.H. Vroom, *Some Personality Determinants of the Effects of Participation* (Englewood Cliffs, NJ: Prentice-Hall, 1960).

42. Hofstede, *The Game of Budget Control*.

43. P. Brownell, "The Role of Accounting Data in Performance Evaluation, Budgetary Participation, and Organizational Effectiveness," *Journal of Accounting Research* (Spring 1982): 12–27.

44. E.A. Locke and D.M. Schweiger, "Participation in Decision-Making: One More Look," in *Research in Organizational Behavior*, vol. 1, ed. B.M. Staw (Greenwich, CT: JAI Press, 1979), 325.

45. Ibid.

46. C. Argyris, *The Impact of Budgets on People* (New York: Controllership Foundation, 1952); S.W. Becker and D. Green, "Budgeting and Employee Behavior," *Journal of Business* (October 1962): 352–402.

47. Ahmed Belkaoui, *Cost Accounting: A Multidimensional Emphasis* (Hinsdale, IL: Dryden Press, 1983); idem, *Conceptual Foundations of Management Accounting* (Reading, MA: Addison-Wesley, 1980); idem, *Handbook of Management Control Systems* (New Haven, CT: Greenwood Press, 1986).

48. Hofstede, *The Game of Budget Control*; D.G. Searfoss, "Some Behavioral Aspects of Budgeting for Control: An Empirical Study," *Accounting, Organizations and Society* (November 1976): 375–85; Kenis, "Effects of Budgetary Goal Characteristics on Managerial Attitudes and Performance"; Searfoss and Monczka, "Perceived Participation in the Budget Process and Motivation to Achieve the Budget"; Kenneth A Merchant, "The Design of the Corporate Budgeting System: Influences on Managerial Behavior and Performance," *The Accounting Review* (October 1981): 813–29.

49. V.H. Vroom, *Work and Motivation* (New York: Wiley, 1964); J.R. Hackman and E.E. Lawler, "Employee Reactions to Job Characteristics," *Journal of Applied Psychology* (June 1971): 259–86; J.R. Hackman and L.W. Porter, "Expectancy Theory Predictions of Work Effectiveness," *Organizational Behavior and Human Performance* (November 1968): 417–26.

50. K.R. Ferris, "A Test of the Expectancy Theory of Motivation in an Accounting

Environment," *The Accounting Review* (July 1977): 605–15; Rockness, "Expectancy Theory in a Budgetary Setting"; Milani, "Relationship of Participation in Budget-Setting to Industrial Supervisor Performance and Attitudes"; T.R. Mitchell, "Expectancy Models of Job Satisfaction, Occupational Preference, and Effort: A Theoretical, Methodological, and Empirical Appraisal," *Psychological Bulletin* (December 1974): 1053–77; M.A. Wahba and R.J. House, "Expectancy Theory in Work and Motivation—Some Logical and Methodological Issues," *Human Relations* (February 1974): 121–47; T. Connolly, "Some Conceptual and Methodological Issues in Expectancy Models of Work Performance Motivation," *Academy of Management Review* (October 1976): 37–47; J.P. Campbell and R.D. Pritchard, "Motivation Theory in Industrial and Organizational Psychology," in *Handbook of Industrial and Organizational Psychology*, ed. M.D. Dunnette (Chicago: Rand McNally, 1976), 63–130; T.R. Mitchell, "Organizational Behavior," *Annual Review of Psychology* (1979); 243–81.

51. P. Brownell and M. McInnes, "Budgetary Participation, Motivation and Managerial Performance," *The Accounting Review* (October 1986): 587–603.

52. R.J. House, "A Path-Goal Theory of Leader Effectiveness," *Administrative Science Quarterly* (September 1971): 321–38; J. Ronen and J.L. Livingstone "An Expectancy Theory Approach to the Motivational Impacts of Budgets," *The Accounting Review* (October 1975): 671–85.

53. Brownell and McInnes, "Budgetary Participation, Motivation and Managerial Performance," 597.

54. Lobeman Mia, "Managerial Attitude, Motivation and the Effectiveness of Budget Participation," *Accounting, Organizations and Society* 13 (1988): 465–75.

55. Argyris, *The Impact of Budgets on People*; D.T. DeCoster and J.P. Fertakis, "Budget-Induced Pressure and Its Relationship to Supervisory Behavior," *Journal of Accounting Research* (Autumn 1968): 237–46.

56. A.G. Hopwood, "An Empirical Study of the Role of Accounting Data in Performance Evaluation," supplement to *Journal of Accounting Research* (1972): 156–82.

57. David T. Otley, "Budget Use and Managerial Performance," *Journal of Accounting Research* (Spring 1978): 122–79.

58. Ibid., 176.

59. Brownell, "Role of Accounting Data in Performance Evaluation, Budgetary Participation, and Organizational Effectiveness."

60. B.F. Skinner, *The Behavior of Organisms* (New York: Appleton-Century-Crofts, 1938).

61. F. Heider, "Attitudes and Cognitive Organization," *Journal of Psychology* (January 1946): 107–12.

62. Ahmed Riahi-Belkaoui, *The New Foundations of Management Accounting* (Westport, CT: Greenwood, 1992).

63. Ahmed Riahi-Belkaoui, *Behavioral Accounting* (Westport, CT: Greenwood, 1989).

64. A. Riahi-Belkaoui, "The Effects of Goal Setting and Task Uncertainty on Task Outcomes," *Management Accounting Research* (June 1992): 91–96.

65. M.K. Hirst, "Reliance on Accounting Performance Measures, Task Uncertainty and Dysfunctional Behavior: Some Extensions," *Journal of Accounting Research* (Autumn 1983), 596–605.

66. P. Brownell and M. Hirst, "Reliance on Accounting Information, Budgetary Participation, and Task Uncertainty: Tests of a Three-Way Interaction," *Journal of Accounting Research* (Autumn 1986), 241–49.

67. P. Brownell and A.S. Dunk, "Task Uncertainty and Its Interaction with Budgetary Participation and Budget Emphasis: Some Methodological Issues and Empirical Investigation," *Accounting, Organizations and Society* 16 (1991): 693–703.

68. R. Kahn, D. Wolfe, R. Quinn, J.D. Snock and R. Rosenthal, *Organization Stress Studies in Role Conflict and Ambiguity* (New York: Wiley, 1964).

69. Hopwood, "Empirical Study of the Role of Accounting Data in Performance Evaluation."

70. D.T. Otley, "Budget Use and Managerial Performance," *Journal of Accounting Research* (Spring 1978): 122–49.

71. I. Kenis, "Effects of Budgetary Goal Characteristics on Managerial Attitudes and Performance," *The Accounting Review* (October 1979): 707–21.

72. Hirst, "Reliance on Accounting Performance Measures, Task Uncertainty and Dysfunctional Behavior."

73. Ibid.

74. Ibid.

75. Galbraith, *Designing Complex Organizations*; M.L. Tushman and D.A. Nadler, "Information Processing as an Integrating Concept in Organizational Design," *Academy of Management Review* (1978): 613–24.

76. Lawrence and Lorsch, *Organization and Environment*.

77. V. Govindarajan, "Impact of Participation in the Budgetary Process on Managerial Attitudes and Performance: Universalistic and Contingency Perspectives," *Decision Sciences* (February 1986): 496–516.

78. Mark K. Hirst, "Accounting Information and the Evaluation of Subordinate Performance: A Situational Approach," *The Accounting Review* (October 1981): 771–84.

79. P. Brownell and M.K. Hirst, "Reliance on Accounting Information, Budgetary Participation, and Task Uncertainty: Tests of a Three-Way Interaction," *Journal of Accounting Research* (Autumn 1986): 841–49.

80. G. Graen, "Role-Making Processes within Complex Organizations," in *Handbook of Industrial Psychology*, ed. M.D. Dunnette (Chicago: Rand McNally, 1976).

81. T.A. Beehr, J.T. Walsh, and T.D. Taber, "Relationship of Stress to Individually and Organizationally Valued States: Higher Order Needs as a Moderator," *Journal of Applied Psychology* (1976): 41–47; R.D. Caplan, S. Cobba, J.R.P. French, R. Van Harrison, and S.R. Pinneas, *Job Demands and Worker Health: Main Effects and Occupational Differences* (Washington, DC: Government Printing Office, 1975): C.N. Greene, "Relationships among Role Accuracy, Compliance, Performance Evaluation and Satisfaction within Managerial Dyads," *Academy of Management Journal* (1972): 205–15; W.C. Hamner and H.W. Tosi, "Relationships of Role Conflict and Role Ambiguity to Job Involvement Measures," *Journal of Applied Psychology* (1974): 497–99; T.W. Johnson and J.E. Stinton, "Role Ambiguity, Role Conflict, and Satisfaction: Moderating Effects of Individual Influences," *Journal of Applied Psychology* (1975): 329–33; R.J. Paul, "Role Clarity as a Correlate of Satisfaction, Job-Related Strain, and Propensity to Leave—Male vs. Female," *Journal of Applied Psychology* (1974): 233–45; J.R. Rizzo, R.J. House, and S.I. Lirtzman, "Role Conflict and Ambiguity in Complex Organizations," *Administrative Service Quarterly* (June 1970): 150–63.

82. Hamner and Tosi, "Relationships of Role Conflict and Role Ambiguity to Job Involvement Measures"; A.D. Brief and R.J Alday, "Correlates of Role Indices," *Journal of Applied Psychology* (1976): 468–72.

83. Beehr, Walsh, and Taber, "Relationship of Stress to Individually and Organizationally Valued States."

84. A.R. Cohen, "Situational Structure, Self-Esteem and Threat Oriented Reactions to Power," in *Studies in Social Power*, ed. D. Cartwright (Ann Arbor: University of Michigan Press, 1959).

85. H. Tosi and D. Tosi, "Some Correlates of Role Conflict and Ambiguity among Public School Teachers," *Journal of Human Relations* (1970): 1068–75; R.S. Schuler, "A Role and Expectancy Perception Model of Participation in Decision Making," *Academy of Management Journal* (June 1980): 331–40.

86. R.H. Chenhall and P. Brownell, "The Effects of Participative Budgeting on Job Satisfaction and Performance: Role Ambiguity as an Intervening Variable," *Accounting, Organizations and Society* 13, no. 3 (1988): 225–33.

87. D.J. Cherrington and J.O. Cherrington, "Appropriate Reinforcement Contingencies in the Budgeting Process," supplement to *Journal of Accounting Research* (1973): 225–53.

88. B.F. Skinner, *Contingencies of Reinforcement* (New York: Appleton-Century-Crofts, 1969).

89. E. Aronson, "Dissonance Theory: Progress and Problems," in *Theories of Cognitive Consistency: A Sourcebook*, ed. R.P. Abelson, E. Aronson, W.J. McGuire, T.M. Newcomb, M.J. Rosenberg, and P.H. Tannenbaum (Chicago: Rand McNally, 1968), 5–6.

90. Michael F. Foran and Don T. DeCoster, "An Experimental Study of the Effects of Participation, Authoritarianism, and Feedback on Cognitive Dissonance in a Standard Setting Situation," *The Accounting Review* (October 1974): 751–63.

91. Ibid., 762.

92. M.G. Tiller, "The Dissonance Model of Participative Budgeting: An Empirical Exploration," *Journal of Accounting Research* (Autumn 1983): 581–95.

93. B.D. Slack and J.O. Cook, "Authoritarian Behavior in a Conflict Situation," *Journal of Personality and Social Psychology* (January 1973): 130–36.

94. Vroom, *Some Personality Determinants of the Effects of Participation*; Hofstede, *The Game of Budget Control*; R.E. Seiler and R.W. Bartlett, "Personality Variables as Predictors of Budget Systems Characteristics," *Accounting, Organizations and Society* (December 1982): 381–403.

95. Foran and DeCoster, "Experimental Study of the Effects of Participation, Authoritarianism, and Feedback on Cognitive Dissonance in a Standard Setting Situation"; A.A. Abdel-Halim and K.M. Rowland, "Some Personality Determinants of the Effects of Participation: A Further Investigation," *Personnel Psychology* (Spring 1976): 16–17; Frank Collins, "The Interaction of Budget Characteristics and Personality Variables with Budgetary Response Attitudes," *The Accounting Review* (April 1978): 324–35.

96. Robert H. Chenhall, "Authoritarianism and Participative Budgeting: A Dyadic Analysis," *The Accounting Review* (April 1986): 263–72.

97. Slack and Cook, "Authoritarian Behavior in a Conflict Situation"; W. Haythorn, A. Conch, D. Haefner, P. Langham, and L. Carter, "The Behavior of Authoritarian and Equalitarian Personalities in Small Groups," *Human Relations* (February 1956): 57–74.

98. M. Deutsch, "Trust, Trustworthiness and the F-Scale," *Journal of Abnormal and Social Psychology* (July 1960): 138–40.

99. J.B. Rolter, M. Seeman, and S. Liverant, "Internal versus External Control of

Reinforcement: A Major Variable in Behavioral Theory" in *Decisions, Values and Groups*, ed. N.F. Washburne (New York: Pergamon Press, 1962), 473–516.

100. H.M. Lefcourt, "Internal versus External Control of Reinforcement: A Review," *Psychological Bulletin* (April 1966): 206–20.

101. Brownell, "Participation in Budgeting, Locus of Control and Organizational Effectiveness."

102. Ibid., 847.

103. D. Pelz, "Influence: A Key to Effective Leadership in the First Line Supervisor," *Personnel* (1952): 209–71.

104. K.H. Roberts and C.A. O'Reilly, "Failures in Upward Communication: Three Possible Culprits," *Academy of Management Journal* (1974): 205–15; A.P. Jones, L.R. James, and J.R. Bruni, "Perceived Leadership Behavior and Employee Confidence in the Leader as Moderated by Job Involvement," *Journal of Applied Psychology* (1978): 146–49; C.A. O'Reilly and K.H. Roberts, "Supervisor Influence and Subordinate Mobility Aspirations as Moderators of Consideration and Initiating Structure," *Journal of Applied Psychology* (1978): 96–102; F.M. Jablin, "Superior's Upward Influence, Satisfaction and Openness in Superior-Subordinate Communication: A Reexamination of the 'Pelz Effect'," *Human Communication Research* (1980): 210–20.

105. Ahmed Belkaoui, "Leadership Style, Dimensions of Superior's Upward Influence and Participative Budgeting," working paper, University of Illinois at Chicago, June 1988.

106. Dennis Murray, "The Performance Effects of Participative Budgeting: An Integration of Intervening and Moderating Variables," *Behavioral Research in Accounting* 2 (1990): 104–23.

107. K. Merchant, "The Design of Corporate Budgeting System: Influences on Managerial Behavior and Performance," *The Accounting Review* 56 (1981): 813–29.

108. K. Merchant, "Influences on Departmental Budgeting: An Empirical Examination of a Contingency Model," *Accounting, Organizations and Society* 9 (1984): 291–310.

109. L. Mia, "Participation in Budgeting Decision Making, Task Difficulty, Locus of Control, and Employee Behavior: An Empirical Study," *Decision Sciences* 18 (1987): 547–61.

110. M. Shields, and S.M. Young, "Antecedents and Consequences of Participative Budgeting: Evidence on the Effects of Asymmetrical Information," *Journal of Management Accounting Research* 5 (1993): 265–80.

111. J.F. Shields and M.D. Shields, "Antecedents of Participative Budgeting," *Accounting, Organizations and Society* 23 (1998): 49–76.

112. Ibid., 49.

113. H. Nomi, and R.J. Parker, "The Relationship between Budget Participation and Job Performance: The Roles of Budget Adequacy and Organizational Commitment," *Accounting, Organizations and Society* 23 (1998): 467–83.

114. J.E. Mathiew and D.M. Zajac, "A Review and Meta-Analysis of the Antecedents, Correlates, and Consequences of Organizational Commitment," *Psychological Bulletin* 1 (1990): 171–94.

115. F.I. Hanson, "The Budgetary Control Function," *The Accounting Review* (April 1966): 241.

116. Nomi and Parker, "Relationship between Budget Participation and Job Performance."

SELECTED BIBLIOGRAPHY

Becker, S.W., and D. Green. "Budgeting and Employee Behavior," *Journal of Business* (October 1962): 352–402.

Belkaoui, Ahmed. "Leadership Style, Dimensions of Superior's Upward Influence and Participative Budgeting." Working paper. University of Illinois at Chicago, June 1988.

Brownell, P. "A Field Study Examination of Budgetary Participation and Locus of Control." *Accounting Review* (October 1982): 766–77.

———. "Participation in Budgeting, Locus of Control and Organizational Effectiveness." *The Accounting Review* (October 1981): 844–60.

———. "Participation in the Budgeting Process: When It Works and When It Doesn't." *Journal of Accounting Literature* (Spring 1982): 124–53.

———. "The Role of Accounting Data in Performance Evaluation, Budgetary Participation, and Organizational Effectiveness." *Journal of Accounting Research* (Spring 1982): 12–27.

Brownell, P., and M.K. Hirst. "Reliance on Accounting Information, Budgetary Participation, and Task Uncertainty: Tests of a Three-Way Interaction." *Journal of Accounting Research* (Autumn 1986): 841–49.

Brownell, P., and M. McInnes. "Budgetary Participation, Motivation and Managerial Performance." *The Accounting Review* (October 1986): 587–603.

Bryan, J.P., and E.A. Locke. "Goal Setting as a Means of Increasing Motivation." *Journal of Applied Psychology* (1967): 274–77.

Burns. W.J., Jr., and J.H. Waterhouse. "Budgetary Control and Organizational Structure." *Journal of Accounting Research* (Autumn 1975): 177–203.

Campbell, J.P., and R.D. Pritchard. "Motivation Theory in Industrial and Organizational Psychology." In *Handbook of Industrial and Organizational Psychology*, ed. M.D. Dunnette. Chicago: Rand McNally, 1976, 63–130.

Chenhall, Robert H. "Authoritarianism and Participative Budgeting: A Dyadic Analysis." *Accounting Review* (April 1986): 263–72.

Chenhall, Robert H., and P. Brownell. "The Effects of Participative Budgeting on Job Satisfaction and Performance: Role Ambiguity as an Intervening Variable." *Accounting, Organizations and Society* 13, no. 3 (1988): 225–33.

Cherrington, D.J., and J.O. Cherrington. "Appropriate Reinforcement Contingencies in the Budgeting Process," Supplement to *Journal of Accounting Research* (1973): 225–53.

Chow, C.W. "The Effects of Job Standard Tightness and Compensation Scheme on Performance: An Exploration of Linkages." *Accounting Review* (October 1983): 667–85.

Coch, L., and J.R.P. French, Jr. "Overcoming Resistance to Change." *Human Relations* (August 1948): 512–32.

Collins, Frank. "The Interaction of Budget Characteristics and Personality Variables with Budgetary Response Attitudes." *The Accounting Review* (April 1978): 324–35.

Connolly, T. "Some Conceptual and Methodological Issues in Expectancy Models of Work Performance Motivation." *Academy of Management Review* (October 1976): 37–47.

DeCoster, D.T., and J.P. Fertakis. "Budget-Induced Pressure and Its Relationship to Supervisory Behavior." *Journal of Accounting Research* (Autumn 1968): 237–46.

Demski, J.S., and G.A. Feltham. "Economic Incentives in Budgetary Control Systems." *The Accounting Review* (April 1978): 336–59.

Ferris, K.R. "A Test of the Expectancy Theory of Motivation in an Accounting Environment." *The Accounting Review* (July 1977): 605–15.

Foran, Michael F., and Don T. DeCoster. "An Experimental Study of the Effects of Participation, Authoritarianism, and Feedback on Cognitive Dissonance in a Standard Setting Situation." *The Accounting Review* (October 1974): 751–63.

French, J.R.P., Jr., J. Israel, and D. Ho. "An Experiment on Participation in a Norwegian Factory: Interpersonal Discussions of Decision-Making." *Human Relations* (February 1960): 3–19.

Govindarajan, V. "Impact of Participation in the Budgetary Process on Managerial Attitudes and Performance: Universalistic and Contingency Perspectives." *Decision Sciences* (February 1986): 496–516.

Griffin, R.W. "Relationships among Individual, Task Design, and Leader Behavior Variables." *Academy of Management Journal* (December 1980): 665–83.

Hackman, J.R., and E.E. Lawler. "Employee Reactions to Job Characteristics." *Journal of Applied Psychology* (June 1971): 259–86.

Hackman, J.R., and L.W. Porter. "Expectancy Theory Predictions of Work Effectiveness." *Organizational Behavior and Human Performance* (November 1968): 417–26.

Halpin, A.W. "The Leadership Behavior and Combat Performance of Airplane Commanders." *Journal of Abnormal and Social Psychology* 10 (1954): 19–22.

Haythorn, W., A. Conch, D. Haefner, P. Langham, and L. Carter. "The Behavior of Authoritarian and Equalitarian Personalities in Small Groups." *Human Relations* (February 1956): 57–74.

Hirst, Mark K. "Accounting Information and the Evaluation of Subordinate Performance: A Situational Approach." *The Accounting Review* (October 1981): 771–84.

———. "The Effects of Setting Budget Goals and Task Uncertainty on Performance: A Theoretical Analysis." *The Accounting Review* (October 1987): 774–84.

Hofstede, G.H. *The Game of Budget Control*. London: Tavistock, 1968.

Hopwood, A.G. "An Empirical Study of the Role of Accounting Data in Performance Evaluation." Supplement to *Journal of Accounting Research* (1972): 156–82.

House, R.J. "A Path-Goal Theory of Leader Effectiveness." *Administrative Science Quarterly* (September 1971): 321–38.

House, R.J., A.C. Filley, and S. Kerr. "Relation of Leader Consideration and Initiating Structure to R.D. Subordinates' Satisfaction." *Administrative Science Quarterly* (March 1971): 19–30.

Industrial Democracy in Europe International Research Group. "Participation: Formal Rules, Influence and Involvement." *Industrial Relations* (Fall 1979): 273–94.

Jablin, F.M. "Superior's Upward Influence, Satisfaction and Openness in Superior-Subordinate Communication: A Reexamination of the 'Pelz Effect.'" *Human Communication Research* (1980): 210–20.

Jones, A.P., L.R. James, and J.R. Bruni. "Perceived Leadership Behavior and Employee Confidence in the Leader as Moderated by Job Involvement." *Journal of Applied Psychology* (1978): 146–49.

Kenis, I. "Effects of Budgetary Goal Characteristics on Managerial Attitudes and Performance." *The Accounting Review* (October 1979): 707–21.

King, C.D., and M. van de Vail. *Models of Industrial Democracy*. New York: Moulton, 1978.

Locke, E.A., K.N. Shaw, L.M. Saari, and G.P. Latham. "Goal Setting and Task Performance: 1969–1980." *Psychological Bulletin* (1981): 15–32.

Melman, S. "Managerial vs. Cooperation Decision in Israel." *Studies in Comparative International Development* 6 (1970–1971): 10–21.

Meyer, H.H. "The Effective Superior: Some Surprising Findings." In *The Failure of Success*, ed. A.J. Marrow. New York: Amacom, 1972.

Milani, K.W. "The Relationship of Participation in Budget-Setting to Industrial Supervisor Performance and Attitudes: A Field Study." *The Accounting Review* (April 1975): 274–85.

Mitchell, T.R. "Expectancy Models of Job Satisfaction, Occupational Preference, and Effort: A Theoretical, Methodological, and Empirical Appraisal." *Psychological Bulletin* (December 1974): 1053–77.

Naylor, J.C., and D.R. Ilgen. "Goal Setting: A Theoretical Analysis of a Motivational Technology." In *Research in Organizational Behavior*, ed. B.M. Staw and L.L. Cummings. Greenwich, CT: JAI Press, 1984, 95–140.

O'Reilly, C.A., and K.H. Roberts. "Supervisor Influence and Subordinate Mobility Aspirations as Moderators of Consideration and Initiating Structure." *Journal of Applied Psychology* (1978): 96–102.

Otley, David T. "Budget Use and Managerial Performance." *Journal of Accounting Research* (Spring 1978): 122–49.

Pelz, D. "Influence: A Key to Effective Leadership in the First Line Supervisor." *Personnel* (1952): 209–71.

Roberts, K.H., and C.A. O'Reilly. "Failures in Upward Communication: Three Possible Culprits." *Academy of Management Journal* (1974): 205–15.

Rockness, H.O. "Expectancy Theory in a Budgetary Setting: An Empirical Examination." *The Accounting Review* (October 1977): 893–903.

Ronen, J., and J.L. Livingstone. "An Expectancy Theory Approach to the Motivational Impacts of Budgets." *The Accounting Review* (October 1975): 671–85.

Searfoss, D. "Some Behavioral Aspects of Budgeting for Control: An Empirical Study." *Accounting Organizations and Society* (November 1976): 375–85.

Searfoss, D., and R. Monczka. "Perceived Participation in the Budget Process and Motivation to Achieve the Budget." *Academy of Management Journal* (December 1973): 541–54.

Seiler, R.E., and R.W. Bartlett. "Personality Variables as Predictors of Budget Systems Characteristics." *Accounting, Organizations and Society* (December 1982): 381–403.

Stedry, A., and E. Kay. "The Effects of Goal Difficulty on Performance: A Field Experiment." *Behavioral Science* (November 1966): 459–70.

Swieringa, R.J., and R.H. Moncur. *Some Effects of Participative Budgeting on Managerial Behavior*. New York: National Association of Accountants, 1974.

Tiller, M.G. "The Dissonance Model of Participative Budgeting: An Empirical Exploration." *Journal of Accounting Research* (Autumn 1983): 581–95.

Tushman, M.L., and D.A. Nadler. "Information Processing as an Integrating Concept in Organizational Design." *Academy of Management Review* (1978): 613–24.

Vroom, V.H. *Some Personality Determinants of the Effects of Participation.* Englewood Cliffs, NJ: Prentice-Hall, 1960.

Wahba, M.A., and R.J. House. "Expectancy Theory in Work and Motivation—Some Logical and Methodological Issues." *Human Relations* (February 1974): 121–47.

9

Behavioral Issues in Control

INTRODUCTION

Control of individual processes and activities in a given period involves mostly (a) a clinical judgment on whether or not to investigate a variance between actual performance and standard performance and (b) actions that reduce and/or correct the problems created by management's attempts to manipulate or normalize accounting data destined for internal or external decision making.

Studies have not been very conclusive in evaluating the accuracy of clinical judgment as an ex ante skill; the results show the correlation between judgment and some standard criterion to be low. In spite of these results, control continues to be practiced without any challenge to the validity of the clinical judgment it is generally based on. This chapter examines the possible threats to the validity of control judgments.

With regard to the manipulation of data, control may be exercised to limit the consequences of both slack budgeting and income smoothing. This chapter elaborates on the nature and causes of these managerial tricks of influencing data.

BASE RATE ISSUES IN CONTROL

The most important information used in any judgment in general and in a control judgment in particular is the *base rate*, which is the probability of the occurrence of an event. Not only is its determination difficult, but evidence shows that people tend to ignore the base rate and focus on positive hits.

Task Structure of Control

The structure of tasks, proposed initially in the accounting literature by H. Bierman and his associates, considers control situations characterized by a *two-state*, two-action problem with these states:

S_1 in control,
S_2 out of control,

and these possible actions:

A_1 = Investigate the variance,
A_2 = Do not investigate the variance.[1]

The structure of tasks, proposed in the psychological literature by H. J. Einhorn and R. M. Hogarth to consider judgments, actions, and outcome feedback and as a criterion for the evaluation of the accuracy of the judgment, is as follows:

1. Denote by x an evaluative judgment and by x_c a cutoff point such that if
   $x \lesssim x_c$, investigate the variance,
   $x \gtrsim x_c$, do not investigate the variance.
2. Consider also the existence of a criterion, y, used to evaluate the accuracy of the judgment x and y_c, a cutoff point, such that if
   $y \geq y_c$, S_1 is assumed,
   $y \leq y_c$, S_2 is assumed.[2]

Two assumptions are necessary at this stage for an application of the items in accounting. First, x_c and y_c are part of the standards set in the budgeting procedure, and x and y are observed outcomes of the process to be controlled.

The combination of the structure of tables in performance evaluation is shown in Exhibit 9.1. The interrelations between the judgment x and the criterion y result in four quadrants:

Quadrant I denotes the false negative rate:

$$p(y \geq y_c/x < x_c) = fn,$$

Quadrant II denotes the positive hit rate:

$$p(y \geq y_c/x \geq x_c) = ph,$$

Quadrant III denotes the false positive rate:

$$p(y < y_c/x < x_c) = fp$$

Exhibit 9.1
Action-Outcome Combinations that Result from Using Judgment Whether or Not to Investigate a Given Variance

y(Performance)	I	II
S_1		
Unfavorable Variance Resulted from Controllable Causes or Process in Control	False Negative Hits	Positive Hits
y_c		
S_2	IV	III
Unfavorable Variance Resulted from Noncontrollable Causes or Process out of Control	Negative Hits	False Positive Hits x
	x_c	
	Do not Investigate $x < x_c$	Investigate (judgement) $x > x_c$

Quadrant IV denotes the negative hit rate:

$$p(y < y_c/x < x_c) = nh.$$

This is obtained by denoting the correct predictions as positive and negative hits and the two types of errors as false positive ($y < y_c/x \geq x_c$) and false negative ($y > y_c/x < x_c$).

Other relevant information includes:

a. The base rate: $p(y \geq y_c) = br$, the unconditional probability of exceeding the criterion
b. The selection ratio: $p(x \geq x_c) = 0$

This structure of tasks, as depicted in Exhibit 9.1., shows three factors affecting the positive hit rate:

1. the correlation between x and y as measured by Px_y;
2. the selection ratio Θ; and
3. the base rate, br.

Evidence of the effects of these three factors on the positive hit rate is also provided by H. C. Taylor and T. T. Russell.[3]

This structure of tasks may also be used to determine the number of positive hits and false positives resulting from making predictions in selection tasks in general and performance evaluation in particular. Hence let:

$\quad N =$ Number of total decisions to be made, or the total
$\qquad$ number of variances to be investigated.
$\quad P_{xy} =$ Correlation between prediction and outcomes.
$\quad N_p =$ Number of positive hits $= N \times p(y \geq y_c, x \geq x_c)$.
$\quad N_f =$ Number of false positives $= N \times p(y < y_c, x \geq x_c)$.

From these definitions it can be shown, after replacing the joint probabilities by conditional probabilities multiplied by their respective marginal probabilities, that

$$N_p = N \times p(y \geq y_c/x \geq x_c)p(x \geq x_c) = Nph0,$$
$$N_f = N \times p(y < y_c/x \geq x_c)p(x \geq x_c) = Nfp0,$$

and since $ph = 1 - fp$,

$$N, = Nph0$$
$$NI = M(1 - ph)0$$

Einhorn maintained that if $\dfrac{N_p}{N_f}$ is used by people to evaluate the feedback effect of outcomes, the positive hit rate determines the sign of the feedback. With $ph > 0.5$, $N_p > N_f$. If people evaluate the same feedback by the difference $N_p - N_f$, then $N_p - N_f - N0$ $(2ph - 1)$ and $N_p > N_f$ if $ph > 0.5$.[4]

The Determination of the Base Rate

In accounting literature, Bierman and his associates were the first use the normative structure of tasks in performance evaluation and introduced the costs and benefits of an investigation in the investigation decision.[5] Given a particular observation on a given activity, the actual base rate, $P_a(y \geq y_c)$, given that the system is in control, is determined. Assuming the cost of the investigation to be the amount c, the cost of correction to be M, and the present value of the savings obtainable from an investigation when the activity is out of control to be $L -$

M, an investigation is signaled if $P_a(y \geq y_c) < 1 - \dfrac{C}{L - M}$. This normative accounting control model rests therefore on a proper estimation of the actual base rate, $P_a(y \geq y_c)$. But can the actual base rate be estimated? From the psychological literature, the answer appears that the base rate is not likely to be known, nor can it be estimated by past data.

The base rate can be expressed as a function of the positive hit rate, the false negative rate, and the selection ratio. From Exhibit 9.1, it may be stated that

$$P(y \geq y_c) = p(y \geq y_c/x \geq x_c)p(x \geq x_c) + p(y \geq y_c/x < x_c)p(x < x_c)$$

In other words, the base rate = positive hit rate × selection ratio + false negative rate (1 − selection ratio). Therefore, the computation of the base rate depends on the availability of (1) the positive hit rate, (2) the selection ratio, and (3) the false negative rate. It may be argued that both the positive hit rate and the selection ratio may be available, but the false negative rate may not be. For example, in a control context the selection ratio may be estimated from past records. It corresponds to the proportion of variances getting investigated as opposed to not getting investigated. Similarly, the positive hit rate may be easily estimated. It corresponds to the proportion of "successes" of those variances that have been investigated. The problem is in the determination of the false negative rate. It corresponds to those variances that have not been investigated; therefore, it would be difficult to estimate how many of those variances not investigated would have been due to controllable causes. The base rate may then be difficult to estimate given the difficulty of estimating the false negative rate.

Ignorance of the Base Rate

Both singular and distributional information are usually available to people when they judge the probability of an event. *Singular information*, or *case data*, refers to evidence on the case under consideration. *Distributional information*, or *base-rate data*, refers to the probability of the occurrence of the event in general. For example, the number of defective items in a sample provides singular information about the probability of the system being in control, and the base-rate *frequency* of the process being in control constitutes distributional information. Research has shown that intuitive judgments are generally influenced by singular evidence and a general neglect of base rates. This ignorance of the base rate was confirmed in a number of replications, varying base rates, problem content, information order, and response mode and using simple experimental tasks and complex realistic problems.[6] More recently, however, A. Tversky and D. Kahneman have shown that base-rate information that is given a casual interpretation affects judgment.[7] The evidence in the accounting literature is mired. Swieringa and associates and M. Gibbins, replicating and extending some of Tversky and Kahneman's work, reported that their subjects, students and practicing auditors did systematically react to base rates.[8] However, E. J. Joyce G. C. Biddle, using between-subject design rather than within-subject design, found that the auditor's probability judgments were slightly regressed toward the base rate.[9] The magnitude of the regression was, however, considered low.

Focus on Positive Hits

Various experiments have shown that people fail to show an intuitive appreciation of correlation or contingency when judging the relations between events on the basis of a serial correlation. Most of these studies show that the judgments are not based on a comparison of conditional probabilities.[10] More explicitly, J. Smedslund showed that people with no statistical training have no adequate concept of a correlation and tend to depend exclusively on the frequency of positive confirming cases.[11] Similarly, H. M. Jenkins and W. C. Ward found also a lack of appreciation of the concept of correlation.[12] Their subjects made judgments of control that bore no relationship to the concept of statistical control. They seemed to perceive a contingency only when favorable events occurred. In a second experiment Jenkins and Ward found that the type of information display may affect the perception of a contingency.[13] However, their results, in general, support the earlier findings that statistically naive subjects lack an abstract concept of contingency that is isomorphic with the statistical concept and tend to rely on rules involving the frequency of positive favorable events. Thus, using the terminology of Exhibit 9.1, these findings imply that people judge the strength of relationships by the frequency of positive hits and disregard the other three informations, namely, the negative hit rate, the false positive hit rate, and the false negative hit rate.[14]

HEURISTIC AND BIAS IN CONTROL JUDGMENTS

Representativeness

Representativeness refers to the heuristic used by people when they judge the probability of an event by its degree of similarity (representativeness) to the category of which it is perceived to be an example. "A person who follows this heuristic evaluates the probability of an uncertain event, or a sample, by the degree to which it is: (i) similar in essential properties to its parent population; and (ii) reflects the salient feature of the process by which it is generated." It is a mental process or strategy of stereotyping by degree of similarity, for example, imagining that someone is an accountant because he exhibits characteristics typical of an accountant. Consequently, people often fail to give enough credence to the possibility of "surprising" or "unusual events." Representativeness may lead to several systematic biases in probability estimation, including (1) insensitivity to prior probabilities, (2) disregard for the impact of sample size on the variance of the sampling distribution, misperception of the likelihood of different sequences resulting from a random process, and (4) insensitivity to the predict-ability of data, which results in unwarranted confidence in judgment and mis-conception of regression toward the mean (for example, that extreme values predictor variables are likely to produce less extreme outcomes).[15]

Availability

Availability refers to the heuristic used by people when they assess the prob-ability of an event by the case with which it comes to mind. "A person is said to employ the availability heuristic whenever he estimates frequency or proba-bility by the case with which instances or associations can be brought to mind."[16] It is a mental process, a strategy related to the case of recollecting specific examples or instances from memory that affects judgments of frequency. As an example, the frequency of well-publicized events like death from terrorism is overestimated, but the frequency of less well-publicized events like death from hunger in America is underestimated. Instances of frequent events are recalled more easily than instances of less frequent events. The availability heuristic depends on familiarity, salience, recency of occurrence, imaginability, or the effectiveness of a search net.

Adjustment and Anchoring

Adjustment and *anchoring* refer to the heuristic used by people when they make estimates by starting from an initial value (anchoring) and then adjusting the values to yield the final answer.[17] For example, this heuristic may lead cost analysts to make a cost forecast by taking last year's costs and adding, say, 10 percent. Last year's cost is taken as an anchor and adjustments are made ac-cording to changes in conditions foreseen by the cost analyst. Adjustment and anchoring imply that availability is necessary. Robin Hogarth stated:

That is, predictions are made by reference to cases that are available [and] adjustments made concerning the particular case to be predicted relative to the cases. Furthermore, availability and adjustment and anchoring are heuristics that both depend heavily upon the initial point in the judgment process: the information that is available and which forms the anchor.[18]

Adjustment and anchoring are more standard procedures in managerial ac-counting decisions and especially in budget behavior and performance evalua-tion.[19]

Hindsight Bias

Hindsight bias means that the knowledge that an event has happened increases its perceived prior probability of occurrence, and the knowledge that an event has not occurred decreases its perceived prior probability of occurrence.[20] In retrospect, people are not "surprised" about a past event. They can easily explain it. A good example is the "Monday morning quarterback phenomena." In addition, people do not realize the impact of outcome knowledge on probability assessment. B. Fischhoff noted that "making sense out of what one is told about the past seems so natural and effortless a response that one may be unaware that outcome knowledge has had any effect at all on him."[21] What may result from the hindsight bias is the observed overconfidence in probability assessments. The presence of hindsight bias raises the following important issues.

1. The judgment of the apparent failures or successes of others may be colored by the hindsight bias.
2. Hindsight bias implies distortion in memory.
3. Overcoming the bias is important to force people to realize the real significance of events.
4. Learning from experience is not evident.[22]

Calibration of Judgments

A probability expresses a degree of belief that an individual associates with a statement whose truth has not been ascertained. When the truth or the falsity of the statement can be verified, the adequacy of probability may be assessed. One way of assessing the adequacy of the probability is to look at the calibration of the confidence statements that reflect the amount of knowledge of the topic area contained in the probability assessments. A judge is considered well calibrated if in the long run, for all propositions assigned a given probability, the proportion that is true is equal to the probability assigned. In general, the calibration of individuals is evaluated by determining their probability assessments, verifying the related statements, and then determining the proportion that is true overall. Individuals who are not calibrated will be underconfident or overconfident. A survey of the growing literature on calibration has been provided by S. Lichtenstein, B. Fischhoff, and L. D. Phillips.[23] The main evidence from the existing research is that people tend to be overconfident. The effect was found to be robust. The calibration of probability is independent of several examined factors, namely, subjects' intelligence, subjects' expertise in the subject matter of the questions, and subjects' reliance on the usual responses of 0.50 and 1.00. It was, however, found to depend on item difficulty. Subjects tend to be overconfident with hard items and underconfident with easy items.

Ignoring and Disconfirming Information

It is an accepted normative view of scientific inference that disconfirmation and testing of alternative hypotheses have major roles. More particularly, K. R. Popper's philosophy of science is based on the concept of disconfirmation or

Exhibit 9.2
Loss of Utility due to Fallibility Judgment in a Performance Evaluation Sample

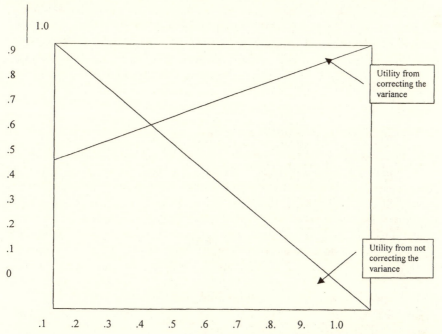

refutation.[24] He maintained that hypotheses can be disconfirmed only by evidence and can never be confirmed. J. R. Platt also argued that successive generations of alternative hypotheses should be disconfirmed—a strategy he labeled "strong inference."[25] The findings in psychological research, however, show that people have difficulty using "disconfirming information." C. R. Mynatt and associates, M. E. Doherty and associates, and P. C. Wason provided evidence of the tendency for people to look only for confirmatory evidence.[26]

Effect on Judgment Fallibility on Control

Control involves a clinical judgment about whether to investigate a given variance. The evidence reviewed shows a general fallibility of judgments. Why should one worry about the fallibility of judgments in control? D. Von Winterfield and W. Edwards argued that, in most real-world decision problems, material errors have a minor impact on the expected gain.[27] A suboptional choice does not seriously hurt the decision maker as long as the alternative selected is not grossly away from the optimum.[28] However, there are situations in which the fallibility of judgment in performance evaluation might make a difference. For example, cost accountants must decide the probability that the process is out of control and should be corrected versus having the process in control and not being corrected. Let us also assume that the utilities to the person investigated are such that the correction of the variance is better if the probability of the process out of control is ≥ 0.35, as shown in Exhibit 9.2. If cost accountants estimate the probability, or in their judgment they should have estimated it, to be 0.30, they would advise for the correction of the variance and create a loss of utility applied to the person investigated. D. G. Fryback has shown similar real-life utility functions.[29]

THE "PELZ EFFECT" AND CONTROL

Researchers of superior-subordinate communication have studied the effects of a superior's upward influence in the organizational hierarchy on his or her relationship with subordinates. The best-known result of this line of research is the so-called Pelz effect. In his seminal study, D. Pelz reported the existence of a positive association between a supervisor's upward hierarchical influence and a subordinate's satisfaction with the performance of the supervisor, provided the superior also exhibited "supportive" leadership style in interactions with the employee.[30] As Pelz noted, "If the supervisor has *little* power or influence, then neither his helpful behavior nor his restraining behavior will have much concrete effect on the employees."[31] L. W. Wager also explored the effects of supervisors' hierarchical influence and of leadership style on the fulfillment of their supervisory role obligations toward others lower in the organization.[32] He found results similar to Pelz's. He also observed that a supportive style of leadership was a more powerful variable than hierarchical influence in contributing to the fulfillment of supervisory-role obligations and that the magnitude of the moderating effect of influence varies markedly with organizational status of the respondent. As Wager noted, *"The more organizationally marginal the status occupied by subordinates, the greater will be the pervasiveness of the effect of a supervisor's influence on his style of leadership as it bears an fulfillment of his supervisory role."*[33]

CONCLUSIONS

This chapter examined both the judgment fallibility in control and the attempts by managers to manipulate accounting data. Both phenomena need to be controlled to secure a *"healthy"* behavioral atmosphere within the organization. With regard to the manipulation of data, control may need to at least correct some of the consequences of slack budgeting and income smoothing. With regard to the fallibility of judgment, negative behavioral effects may have resulted in the implementation of control in corporations. To alleviate the situation, controllers may have to exhibit appropriate caution concerning their judgment ability in performance evaluation, especially in view of the evidence of the use of heuristics and bias in judgment.

NOTES

1. H. Bierman, Jr., L.E. Fourakeer, and R.K. Jaedicke, "A Use of Probability and Statistics in Performance Evaluation," *The Accounting Review* (July 1961):409–17.

2. H.J. Einhom and R.M. Hogarth, "Confidence in Judgment: Persistence of the Illusion of Validity," *Psychological Review* 85 (1978): 395–416.

3. H.C. Taylor and T.T. Russell, "The Relationship of Validity Coefficients to the Practical Effectiveness of Tests in Selection: Discussion and Tables,"*Journal of Applied Psychology* 23 (1939): 565–78.

4. H.J. Einhorn, "Learning from Experience and Suboptimal Rules in Decision Making," in *Cognitive Processes in Choice and Decision Behavior*, ed. T. Wallsten (Hillsdale, NJ: Erlbaum, 1980).

5. Bierman, Fourakeer, and Jaedicke, "Use of Probability and Statistics in Performance Evaluation," 409–17.

6. I. Ajzen, "Intuitive Theories of Events and the Effects of Base-Rate Information on Prediction," *Journal of Personality and Social Psychology* 101 (1977): 377–83; M. Hammerton, "A Case of Radical Probability Estimation," *Journal of Experimental Psychology* 101 (1973): 252–54; D. Kahneman and A. Tversky, "On the Psychology of Prediction," *Psychological Review* 80 (1973), 237–251; D. Lyon and P. Slovic, "Dominance of Accuracy Information and Neglect of Base Rates in Probability Estimation," *Acta Psychologica* 9 (1976): 287–98; R.E. Nisbett and E. Borgida, "Attribution and the Psychology of Prediction," *Journal of Personality and Social Psychology* 11 (1975): 932–43; R.E. Nisbett, E. Borgida, E. Crandall, and H. Reed, "Popular Induction: Information Is Not Necessarily Informative," in *Cognition and Social Behavior*, ed. J.S. Carroll and T.W. Payne (Hillsdale, NJ: Erlbaum, 1976).

7. A. Tversky and D. Kahneman, "Causal Schemata in Judgments under Uncertainty," in *Progress in Social Psychology*, ed. M. Fishbein (Hillsdale, NJ: Erlbaum, 1977).

8. R. Swieringa, M. Gibbins, L. Larson, and J.L. Sweeny, "Experiments in the Heuristics of Human Information Processing," *Studies on Human Information Processing in Accounting*, Supplement to the *Journal of Accounting Research* (1976): 207–32; M. Gibbins, "Human Inference, Heuristics, and Auditor's Judgment Processes," *CICA Audit Research Symposium* (Toronto: Canadian Institute of Chartered Accountants, 1977).

9. E.J. Joyce and G.C. Biddle, "Are Auditors' Judgments Sufficiently Regressive?" (Manuscript, University of Chicago, October 1979).

10. J. Smedslund, "The Concept of Correlation in Adults," *Scandinavian Journal of Psychology* 4 (1963): 165–73; E.D. Neimark and E.H. Shuford, "Comparison of Predictions and Estimates in a Probability Learning Situation," *Journal of Experimental Psychology* 57 (1959): 254–58.

11. Smedslund, "Concept of Correlation in Adults," 165–73.

12. H.M. Jenkins and W.C. Ward, "The Judgment of Contingency between Responses and Outcomes," *Psychological Monographs* 79 (1965): 16–25.

13. Ibid.

14. D. Kahneman and A. Tversky, "Subjective Probability: A Judgment of Representativeness," *Cognitive Psychology* (July 3, 1972): 430–54.

15. Robert Libby, *Accounting and Human Information Processing: Theory and Applications* (Englewood Cliffs, NJ: Prentice-Hall, 1981), 58.

16. A. Tversky and D. Kahneman, "Availability: A Heuristic for Judging Frequency and Probability," *Cognitive Psychology* (September 1973): 207–32.

17. A. Tversky and D. Kahneman, "Judgment under Uncertainty: Heuristics and Biases," *Science* (September 1974): 1124–31.

18. Robin Hogarth, *Judgment and Choice* (New York: Wiley, 1980), 47.

19. Ahmed Belkaoui, "Judgment-Related Issues in Performance Evaluation," *Journal of Business Finance and Accounting* (Winter 1982): 489–500.

20. B. Fischhoff, "Perceived Informativeness of Facts," *Journal of Experimental Psychology: Human Perception and Performance* (May 1977): 349–58; B. Fischhoff and R. Beyth, " 'I Knew It Would Happen'—Remembered Probabilities of Once-Future Things," *Organizational Behavior and Human Performance* (February 1975): 1–16.

21. B. Fischhoff, "Hindsight/Foresight: The Effect of Outcome Knowledge on Judgment under Uncertainty," *Journal of Experimental Psychology: Human Perception and Performance* May 1975): 288–99.

22. Hogarth, *Judgment and Choice*, 103.

23. S. Lichtenstein, B. Fischhoff, and L.D. Philips, "Calibration of Probabilities: The State of the Art," in *Decision Making and Change in Human Affairs*, ed. H. Jungeman and G. de Zeew (Amsterdam: Reidel, 1977), 325–30.

24. K.R. Popper, *The Logic of Scientific Discovery* (London: Hutchinson, 1959); idem, *Conjectures and Refutations* (New York: Basic Books, 1962).

25. J.R. Platt, "Strong Influence," *Science* 146 (1964): 347–53.

26. C.R. Mynatt, M.E. Doherty, and R.D. Tweeny, "Confirmation Bias in a Simulated Research Environment: An Experimental Study of Scientific Influence," *Quarterly Journal of Experimental Psychology* 29 (1977): 85–95; M.E. Doherty, C.R. Mynatt, R.D. Tweeny, and M. Schiavo, "Pseudodiagnosticity," *Acta Psychologica*, in press; P.C. Wason, "On the Failure to Eliminate Hypotheses in a Conceptual Task," *Quarterly Journal of Experimental Psychology* 12 (1960): 15–25; idem, "Reasoning about a Rule," *Quarterly Journal of Experimental Psychology* 20 (1968): 273–81.

27. D. Von Winterfield and W. Edwards, *Flat Maxima in Linear Optimization Models*, in *Progress in Social Psychology*, ed. M. Fishhein (Hillsdale, NJ: Erlbaum, 1977).

28. Ibid., 1.

29. D.G. Fryback, *Use of Radiologists' Subjective Probability Estimates in a Medical Decision-Making Problem*, Michigan Mathematical Psychology Program, Report 74–14 (Ann Arbor: University of Michigan, 1974).

30. D. Pelz, "Influence; A Key to Effective Leadership in the First Line Supervision," *Personnel* 29 (1952): 209–71.

31. Ibid., 213.

32. L.W. Wager, "Leadership Style, Influence, and Supervisory Obligations," *Administrative Science Quarterly* 9 (1965): 391–420.

33. Ibid., 418.

SELECTED BIBLIOGRAPHY

Ajzen, I. "Intuitive Theories of Events and the Effects of Base-Rate Information Prediction." *Journal of Personality and Social Psychology* 101 (1977): 377–83.

Argyris, C. *The Impact of Budgets on People*. New York: The Controllership Foundation, 1952.

Aronson, E., and D.R. Mettee. "Dishonest Behavior as a Function of Differential Levels of Induced Self-Esteem." *Journal of Personality and Social Psychology* (January 1968): 121–27.

Bar-Hillel, M. "The Base-Rate Fallacy in Probability Judgments," *Acta Psychologica*, in press.

Barefield, R.M. "A Model of Forecast Biasing Behavior." *The Accounting Review* (July 1970): 490–501.

Barefield, R.M., and E.E. Comiskey. "The Smoothing Hypothesis: An Alternative Test." *The Accounting Review* (April 1972): 291–98.

Barnea, A., J. Ronen, and S. Sadan. "Classificatory Smoothing of Income with Extraordinary Items." *The Accounting Review* (January 1976): 110–22.

Beach, L.R., and T.S. Scopp. "Intuitive Statistical Inferences about Variances." *Organizational Behavior and Human Performance* 3 (May 1968): 109–83.

Beidleman, C.R. "Income Smoothing: The Role of Management." *The Accounting Review* (October 1973): 653–67.

Belkaoui, A. *Conceptual Foundations of Management Accounting.* Reading, MA: Addison-Wesley, 1980.

———. *Cost Accounting: A Multidimensional Emphasis.* Hinsdale, IL: Dryden Press, 1983.

———. "The Relationships between Self-Disclosure Style and Attitudes to Responsibility of Accounting." *Accounting, Organizations and Society* (December 1981): 281–89.

Bierman, H., Jr., L.E. Fouraker, and R.K. Jaedicke. "A Use of Probability and Statistics in Performance Evaluation." *The Accounting Review* (July 1961): 409–17.

Caplan, E.H. *Management Accounting and Behavioral Sciences.* Reading, MA: Addison-Wesley, 1971.

Cohen, J., and C.E.M. Hansel. "The Idea of a Distribution." *British Journal of Psychology* 46 (May 1955): 11–12.

———. "The Idea of Independence." *British Journal of Psychology* 46 (August 1955): 178–90.

Collins, F. "Managerial Accounting Systems and Organizational Control: A Role Perspective." *Accounting, Organizations and Society* (May 1982): 107–22.

Copeland, R.M. "Income Smoothing," Empirical Research in Accounting: Selected Studies, 1968." Supplement to *Journal of Accounting Research* 6 (1968): 101–16.

Copeland, R.M., and R.D. Licastro. "A Note on Income Smoothing." *The Accounting Review* (July 1968): 540–46.

Cushing, B.E. "An Empirical Study of Changes in Accounting Policy." *Journal of Accounting Research* (Autumn 1969): 196–203.

Dasher, B.E., and R.E. Malcolm. "A Note on Income Smoothing in the Chemical Industry." *Journal of Accounting Research* (Autumn 1970): 253–59.

Doherty, M.E., C.R. Mynatt, R.D. Tweeny, and M. Schiavo. "Pseudodiagnosticity." *Acta Psychologica*, in press.

Edwards, W. "Conservatism in Human Information Processing." In *Formal Representation of Human Judgment*, ed. B. Kleinmuntz. New York: Wiley, 1968.

Einhorn, H.J. "Learning from Experience and Suboptional Rules in Decision Making." In *Cognitive Processes in Choice and Decision Behavior*, ed. T. Wallsten. Hillsdale, NJ: Erlbaum, in press.

Einhorn, H.J., and R.M. Hogarth. "Confidence in Judgment: Persistence of the Illusion of Validity." *Psychological Review* 85 (1978): 395–416.

Einhorn, H.J., and S. Schacht. "Decision Based on Fallible Clinical Judgment." In *Judgment and Decision Processes in Applied Settings*, ed. M. Kaplan and S. Schwartz. New York: Academic Press, 1977.

Fryback, D.G. *Use of Radiologists' Subjective Probability Estimates in a Medical Decision-Making Problem*. Michigan Mathematical Psychology Program, Report 74–14. Ann Arbor: University of Michigan, 1974.

Gibbins, M. "Human Inference, Heuristics, and Auditor's Judgment Processes." *CICA Audit Research Symposium*. Toronto: Canadian Institute of Chartered Accountants, 1977.

Goldberg, L.R. "Diagnosticians versus Diagnostic Signs: The Diagnosis of Psychosis versus Neurosis." *M.M.P.I. Psychological Monographs* 79 (1965).

Gordon, M.J. "Postulates, Principles, and Research in Accounting." *The Accounting Review* (April 1964): 251–63.

Gordon, M.T., B.N. Horwitz, and E.T. Meyers. "Accounting Measurements and Normal Growth of the Firm." In *Research and Accounting Measurement*, ed. R.K. Jaedicke, Y, Ijiri, and O. Nielson. Sarasota, FL: American Accounting Association, 1966, 221–31.

Hammerton, M. "A Case of Radical Probability Estimation." *Journal of Experimental Psychology* 101 (1973): 252–54.

Hofstatter, P.R. "Uber die Schatzung von Gruppeneigenschaften." *Zeitschrift fur Psychologie* 145 (February 1939): 1–44.

Hogarth, R.M. "Cognitive Processes and the Assessment of Subjective Probability Distributions." *Journal of the American Statistical Association* 70 (1975): 271–89.

Hopwood, A.G. "An Empirical Study of the Role of Accounting Data in Performance Evaluation." Empirical Research Studies: Selected Studies, 1972. Supplement to *Journal of Accounting Research* 10 (1972): 194–209.

Huber, G.P. "Methods for Quantifying Subjective Probabilities and Multiattribute Utilities." *Decision Sciences* 5 (1974): 430–58.

Jenkins, H.M., and W.C. Ward. "The Judgment of Contingency between Responses and Outcomes." *Psychological Monographs* 79 (1965).

Joyce, E.J., and G.C. Biddle. "Are Auditors' Judgments Sufficiently Regressive?" Manuscript, University of Chicago, October 1979.

Kahneman, D., and A. Tversky. "On the Psychology of Prediction." *Psychological Review* 80 (1973): 237–251.

———. "Subjective Probability: A Judgment of Representativeness." *Cognitive Psychology* 3 (July 1972): 430–54.

Kamin, J.Y., and J. Ronen. "The Smoothing of Income Numbers: Some Empirical Evidence on Systematic Differences among Management-Controlled and Owner-Controlled Firms." *Accounting, Organizations and Society* 3, no. 2 (1978): 141–53.

Lathrop, R.G. "Perceived Variability." *Journal of Experimental Psychology* 73 (April 1967): 498–502.

Lichtenstein, S., B. Fischhoff, and L.D. Philipps. "Calibration of Probabilities: The State of the Art." In *Decision Making and Change in Human Affairs*, ed. H. Jungeman and G. de Zeew. Amsterdam: Reidel, 1977, 325–30.

Lowe, A.E., and R.W. Shaw. "An Analysis of Managerial Biasing: Evidence from a

Company's Budgeting Process." *Journal of Management Studies* (October 1968): 304–15.

Lyon, D., and P. Slovic. "Dominance of Accuracy Information and Neglect of Base Rates in Probability Estimation." *Acta Psychologica* 10 (1976): 287–98.

Meehl, P.E. *Clinical versus Statistical Prediction*. Minneapolis: University of Minnesota Press, 1954.

Mynatt, C.R., M.E. Doherty, and R.D. Tweeny. "Confirmation Bias in a Simulated Research Environment: An Experimental Study of Scientific Inference." *Quarterly Journal of Experimental Psychology* 29 (1977): 85–95.

Niemark, E.D., and E.H. Shuford. "Comparison of Predictions and Estimates in a Probability Learning Situation." *Journal of Experimental Psychology* 57 (1959): 294–98.

Nisbett, R.E., and E. Borgida. "Attribution and the Psychology of Prediction." *Journal of Personality and Social Psychology* 9 (1975): 932–43.

Nisbett, R.E., E. Borgida, R. Crandall, and H. Reed. "Popular Induction: Information Is Not Necessarily Informative." In *Cognition and Social Behavior*, ed. J.S. Carroll and T.W. Payne. Hillsdale, NJ: Erlbaum, 1976.

Onsi, M. "Factor Analysis of Behavioral Variables Affecting Budgetary Slack." *The Accounting Review* (July 1973): 535–48.

Parker, L.D. "Goal Congruence: A Misguided Accounting Concept." *ABACUS* (June 1976): 3–13.

Peterson, C.R., and L.R. Beach. "Man as an Intuitive Statistician." *Psychological Bulletin* 78 (1967): 231–48.

Platt, J.R. "Strong Inference." *Science* 146 (1964): 347–53.

Popper, K.R. *Conjectures and Refutations*. New York: Basic Books, 1962.

———. *The Logic of Scientific Discovery*. London: Hutchinson, 1959.

Ronen, J. *Smoothing Income Numbers: Objectives, Means, and Implications*. Reading, MA: Addison-Wesley, 1981.

Ronen, J., and S. Sadan. *Smoothing Income Numbers: Objectives, Reasons, and Implications*. Reading, MA: Addison-Wesley, 1981.

Sawyer, J. "Measurement and Prediction: Clinical and Statistical." *Psychological Bulletin* 66 (1966): 178–200.

Schiff, M., and A.Y. Lewin. "The Impact of People on Budgets." *The Accounting Review* (April 1970): 259–68.

———. "Where Traditional Budgeting Fails." *Financial Executive* (May 1968): 57–62.

Slovic, P., and S. Lichtenstein. "Comparison of Bayesian and Regression Approaches to the Study of Information Processing in Judgment." *Organizational Behavior and Human Performance* 6 (1971): 649–744.

Smedslund, J. "The Concept of Correlation in Adults." *Scandinavian Journal of Psychology* 4 (1963): 165–73.

Spencer, J.A. "A Further Study of Estimating Averages." *Ergonomics* 6 (1963): 255–65.

Swieringa, R.J., and R.H. Moncur. "The Relationship between Managers' Budget-Oriented Behavior and Selected Attitudes, Position, Size, and Performance Measures." Empirical Research Studies: Selected Studies, 1972. Supplement to *Journal of Accounting Research* 10 (1972): 19.

Swieringa, R., M. Gibbins, L. Larson, and J.L. Sweeny. "Experiments in the Heuristics of Human Information Processing." *Studies on Human Information Processing in Accounting*. Supplement to *Journal of Accounting Research* (1976): 207–32.

Taylor, H.C., and T.T. Russell. "The Relationship of Validity Coefficients to the Practical Effectiveness of Tests in Selection: Discussion and Tables." *Journal of Applied Psychology* 23 (1939): 565–78.

Tversky, A., and D. Kahneman. "Causal Schemata in Judgments under Uncertainty." In *Progress in Social Psychology*, ed. M. Fishbein. Hillsdale, NJ: Erlbaum, 1977.

———. "Judgment under Uncertainty: Heuristics and Biases." *Science* 185 (1974): 1124–31.

Von Winterfield, D., and W. Edwards. *Flat Maxima in Linear Optimization Models.* Technical Report 011313–4-T. Ann Arbor: Engineering Psychology Laboratory, University of Michigan, 1973.

Wagenaar, W.A. "Appreciation of Conditional Probabilities in Binary Sequences." *Acta Psychologica* 34 (December 1970): 348–56.

———. "Generation of Random Sequences by Human Subjects: A Critical Survey of the Literature." *Psychological Bulletin* 77 (January 1972): 65–72.

Ward, W.C., and H.M. Jenkins. "The Display of Information and the Judgment of Contingency." *Canadian Journal of Psychology* 19 (1965): 231–41.

Wason, P.C. "On the Failure to Eliminate Hypotheses in a Conceptual Task." *Quarterly Journal of Experimental Psychology* 12 (1960): 16–31

———. "Reasoning about a Rule." *Quarterly Journal of Experimental Psychology* 20 (1968): 273–81.

White, C.E. "Discretionary Accounting Decisions and Income Normalization." *Journal of Accounting Research* (Autumn 1970): 260–73.

Williamson, O.E. *The Economy of Discretionary Behavior: Managerial Objectives in the Theory of the Firm.* Englewood Cliffs, NJ.: Prentice-Hall, 1964.

10

Planning, Budgeting, and Information Distortion

INTRODUCTION

In both the process of planning and budgeting, managers may be tempted to distort the information in a process better known as slack behavior. Richard M. Cyert and James G. March advanced the concept of organizational slack as a hypothetical construct to explain overall organizational phenomena.[1] Arie Y. Lewin and Carl Wolf, on the other hand, have made the following warning: "Slack is a seductive concept; it 'explains' too much and 'predicts' too little."[2] Indeed, slack research needs to be categorized along more precise dimensions that better explain its nature and its impact. Accordingly, this chapter reviews the research on slack by differentiating between *organizational slack* and *budgetary slack*.

VIEWS OF SLACK

Slack arises from the tendency of organizations and individuals to refrain from using all the resources available to them. It describes a tendency to not operate at peak efficiency. In general, two types of slack have been identified in the literature, namely organizational slack and budgetary slack. Organizational slack basically refers to an unused capacity, in the sense that the demands put on the resources of the organization are less than the supply of these resources. Budgetary slack is found in the budgetary process and refers to the intentional distortion of information that results from an understatement of budgeted sales and an overstatement of budgeted costs.

The concepts of organizational slack and budgetary slack appear in other literature under different labels. Economists refer to an X-inefficiency in instances where resources are either not used to their full capacity or effectiveness or are used in an extremely wasteful manner, as well as in instances where managers fail to make costless improvements. X-inefficiency is to be differentiated from allocative inefficiency, which refers to whether or not prices in a market are of the right land, that is, whether they allocate input and output to those users who are willing to pay for them.[3] Categories of inefficiency of a nonallocative nature, or X-inefficiency, include inefficiency in (1) labor utilization, (2) capital utilization, (3) time sequence, (4) extent of employee cooperation, (5) information flow, (6) bargaining effectiveness, (7) credit availability utilization, and (8) heuristic procedures.[4]

Agency theory also refers to slack behavior. The problem addressed by the agency theory literature is how to design an incentive contract such that the total gains can be maximized, given (1) information asymmetry between principal and agent, (2) pursuit of self-interest by the agent, and (3) environmental uncertainty affecting the outcome of the agent's decisions.[5] Slack can occur when managers dwell in an "excess consumption of perquisites" or in a "tendency to shrink." Basically, slack is the possible "shrinking" behavior of an agent.[6]

The literature in organizational behavior refers to slack in terms of defensive tactical responses and deceptive behavior. By viewing organizations as political environments, the deceptive aspects of individual power-acquisition behavior become evident.[7] A variety of unobtrusive tactics in the operation of power,[8] covert intents and means of those exhibiting power-acquisition behaviors,[9] and a "wolf in sheep's clothing" phenomenon, whereby individuals profess a mission or goal strategy while practicing an individual-maximization strategy,[10] characterize these deceptive behaviors, which are designed to present an illusionary or false impression. V. E. Schein has provided the following examples of deceptive behaviors in communication, decision making, and presentation of self.

Communication. With regard to written or oral communications, there may be an illusion that these communications include all the information or that these communications are true, which masks the reality of either of them consisting of only partial information or of their actually distorting the information.

Decision making. A manager may present the illusion that he is actually compromising or giving in with regard to a decision, whereas in reality he is purposely planning to lose this particular battle with the long-range objective of winning the war. Or a manager or a subunit may initiate a particular action and then work on plans and activities for implementing a program. This intensive planning and studying, however, may in reality be nothing more than a delaying tactic, during which delay the actual program will die or be forgotten. Underlying this illusion that one is selecting subordinates, members of boards of directors, or successors on the basis of their competency may be the reality that these individuals are selected for loyalty, compliancy, or conformity to the superior's image.

Presentation of self. Many managers exude an apparent confidence, when in reality they are quite uncertain. Still other managers are skilled in organizing participatory group decision-making sessions, which in reality have been set up to produce a controlled outcome.[11]

Schein then hypothesized that the degree to which these behaviors are deceptive seems to be a function of both the nature of the organization and the lands of power exhibited (work-related or personal).[12] She relied on Cyert and March's dichotomization of organizations as either low- or high-slack systems.[13] Low-slack systems are characterized by a highly competitive environment that requires rapid and nonroutine decision making on the part of its members and a high level of productive energy and work outcomes to secure an effective performance. High-slack systems are characterized by a reasonably stable environment that requires routine decision making to secure an effective performance. Given these dichotomizations, Schein suggested that:

1. The predominant form of power acquisition behavior is personal in a high-slack organization and work-related in a low-slack organization.

2. The underlying basis of deception is an inherent covert nature of personal power acquisition behaviors in a high-slack organization and an organization['s] illusion as to how work gets done in a low-slack organization.

3. The benefits of deception to members are the provisions of excitement and personal rewards in a high-slack organization and the facilitation of work accomplishment and organizational rewards in a low-slack organization.

4. The benefits of deception to organization are to foster [the] illusion of a fast-paced, competitive environment in a high-slack organization and to maintain an illusion of workability of the formal structure in a low-slack organization.[14]

ORGANIZATIONAL SLACK

Nature of Organizational Slack

There is no lack of definitions for organizational slack, as can be seen from the definitions provided by Cyert and March,[15] Child,[16] M. D. Cohen, March, and J. P. Olsen,[17] March and Olsen,[18] D. E. Dimmick and V. V. Murray,[19] R. J. Litschert and T. W. Bonham,[20] and March.[21]

What appears from these definitions is that organizational slack is a buffer created by management in its use of available resources to deal with internal as well as external events that may arise and threaten an established coalition. Slack, therefore, is used by management as an agent of change in response to changes in both the internal and external environments.

Cyert and March's model explains slack in terms of cognitive and structural factors.[22] It provides the rationale for the unintended creation of slack. Individuals are assumed to "satisfice," in the sense that they set aspiration levels for performance rather than a maximization goal. These aspirations adjust upward or downward, depending on actual performance, and in a slower fashion than actual changes in performance. It is this lag in adjustment that allows excess resources from superior performance to accumulate in the form of organizational slack. This slack is then used as a stabilizing force to absorb excess resources in good times without requiring a revision of aspirations and intentions regarding the use of these excess resources. "By absorbing excess resources it retards upward adjustment of aspirations during relatively good times . . . by providing a pool of emergency resources, it permits aspirations to be maintained during relatively bad times."[23]

Oliver E. Williamson has proposed a model of slack based on managerial incentives.[24] This model provides the rationale for managers' motivation and desire for slack resources. Under conditions where managers are able to pursue their own objectives, the model predicts that the excess resources available after target levels of profit have been reached are not allocated according to profit-maximization rules. Organizational slack becomes the means by which a manager achieves his or her personal goals, as characterized by four motives: income, job security, status, and discretionary control over resources. Williamson makes the assumption that the manager is motivated to maximize his or her personal goals subject to satisfying organizational objectives and that the manager achieves this by maximizing slack resources under his or her control. Williamson has suggested that there are four levels of profits: (1) a maximizing profit equal to the profit the firm would achieve when marginal revenue equals marginal cost, (2) actual profit equal to the true profit achieved by the firm, (3) reported profit equal to the accounting profit reported in the annual report, and (4) minimum profit equal to the profit needed to maintain the organizational coalition. If the market is noncompetitive, various forms of slack emerge: (1) *slack absorbed as staff* equal to the difference between maximum profit and actual profit, (2) *slack in the form of cost* equal to the difference between reported and minimum profits, and (3) *discretionary spending for investment* equal to the difference between reported and minimum profits.

Income smoothing can be used to substantiate the efforts of management to neutralize environmental uncertainty and to create organizational slack by means of an accounting manipulation of the level of earnings. J. Y. Kamin and J. Ronen have related organizational slack to income smoothing by reasoning that the decisions that affect the allocation of costs—such as budget negotiations, which often result in slack accumulation—are aimed at smoothing earnings.[25] They hypothesized that management-controlled firms were more likely to be engaged in smoothing as a manifestation of managerial discretion and slack. "Accounting" and "real" smoothing were tested by observing the behavior of discretionary expenses vis-à-vis the behavior of income numbers. Their results showed that (1) a majority of the firms behaved as if they were income smoothers and (2) a particularly strong majority was found among management-controlled firms with high barriers to entry. This line of reasoning was pursued by Ahmed Bel-kaoui and R. D. Picur.[26] Their study tested the effects of the dual economy on income-smoothing behavior. It was hypothesized that a higher degree of smoothing of income numbers would be exhibited by firms in the periphery sector than by firms in the core sector in reaction to different opportunity structures and experiences. Their results indicated that a majority of the firms may have been resorting to income smoothing. A higher number were found among firms in the periphery sector.

Lewin and Wolf proposed the following statements as a theoretical framework for understanding the concept of slack:

1. Organizational slack depends on the availability of excess resources.
2. Excess resources occur when an organization generates or has the potential to generate resources in excess of what is necessary to maintain the organizational coalition.
3. Slack occurs unintentionally as result of the imperfection of the resource allocation decision-making process.
4. Slack is created intentionally because managers are motivated to maximize slack resources under their control to ensure achievement of personal goals subject to the achievement of organizational goals.
5. The disposition of slack resources is a function of a manager's expense preference function.
6. The distribution of slack resources is an outcome of the bargaining process setting organization and reflects the discretionary power of organization members in allocating resources.
7. Slack can be present in a distributed or concentrated form.
8. The aspiration of organizational participants for slack adjusts upward as resources become available. The downward adjustment of aspirations for slack resources, when resources become scarce, is resisted by organizational participants.
9. Slack can stabilize short-term fluctuations in the firm's performance.
10. Beyond the short term, the reallocation of slack requires a change in organizational goals.
11. Slack is directly related to organizational size, maturity, and stability of the external environment.[27]

Functions of Organizational Slack

Because the definition of slack is often intertwined with a description of the functions that slack serves, L. J. Bourgeois discussed these functions as a means of making palpable the ways of measuring slack.[28] From a review of the administrative theory literature, he identified organizational slack as an independent variable that either "causes" or serves four primary functions: "(1) as an inducement for organizational actors to remain in the system, (2) as a resource for conflict resolution, (3) as a buffering mechanism in the work flow process, or (4) as a facilitator of types or creative behavior within the organization."[29]

The concept of slack as an inducement to maintain the coalition was first introduced by C. I. Barnard in his treatment of the inducement/contribution ratio (I/C) as a way of attracting organizational participants and sustaining their membership.[30] March and H. A. Simon later described slack resources as the source of inducements through which the inducement/contribution ratio might exceed a value of one, which is equivalent to paying an employee more than would be required to retain his or her services.[31] This concept of slack was then explicitly introduced by Cyert and March as consisting of payments to members of the coalition in excess of what is required to maintain the organization.[32]

Slack as a resource for conflict resolution was introduced in L. R. Pondy's goal model.[33] In this model subunit goal conflicts are resolved partly by sequential attention to goals and partly by adopting a decentralized organizational structure. A decentralized structure is made possible by the presence of organizational slack.

A notion of slack as a technical buffer from the variances and discontinuities caused by environmental uncertainty was proposed by J. D. Thompson.[34] It was also acknowledged in Pondy's system model, which described conflict as a result of the lack of buffers between interdependent parts of an organization.[35] Jay Galbraith saw buffering as an information-processing problem: "Slack resources are an additional cost to the organization or the customer. . . . The creation of slack resources, through reduced performance levels, reduces the amount of information that must be processed during task execution and prevents the over loading of hierarchical channels."[36]

According to Bourgeois, slack facilitates three types of strategic or creative behavior within the organization: (1) providing resources for innovative behavior, (2) providing opportunities for a satisficing behavior, and (3) affecting political behavior.[37]

First, as a facilitator of innovative behavior, slack tends to create conditions that allow the organization to experiment with new strategies[38] and introduce innovation.[39] Second, as a facilitator of suboptimal behavior, slack defines the threshold of acceptability of a choice, or "bounded search,"[40] by people whose bounded rationality leads them to satisfice.[41] Third, the notion that slack affects political activity was advanced by Cyert and March, who argued that slack reduces both political activity and the need for bargaining and coalition-forming activity.[42] Furthermore, W. G. Astley has argued that slack created by success results in self-aggrandizing behavior by managers who engage in political behavior to capture more than their fair share of the surplus.[43]

W. Richard Scott argued that lowered standards create slack—unused resources—that can be used to create ease in the system.[44] Notice the following comment: "Of course, some slack in the handling of resources is not only inevitable but essential to smooth operations. All operations require a margin of error to allow for mistakes, waste, spoilage, and similar unavoidable accompaniments of work."[45] But the inevitability of slack is not without consequences:

The question is not whether there is to be slack but how much slack is permitted. Excessive slack resources increase costs for the organization that are likely to be passed on to the consumer. Since creating slack resources is a relatively easy and painless solution available to organizations, whether or not it is employed is likely to be determined by the amount of competition confronting the organization in its task environment.[46]

Measurement of Organizational Slack

One problem in investing empirically the presence of organizational slack relates to the difficulty of securing an adequate measurement of the phenomenon. Various methods have been suggested. In addition to these methods, eight variables that appear in public data, whether they are created by managerial actions or made available by environment, may explain a change in slack.[47] The model, suggested by Bourgeois, is as follows:

$$\text{Slack} = f \text{ (RE, DP, G\&A WC/S, D/E, CR, I/P, P/E)}$$

where:

$$
\begin{aligned}
\text{RE} &= \text{Retained earnings} \\
\text{DP} &= \text{Dividend payout} \\
\text{G\&A} &= \text{General and administrative expense} \\
\text{WC/S} &= \text{Working capital as a percentage of sales} \\
\text{D/E} &= \text{Debt as a percentage of equity} \\
\text{CR} &= \text{Credit rating} \\
\text{I/P} &= \text{Short-term loan interest compared to prime rate} \\
\text{P/E} &= \text{Price/earnings ratio.}
\end{aligned}
$$

Here RE, G&A, WC/S, and CR are assumed to have a positive effect on changes in slack, whereas DP, D/E, P/E, and I/P are assumed to have a negative effect on changes in slack.

Some of these measures have also been suggested by other researchers. For example, Martin M. Rosner used profit and excess capacity as slack measures,[48] and Lewin and Wolf used selling, general, and administrative expenses as surrogates for slack.[49] Bourgeois and Jitendra V. Singh refined these measures by suggesting that slack could be differentiated on an "ease-or-recovery" dimension.[50] Basically, they considered excess liquidity to be *available slack*, not yet earmarked for particular uses. Overhead costs were termed *recoverable slack*, in the sense that they are absorbed by various organizational functions but can be recovered when needed elsewhere. In addition, the ability of a firm to generate resources from the environment, such as the ability to raise additional debt or equity capital, was considered *potential slack*. All of these measures were divided by sales to control for company size.

Building on Bourgeois and Singh's suggestions, Theresa K. Lant opted for the four following measures:

1. Administrative slack = (General and administrative expenses)/cost of goods sold
2. Available liquidity = (Cash + marketable securities − current liabilities)/sales
3. Recoverable liquidity = (Accounts receivable + inventory)/sales
4. Retained earnings = (Net profit − dividends)/sales[51]

Lant used these measures to show empirically that (1) available liquidity and general and administrative expenses have significantly higher variance than profit across firms and across time and (2) the mean change in slack is significantly greater than the mean change in profit. She concluded as follows:

These results are logically consistent with the theory that slack absorbs variance in actual profit. They also suggest that the measures used are reasonable measures for slack. Thus, it supports prior work which has used these measures, and implies that further large sample models using slack as a variable is feasible since financial information is readily available for a large number of firms. Before these results can be generalized, however, the tests conducted here should be replicated using different samples of firms from a variety of industries.[52]

BUDGETARY SLACK

Nature of Budgetary Slack

The literature on organizational slack shows that managers have the motives necessary to desire to operate in a slack environment. The literature on budgetary slack considers the budget as the embodiment of that environment and, therefore, assumes that managers will use the budgeting process to bargain for slack budgets. As stated by Schiff and Lewin, "Managers will create slack in budgets through a process of *understating revenues and over-stating costs.*"[53] The general definition of budgetary slack, then, is the understatement of revenues and the overstatement of costs in the budgeting process. A detailed description of the creation of budgetary slack by managers was reported by Schiff and Lewin in their study of the budget process of three divisions of multidivision companies.[54] They found evidence of budgetary slack through underestimation of gross revenue, inclusion of discretionary increases in personnel requirements, establishment of marketing and sales budgets with internal limits on funds to be spent, use of manufacturing costs based on standard costs that do not reflect process improvements operationally available at the plant, and inclusion of discretionary "special projects."

Evidence of budgetary slack has also been reported by others. A. E. Lowe and R. W. Shaw found a downward bias, introduced through sales forecasts by line managers, which assumed good performance where rewards were related to forecasts.[55] M. Dalton reported various examples of department managers allocating resources to what they considered justifiable purposes even though such purposes were not authorized in their budgets.[56] G. Shillinglaw noted the extreme vulnerability of budgets used to measure divisional performance given the great control exercised by divisional management in budget preparation and the reporting of results.[57]

Slack creation is a generalized organizational phenomenon. Many different organizational factors have been used to explain slack creation, in particular, organizational structure, goal congruence, control system, and managerial behavior. Slack creation is assumed to occur in cases where a Tayloristic organizational structure exists,[58] although it is also assumed to occur in a participative organizational structure.[59] It may be due to conflicts that arise between the individual and organizational goals, leading managers intentionally to create slack. It may also be due to the attitudes of management toward the budget and to workers' views of the budgets as a device used by management to manipulate them.[60] Finally, the creation of slack may occur whether or not the organization is based on a centralized or decentralized structure.[61] With regard to this last issue, Schiff and Lewin have reported that the divisional controller appears to have undertaken the tasks of creating and managing divisional slack and is most influential in the internal allocation of slack.

Budgeting and the Propensity to Create Budgetary Slack

The budgeting system has been assumed to affect a manager's propensity to create budgetary slack, in the sense that this propensity can be increased or decreased by the way in which the budgeting system is designed or complemented. Mohamed Onsi was the first to investigate empirically the connections between the type of budgeting system and the propensity to create budgetary slack.[62] From a review of the literature, he stated the following four assumptions:

1. Managers influence the budget process through bargaining for slack by understating revenues and overstating costs. . . .
2. Managers build up slack in "good years" and reconvert slack into profit in "bad years."
3. Top management is at a "disadvantage" in determining the magnitude of slack. . . .
4. The divisional controller in decentralized organizations participates in the task of creating and managing divisional slack.[63]

Personal interviews of thirty-two managers of five large national and international companies and statistical analysis of a questionnaire were used to identify the important behavioral variables that influence slack buildup and utilization. The questionnaire's variables were grouped into the following eight dimensions:

1. *Slack attitude* described by the variables indicating a manager's attitude to slack.
2. *Slack manipulation* described by the variables indicating how a manager builds up and uses slack.
3. *Slack institutionalization* described by the variables that make a manager less inclined to reduce his slack.
4. *Slack detection* described by the variables indicating the superior's ability to detect slack based on the amount of information he receives.
5. *Attitude toward the top management control system* described by the variables indicating an authoritarian philosophy toward budgeting being attributed to top management by divisional managers.
6. *Attitudes toward the divisional control system* described by variables on attitudes toward subordinates, sources of pressure, budget autonomy, budget participation, and supervisory uses of budgets.
7. *Attitudes toward the budget* described by variables on attitude toward the level of standards, attitude toward the relevancy of budget attainment to valuation of performance, and the manager's attitude (positive or negative) toward the budgetary system in general, as a managerial tool.
8. *Budget relevancy* described by variables indicating a manager's attitudes toward the relevancy of standards for his department's operation.[64]

Factor analysis reduced these dimensions to seven factors and showed a relationship between budgetary slack and what Onsi called "an authoritarian top management budgetary control system." Thus, he stated: "Budgetary slack is created as a result of pressure and the use of budgeted profit attainment as a basic criterion in evaluating performance. Positive participation could encourage less need for building-up slack. However, the middle managers' perception of pressure was an overriding concern. The positive correlation between managers' attitudes and attainable level of standards is a reflection of this pressure."[65]

Cortlandt Cammann explored the moderating effects of subordinates' participation in decision making and the difficulty of subordinates' jobs based on their responses to different uses of control systems by their superiors.[66] His results showed that the use of control systems for contingent reward allocation produced defensive responses by subordinates under all conditions, which included the creation of budgetary slack. Basically, when superiors used budgeting information as a basis for allocating organizational rewards, their subordinates' responses were defensive. Allowing participation in the budget processes reduced this defensiveness.

Finally, Kenneth A. Merchant conducted a field study designed to investigate how managers' propensities to create budgetary slack are affected by the budgeting system and the technical context.[67] He hypothesized that the propensity to create budgetary slack is positively related to the importance placed on meeting budget targets and negatively related to the extent of participation allowed in budgeting processes, the degree of predictability in the production process, and the superiors' abilities to create slack. Unlike earlier studies that had drawn across functional areas, 170 manufacturing managers responded to a questionnaire measuring the propensity to create slack, the importance of meeting the budget, budget participation, the nature of technology in terms of work-flow integration and product standardization, and the ability of superiors to detect slack. The results suggested that managers' propensities to create slack (1) do vary with the setting and with how the budgeting system is implemented; (2) are lower where managers actively participate in budgeting, particularly when technologies are relatively predictable; and (3) are higher when a tight budget requires frequent tactical responses to avoid overruns.

The three studies by Onsi, Cammann, and Merchant provide evidence that participation may lead to positive communication between managers so that subordinates feel less pressure to create slack. This result is, in fact, contingent on the amount of information asymmetry existing between the principals (superiors) and the agents (the subordinates). Although participation in budgeting leads subordinates to communicate or reveal some of their private information, agents may still misrepresent or withhold some of their private information, leading to budgetary slack. Accordingly, Alan S. Dunk proposed a link between participation and budgetary slack through two variables: superiors' budget emphasis in their evaluation of subordinate performance and the degree of information asymmetry between superiors and subordinates:[68] "When participation, budget emphasis, and information asymmetry are high (low), slack will be high (low)." The results, however, showed that low (high) slack is related to high (low)[69] participation, budget emphasis, and information asymmetry. The results are stated as follows: The results of this study show that the relation between participation and slack is contingent upon budget emphasis and information asymmetry, but in a direction contrary to expectations.

The results provide evidence for the utility of participative budgeting, and little support for the view that high participation may result in increased slack when the other two predictors are high. Although participation may induce subordinates to incorporate slack in budgets, the results suggest that participation alone may not be sufficient. The findings suggest that slack reduction results from participation, except when budget emphasis is low.[70]

Budgetary Slack, Information Distortion, and Truth-Inducing Incentives Schemes

Budgetary slack involves a deliberate distortion of input information. Distortion of input information in a budget setting arises, in particular, from the need of managers to accommodate their expectations about the kinds of payoffs associated with different possible outcomes. Several experiments have provided evidence of such distortion of input information. Cyert, March, and W. H. Star-buck showed in laboratory experiments that subjects adjusted the information they transmitted in a complex decision-making system to control their payoffs.[71] Similarly, Lowe and Shaw have shown that in cases where rewards were linked to forecasts, sales managers tended to distort the input information and to induce biases in their sales forecast.[72] Dalton also provided some rich situational descriptions of information distortion in which lower-level managers distorted the budget information and allocated resources to what were perceived to be justifiable objectives.[73] Finally, given the existence of a payoff structure that can induce a forecaster to bias intentionally his or her forecast, R. M. Barefield provided a model of forecast behavior that showed a "rough" formulation of a possible link between a forecasters' biasing and the quality of the forecaster as a source of data for an accounting system.[74]

Taken together, these studies suggest that budgetary slack, through systematic distortion of input information, can be used to accommodate the subjects' expectations about the payoffs associated with various possible outcomes. They fail, however, to provide a convincing rationalization of the link between distortion of input information and the subjects' accommodation of their expectations. Agency theory and issues related to risk aversion may provide such a link. Hence, given the existence of divergent incentives and information asymmetry between the controller (or employer) and the controllee (or employee) and the high cost of observing employee skill or effort, a budget-based employment contract (that is, where employee compensation is contingent on meeting the performance standard) can be Pareto-superior to fixed-pay or linear-sharing rules (where the employer and employee split the output).[75] However, these budget-based schemes impose a risk on the employee, as job performance can be affected by a host of uncontrollable factors. Consequently, risk-averse individuals may resort to slack budgeting through systematic distortion of input information. In practice, moreover, any enhanced (increased) risk aversion would lead the employee to resort to budgetary slack. One might hypothesize that, without proper incentives for truthful communication, the slack budgeting behavior could be reduced. One suggested avenue is the use of truth-inducing, budget-based schemes.[76] These schemes, assuming risk neutrality, motivate a worker to reveal private information truthfully about future performance and to maximize performance regardless of the budget.

Accordingly, Mark S. Young conducted an experiment to test the effects of risk aversion and asymmetrical information on slack budgeting.[77] Five hypotheses related to budgetary slack were developed and tested using a laboratory experiment. The hypotheses were as follows:

Hypothesis 1: A subordinate who participates in the budgeting process will build slack into the budget. . . .

Hypothesis 2: A risk-averse subordinate will build in more budget slack than a non-risk-averse subordinate. . . .

Hypothesis 3: Social pressure not to misrepresent productive capability will be greater for a subordinate whose information is known by management than for a subordinate having private information. . . .

Hypothesis 4: As social pressure increases for the subordinate, there is a lower degree of budgetary slack. . . .

Hypothesis 5: A subordinate who has private information builds more slack into the budget than a subordinate whose information is known by management.[78]

The results of the experiment confirmed the hypothesis that a subordinate who participates builds in budgetary slack and that slack is, in part, attributable to a subordinate's risk preferences. Given state uncertainty and a worker-manager information asymmetry about performance capability, the subjects in the experiment created slack even in the presence of a truth-inducing scheme. In addition, risk-averse workers created more slack than non-risk-averse workers did. Similarly, C. Chow, J. Cooper, and W. Waller provided evidence that, given a worker-manager information asymmetry about performance capability, slack is lower under a truth-inducing scheme than under a budget-based scheme with an incentive to create slack.[79]

Both Young's and Chow, Cooper, and Waller's studies were found to have limitations.[80] With regard to Young's study, William S. Waller found three limitations: "First, unlike the schemes examined in the analytical research, the one used in his study penalized outperforming the budget, which limits its general usefulness. Second, there was no manipulation of incentives, so variation in slack due to incentives was not examined. Third, risk performances were measured using the conventional lottery technique of which the validity and reliability are suspect."[81] With regard to Chow, Cooper, and Waller's study. Waller found the limitations to be the assumption of state certainty and the failure to take risk preference into account. Accordingly, Waller conducted an experiment under which subjects participatively set budgets under either a scheme with an incentive for creating slack or a truth-incentive scheme like those examined in the analytic research. In addition, risk neutrality was induced for one half of the subjects and constant, absolute risk aversion for the rest, using a technique discussed by J. Berg, L. Daley, J. Dickhaut, and J. O'Brien that allows the experimenter to induce (derived) utility functions with any shape.[82] The results of the experiment show that when a conventional truth-inducing scheme is introduced, slack decreases for risk-neutral subjects but not for risk-averse subjects. Added to the evidence provided by the other studies, this study indicates that risk preference is an important determinant of slack, especially in the presence of a truth-inducing scheme.

Basically, there is preliminary evidence that risk-averse workers create more budgetary slack than risk-neutral ones. In addition, "truth-inducing incentive schemes" reduce budgetary slack for risk-neutral subjects but not for risk-averse subjects. It seems that resource allocations within organizations are mediated by perceptions of risk, where risk is a stable personal trait. Accordingly, D. C. Kim tested whether risk preferences are domain-specific; that is, latent risk preferences translate into differing manifest risk preferences according to the context.[83] He relied on an experiment simulating the public accountants' budgeting of billable bonus to test the hypothesis that subject preference for tight or safe budget behavior depends on the performance of co-workers and domain-specific risk preferences. The results supported the view that subordinates' risk preferences are influenced by a situation-dependent variable. As stated by Kim: "The reversal of risk preferences around a neutral reference point is statistically significant for both dispositionally risk-averse and dispositionally risk-seeking subjects. The dispositional variable also contributes to the explanation of variation in subjects' manifest risk preferences. Thus the propensity to induce budgetary slack seems to be a joint function of situations and dispositions."[84]

Budgetary Slack and Self-Esteem

The enhancement of risk aversion and the resulting distortion of input information can be more pronounced when self-esteem is threatened. It was found that persons who have low opinions of themselves are more likely to cheat than persons with higher self-esteem.[85] A situation of dissonance was created in an experimental group by giving out positive feedback about a personality test to some participants and negative feedback to others. All the participants were then asked to take part in a competitive game of cards. The participants who received a blow to their self-esteem cheated more often than those who had received positive feedback about themselves. Could it also be concluded that budgetary slack through information distortion may be a form of dishonest behavior, arising from the enhancement of risk aversion caused by a negative feedback on self-esteem? A person's expectations can be an important determinant of his or her behavior. A negative impact on self-esteem can lead an individual to develop an expectation of poor performance. At the same time, the individual who is given negative feedback about his or her self-esteem would be more risk averse than others and would be ready to resort to any behavior to cover the situation. Consequently, the person may attempt to distort the input information in order to have an attainable budget. Belkaoui accordingly tested the hypothesis that individuals given negative feedback about their self-esteem would introduce more bias into estimates than individuals given positive or neutral feedback about their self-esteem.[86] One week after taking a self-esteem test, subjects were provided with false feedback (either positive or negative) and neutral feedback about their self-esteem score. They were then asked to make two budgeting decisions, first one cost estimate and then one sales estimate for a fictional budgeting decision. The results showed that, in general, the individuals who were provided with information that temporarily caused them to lower their self-esteem were more apt to distort input information than those who were made to raise their self-esteem. It was concluded that whereas slack budgeting may be consistent with generally low self-esteem feedback, it is inconsistent with generally high or neutral self-esteem feedback.

Toward a Theoretical Framework for Budgeting

A theoretical framework aimed at structuring knowledge about biasing behavior was proposed by Kari Lukka.[87] It contains an explanatory model for budgetary biasing and a model for budgetary biasing at the organizational level.

The explanatory model of budgetary biasing at the individual level draws from the management accounting and organizational behavior literature and related behavioral research to suggest a set of intentions and determinants of budgetary biasing. Budgetary biasing is at the center of many interrelated and sometimes contradictory factors with the actor's intentions as the synthetic core of his or her behavior.

The model for budgetary biasing at the organizational level shows that the "bias contained in the final budget is not the result of one actor's intentional behavior, but rather the result of the dialectics of the negotiations."[88] Whereas budgetary biases 1 and 2 are the original biases created in the budget by the controlling unit and the controlled unit, biases 3 and 4 are the final biases to end up in the budget after the budgetary negotiations, which are characterized by potential conflicts and power factors. The results of semistructured interviews at different levels of management of a large decentralized company verified the theoretical framework. The usefulness of this theoretical framework rests on further refinements and empirical testing.

Positive versus Negative Slack

Although the previous sections have focused on budgetary, or positive, slack, budgetary bias is, in fact, composed of both budgetary slack and an upward bias, or a negative slack. Whereas budgetary slack refers to bias in which the budget is designed intentionally so as to make it easier to achieve the forecast, upward bias refers to overstatement of expected performance in the budget. David T. Otley has described the difference as follows: "Managers are therefore likely to be conservative in making forecasts when future benefits are sought (positive slack) but optimistic when their need for obtaining current approval dominates (negative slack)."[89]

Evidence for negative slack was first provided by W. H. Read, who showed that managers distort information to prove to their superiors that all is well.[90] He cited several empirical studies of budgetary control that indicated that managers put a lot of effort and ingenuity into assuring that messages conveyed by budgetary information serve their own interests.[91] Following earlier research by Barefield, Otley argued that forecasts may be the mode, rather than the means, of peoples' intuitive probability distributions.[92] Given that the distribution of cost and revenue is negatively skewed, there will be a tendency for budget forecasts to become unintentionally biased in the form of negative slack. Data collected from two organizations verified the presence of negative slack.

Reducing Budgetary Slack: A Bonus-Based Technique

In general, firms use budgeting and bonus techniques to overcome slack budgeting. One such approach consists of paying higher rewards when budgets are set high and achieved, and lower rewards when budgets are either set high but not met or set low and achieved. G. S. Mann presented a bonus system that gave incentives for managers to set budget estimates as close to achievable levels as possible.[93] The following two formulas were proposed:

Formula 1 applies for bonus if actual performance is equal to or greater than budget.

(multiplier no. 2 × budget goal) + [multiplier no. 1 × (actual level achieved budget goal)]

Formula 2 applies for bonus if actual performance is less than budget.

(multiplier no. 2 × budget goal) + [multiplier no. 3 × (actual level achieved − budget goal)]

The three multipliers set by management served as factors in calculating different components of bonuses. They were defined as follows:

Multiplier no. 1 (which must be less than multiplier no. 2, and which in turn must be less than multiplier no. 3) is used when actual performance is greater than budget. It provides a smaller bonus per unit for the part of actual performance that exceeds the budgeted amount. . . .

Multiplier no. 2 is the rate per unit used to determine the basic bonus component. It is based on the budgeted level of activity which equals multiplier no. 2 times the budgeted level.

Multiplier no. 3 is the rate used to reduce the bonus when the achieved level is less than the budget (multiplier no. 3 times work of units by which actual performance fell short of budget).[94]

Exhibit 10.1 shows an illustration of the application of the method and the effect of variations in multipliers or bonuses. As the exhibit shows, the manager will be rewarded for accurate estimation of the level of rates. In addition, the multipliers can be set with greater flexibility for controlling the manager's estimates.

CONCLUSIONS

Organizational slack and budgetary slack are two hypothetical constructs to explain organizational phenomena that are prevalent in all forms of organizations. Evidence linking both constructs to organizational, individual, and con-

Exhibit 10.1
Reducing Slack through a Bonus System

(1)	(2)	(3)	(4) Bonus I	(5) Bonus II
Budget Sales	Actual Sales	State of Nature	Multiple No. 1 = $.05 Multiple No. 2 = $.10 Multiple No.3 = $.15	Multiple no. 1 = .01 Multiple no. 2 = .10 Multiple no. 3 = .30
200,000	180,000	Over estimation	$17,000	$14,000
200,000	200,000	Actual = Budget	20,000	20,000
200,000	220,000	Under estimation	21,000	22,000

textual factors is growing and in the future may contribute to an emerging theoretical framework for an understanding of slack. Further investigation into the potential determinants of organizational and budgetary slack remains to be done. This effort is an important one because the behavior of slack is highly relevant to the achievement of internal economic efficiency in organizations. Witness the following comment: "The effective organization has more rewards at its disposal, or more organizational slack to play with, and thus can allow all members to exercise more discretion, obtain more rewards, and feel that their influence is higher."[95]

NOTES

1. Richard M. Cyert and James G. March, eds., *A Behavioral Theory of the Firm* (Englewood Cliffs, NJ: Prentice-Hall, 1963).

2. Arie Y. Lewin and Carl Wolf, "The Theory of Organizational Slack: A Critical Review," *Proceedings: Twentieth International Meeting of TIMS* (1976): 648–54.

3. Harvey Leibenstein, "Allocative Efficiency vs. 'X-Efficiency,' " *American Economic Review* (June 1966): 392–415.

4. Harvey Leibenstein, "X-Efficiency: From Concept to Theory," *Challenge* (September–October 1979): 13–22.

5. Nandan Choudhury, "Incentives for the Divisional Manager," *Accounting and Business Research* (Winter 1985): 11–21.

6. S. Baiman, "Agency Research in Managerial Accounting: A Survey," *Journal of Accounting Literature* (Spring 1982): 154–213.

7. D. Packard, *The Pyramid Climber* (New York: McGraw-Hill, 1962); E.A. Buttler, "Corporate Politics: Monster or Friend?" *Generation* 3 (1971): 54–58, 74; A.N. Schoo-

maker, *Executive Career Strategies* (New York: American Management Association, 1971).

8. J. Pfeffer, "Power and Resources Allocation in Organizations," in *New Directions in Organizational Behavior*, ed. B.M. Shaw and G.R. Salancik (Chicago: St. Clair Press, 1977).

9. V.E. Schein, "Individual Power and Political Behaviors in Organizations: An Inadequately Explored Reality," *Academy of Management Review* (January 1977): 64–72.

10. B. Bozeman and W. Malpive, "Goals and Bureaucratic Decision-Making: An Experiment," *Human Relations* (June 1977): 417–29.

11. V.E. Schein, "Examining an Illusion: The Role of Deceptive Behaviors in Organizations," *Human Relations* (October 1979): 288–89.

12. Ibid., 290.

13. Cyert and March, *A Behavioral Theory of the Firm.*

14. Schein, "Examining an Illusion," 293.

15. Cyert and March, *A Behavioral Theory of the Firm.*

16. John Child, "Organizational Structure, Environment, and Performance: The Role of Strategic Choice," *Sociology* 6, no. 1 (1972): 2–22.

17. M.D. Cohen, J.G. March, and J.P. Olsen, "A Garbage Can Model of Organizational Choice," *Administrative Science Quarterly* 17, no. 1 (1972): 1–25.

18. J.G. March and J.P. Olsen, *Ambiguity and Choice* (Bergen, Ger.: Universitetsforlagt, 1976).

19. D.E. Dimmick and V.V. Murray, "Correlates of Substantive Policy Decisions in Organizations; The Case of Human Resource Management," *Academy of Management Journal* 21, no. 4 (1978): 611–23.

20. R.J. Litschert and T.W. Bonham, "A Conceptual Model of Strategy Formation," *Academy of Management Review* 3, no. 2 (1978): 211–19.

21. James G. March, interview by Stanford Business School Alumni Association, *Stanford GSB* 47, no. 3 (1978–79): 16–19.

22. Cyert and March, *A Behavioral Theory of the Firm.*

23. Ibid.

24. Oliver E. Williamson, "A Model of Rational Managerial Behavior," in *A Behavioral Theory of the Firm* ed. Richard M. Cyert and James G. March (Englewood Cliffs, NJ: Prentice-Hall, 1963); idem, *The Economics of Discretionary Behavior: Managerial Objectives in a Theory of the Firm* (Englewood Cliffs, NJ: Prentice-Hall, 1964).

25. J.Y. Kamin and J. Ronen, "The Smoothing of Income Numbers: Some Empirical Evidence on Systematic Differences among Management-Controlled and Owner-Controlled Firms," *Accounting, Organizations and Society* (October 1978): 141–57.

26. Ahmed Belkaoui and R.D. Picur, "The Smoothing of Income Numbers: Some Empirical Evidence on Systematic Differences between Core and Periphery Industrial Sector," *Journal of Business Finance and Accounting* (Winter 1984): 527–45.

27. Lewin and Wolf, "Theory of Organizational Slack," 653.

28. L.J. Bourgeois, "On the Measurement of Organizational Slack," *Academy of Management Review* 6, no. 1 (1982): 29–39.

29. Ibid., 31.

30. C.I. Barnard, *Functions of the Executive* (Cambridge, MA: Harvard University Press, 1938).

31. James G. March and H.A. Simon, *Organizations* (New York: Wiley, 1958).

32. Cyert and March, *A Behavioral Theory of the Firm*, 36.

33. L.R. Pondy, "Organizational Conflict: Concepts and Models," *Administrative Science Quarterly* 12, no. 2 (1967): 296–320.

34. J.D. Thompson, *Organizations in Action* (New York: McGraw-Hill, 1967).

35. Pondy, "Organizational Conflict."

36. Jay Galbraith, *Designing Complex Organizations* (Reading, MA: Addison-Wesley, 1973), 15.

37. Bourgeois, "On the Measurement of Organizational Slack," 34.

38. D.C. Hambrick and C.C. Snow, "A Contextual Model of Strategic Decision Making in Organizations," in *Academy of Management Proceedings*, ed. R.L. Taylor, J.J. O'Connell, R.A. Zawala, and D.D. Warrick (1977): 109–12.

39. Cyert and March, *A Behavioral Theory of the Firm.*

40. March and Simon, *Organizations.*

41. H.A. Simon, *Administrative Behavior* (New York: Free Press, 1957).

42. Cyert and March, *A Behavioral Theory of the Firm.*

43. W.G. Astley, "Sources of Power in Organizational Life," Ph.D. diss., University of Washington, 1978.

44. W. Richard Scott, *Organizations: Rational, Natural and Open Systems* (Englewood Cliffs, NJ: Prentice-Hall, 1981), 216.

45. Ibid.

46. Ibid.

47. Bourgeois, "On the Measurement of Organizational Slack," 38.

48. Martin M. Rosner, "Economic Determinant of Organizational Innovation," *Administrative Science Quarterly* 12 (1968): 614–25.

49. Arie Y. Lewin and Carl Wolf, "Organizational Slack: A Test of the General Theory," *Journal of Management Studies* (forthcoming).

50. L.J. Bourgeois and Jitendra V. Singh, "Organizational Slack and Political Behavior within Top Management Teams," working paper, Graduate School of Business, Stanford University, 1983.

51. Theresa K. Lant, "Modeling Organizational Slack: An Empirical Investigation," Stanford University Research Paper, no. 856, July 1986.

52. Ibid., 14.

53. Michael Schiff and Arie Y. Lewin, "The Impact of People on Budgets," *Accounting Review* (April 1970): 259–68.

54. Michael Schiff and Arie Y. Lewin, "Where Traditional Budgeting Fails," *Financial Executive* (May 1968): 51–62.

55. A.E. Lowe and R.W. Shaw, "An Analysis of Managerial Biasing: Evidence from a Company's Budgeting Process," *Journal of Management Studies* (October 1968): 304–15.

56. M. Dalton, *Men who Manage* (New York: Wiley, 1961), 36–38.

57. G. Shillinglaw, "Divisional Performance Review: An Extension of Budgetary Control," in *Management Controls: New Directors in Basic Research*, ed. C.P. Bonini, R.K. Jaedicke, and H.M. Wagner (New York: McGraw-Hill, 1964), 149–63.

58. C. Argyris, *The Impact of Budgets on People* (New York: Controllership Foundation, 1952), 25.

59. E.H. Caplan, *Management Accounting and Behavioral Sciences* (Reading, MA: Addison-Wesley, 1971).

60. Argyris, *The Impact of Budgets on People.*

61. Schiff and Lewin, "Where Traditional Budgeting Fails," 51–62.

62. Mohamed Onsi, "Factor Analysis of Behavioral Variables Affecting Budgetary Slack," *The Accounting Review* (July 1973): 535–48.

63. Ibid., 536.

64. Ibid., 539.

65. Ibid., 546.

66. Cortlandt Cammann, "Effects of the Use of Control Systems," *Accounting, Organizations and Society* (January 1976): 301–13.

67. Kenneth A. Merchant, "Budgeting and the Propensity to Create Budgetary Slack," *Accounting, Organizations and Society* (May 1985): 201–10.

68. Alan S. Dunk, "The Effect of Budget Emphasis and Information Asymmetry on the Relation between Budgetary Participation and Slack," *The Accounting Review* (April 1993): 400–410.

69. Ibid., 400.

70. Ibid., 408–9.

71. Richard M. Cyert, J.G. March, and W.H. Starbuck, "Two Experiments on Bias and Conflict in Organizational Estimation," *Management Science* (April 1961): 254–64.

72. Lowe and Shaw, "Analysis of Managerial Biasing."

73. Dalton, *Men who Manage*.

74. R.M. Barefield, "A Model of Forecast Biasing Behavior," *The Accounting Review* (July 1970): 490–501.

75. J.S. Demski and G.A. Feltham, "Economic Incentives in Budgetary Control Systems," *The Accounting Review* (April 1978): 336–59.

76. Y. Ijiri, J. Kinard, and F. Putney, "An Integrated Evaluation System for Budget Forecasting and Operating Performance with a Classified Budgeting Bibliography," *Journal of Accounting Research* (Spring 1968): 1–28; M. Loeb and W. Magat, "Soviet Success Indicators and the Evaluation of Divisional Performance," *Journal of Accounting Research* (Spring 1978): 103–21; P. Jennergren, "On the Design of Incentives in Business Firms—A Survey of Some Research," *Management Science* (February 1980): 180–20; M. Weitzman, "The New Soviet Incentive Model," *Bell Journal of Economics* (Spring 1976): 251–57.

77. Mark S. Young, "Participative Budgeting: The Effects of Risk Aversion and Asymmetric Information on Budgetary Slack," *Journal of Accounting Research* (Autumn 1985): 829–42.

78. Ibid., 831–32.

79. C. Chow, J. Cooper, and W. Waller, "Participative Budgeting: Effects of a Truth-Inducing Pay Scheme and Information Asymmetry on Slack and Performance," working paper. University of Arizona, Tucson, 1986.

80. William S. Waller, "Slack in Participative Budgeting: The Joint Effect of a Truth-Inducing Pay Scheme and Risk Preferences," *Accounting Organizations and Society* (December 1987): 87–98.

81. Ibid., 88.

82. J. Berg, L. Daley, J. Dickhaut, and J. O'Brien, "Controlling Preferences for Lotteries on Units of Experimental Exchange," *Quarterly Journal of Economics* (May 1986): 281–306.

83. D.C. Kim, "Risk Preferences in Participative Budgeting," *The Accounting Review* (April 1992): 303–18.

84. Ibid., 304.

85. E. Aronson and D.R. Mettee, "Dishonest Behavior as a Function of Differential

Levels of Induced Self-Esteem," *Journal of Personality and Social Psychology* (January 1968): 121–27.

86. Ahmed Belkaoui, "Slack Budgeting, Information Distortion and Self-Esteem," *Contemporary Accounting Research* (Fall 1985): 111–23.

87. Kari Lukka, "Budgetary Biasing in Organizations: Theoretical Framework and Empirical Evidence," *Accounting Organizations and Society* (February 1988): 281–301.

88. Ibid., 292.

89. David T. Otley, "The Accuracy of Budgetary Estimates: Some Statistical Evidence," *Journal of Business Finance and Accounting* (Fall 1985): 416.

90. W.H. Read, "Upward Communication in Industrial Hierarchies," *Human Relations* (1962): 3–16.

91. G.H. Hofstede, *The Game of Budget Control* (London: Tavistock, 1968); A.G. Hopwood, "An Empirical Study of the Role of Accounting Data in Performance Evaluation," supplement to *Journal of Accounting Research* (1972): 156–82; David T. Otley, "Budget Use and Managerial Performance," *Journal of Accounting Research* (Spring 1978): 122–49.

92. R.M. Barefield, "Comments on a Measure of Forecasting Performance," *Journal of Accounting Research* (Autumn 1969): 324–27; Otley, "Accuracy of Budgetary Estimates."

93. G.S. Mann, "Reducing Budget Slack," *Journal of Accountancy* (August 1988): 118–22.

94. Ibid., 119.

95. Charles Perrow, *Complex Organizations: A Critical Essay* (Glenview, IL: Scott, Foresman, 1972), 140.

SELECTED BIBLIOGRAPHY

Antle, R., and G. Eppen. "Capital Rationing and Organizational Slack in Capital Budgeting." *Management Science* (February 1985): 163–74.

Argyris, C. *The Impact of Budgets on People.* New York: Controllership Foundation, 1952.

Aronson, E., and D.R. Mettee. "Dishonest Behavior as a Function of Differential Levels of Induced Self-Esteem." *Journal of Personality and Social Psychology* (January 1968): 121–27.

Astley, W.G. "Sources of Power in Organizational Life." Ph.D. diss., University of Washington, 1978.

Barefield, R.M. "A Model of Forecast Biasing Behavior." *The Accounting Review* (July 1970): 490–501.

Barnard, C.I. *Functions of the Executive.* Cambridge, MA: Harvard University Press, 1937.

Barnea, A., J. Ronen, and S. Sadan. "Classifactory Smoothing of Income with Extraordinary Items." *The Accounting Review* (January 1976): 110–22.

Belkaoui, Ahmed. *Conceptual Foundations of Management Accounting.* Reading, MA: Addison-Wesley, 1980.

———. *Cost Accounting: A Multidimensional Emphasis.* Hinsdale, IL.: Dryden Press, 1983.

———. "The Relationships between Self-Disclosure Style and Attitudes to Responsibility Accounting." *Accounting, Organizations and Society* (December 1981): 281–89.

———. "Slack Budgeting, Information Distortion and Self-Esteem." *Contemporary Accounting Research* (Fall 1985): 111–23.

Belkaoui, Ahmed, and R.D. Picur. "The Smoothing of Income Numbers: Some Empirical Evidence of Systematic Differences between Core and Periphery Industrial Sector." *Journal of Business Finance and Accounting* (Winter 1984): 527–45.

Berg, J., L. Daley, J. Dickhaut, and J. O'Brien. "Controlling Preferences for Lotteries on Units of Experimental Exchange." *Quarterly Journal of Economics* (May 1986): 281–306.

Bonin, J.P. "On the Decision of Managerial Incentive Structures in a Decentralized Planning Environment." *American Economic Review* (September 1976): 682–87.

Bonin, J.P., and A. Marcus. "Information, Motivation, and Control in Decentralized Planning: The Case of Discretionary Managerial Behavior." *Journal of Comparative Economics* (September 1979): 235–53.

Bourgeois, L.J. "On the Measurement of Organizational Slack." *Academy of Management Review* 6, no. 1 (1981): 29–39.

Bourgeois, L.J., and W.G. Astley. "A Strategic Model of Organizational Conduct and Performance." *International Studies of Management and Organization* 9, no. 3 (1979): 40–66.

Bourgeois, L.J., and Jitendra V. Singh. "Organizational Slack and Political Behavior within Top Management Teams." Working paper. Graduate School of Business, Stanford University, 1983.

Brownell, P. "Participation in the Budgeting Process—When It Works and When It Doesn't." *Journal of Accounting Literature* (Spring 1982): 124–53.

Caplan, E.H. *Management Accounting and Behavioral Sciences.* Reading, MA: Addison-Wesley, 1971.

Carter, E. "The Behavioral Theory of the Firm and Top-Level Corporate Decisions." *Administrative Science Quarterly* 16, no. 4 (1971): 413–28.

Child, John. "Organizational Structure, Environment, and Performance: The Role of Strategic Choice." *Sociology* 6, no. 4 (1972): 2–22.

Chow, C., J. Cooper, and W. Waller. "Participative Budgeting: Effects of a Truth-Inducing Pay Scheme and Information Asymmetry on Slack and Performance." Working paper. University of Arizona, Tucson, 1986.

Chow, D. "The Effects of Job Standard Tightness and Compensation Scheme on Performance: An Exploration of Linkages." *The Accounting Review* (October 1983): 667–85.

Christensen, J. "The Determination of Performance Standards and Participation." *Journal of Accounting Research* (Autumn 1982): 589–603.

Cohen, M.D., J.G. March, and J.P. Olsen. "A Garbage Can Model of Organizational Choice." *Administrative Science Quarterly* 17, no. 1 (1972): 1–25.

Collins, F. "Managerial Accounting Systems and Organizational Control: A Role Perspective." *Accounting, Organizations and Society* (May 1982): 107–22.

Conn, D. "A Comparison of Alternative Incentive Structures for Centrally Planned Economic Systems." *Journal of Comparative Economics* (September 1979): 261–78.

Cyert, Richard M., ed. *A Behavioral Theory of the Firm.* Englewood Cliffs, NJ: Prentice-Hall, 1963.

Cyert, Richard M., and James G. March. "Organizational Factors in the Theory of Oligopoly." *Quarterly Journal of Economics* (April 1956): 44–66.

Cyert, Richard M., J.G. March, and W.H. Starbuck. "Two Experiments on Bias and Conflict in Organizational Estimation." *Management Science* (April 1961): 254–64.

Dalton, M. *Men who Manage.* New York: Wiley, 1961.

Demski, J.S., and G.A. Feltham. "Economic Incentives in Budgetary Control Systems." *The Accounting Review* (April 1978): 336–59.

Dimmick, D.E., and V.V. Murray. "Correlates of Substantive Policy Decisions in Organizations: The Case of Human Resource Management." *Academy of Management Journal* 21, no. 4 (1978): 611–23.

Dunk, Alan S. "The Effect of Budget Emphasis and Information Asymmetry on the Relation between Budgetary Participation and Slack." *The Accounting Review* (April 1993): 400–410.

Fitts, W.F. *Manual for the Tennessee Self-Concept Scale.* Nashville, TN: Counselor Recording and Tests, 1965.

———. *Interpersonal Competence: The Wheel Model.* Nashville, TN: Counselor Recording and Tests, 1970.

———. *The Self-Concept and Behavior: Overview and Supplement.* Nashville, TN: Counselor Recording and Tests, 1972.

———. *The Self-Concept and Performance.* Nashville, TN: Counselor Recording and Tests, 1972.

———. *The Self-Concept and Psychopathology.* Nashville, TN: Counselor Recording and Tests, 1972.

Fitts, W.F., J.L. Adams, G. Radford, W.C. Richard, B.K. Thomas, M.M. Thomas, and W. Thompson. *The Self-Concept and Self-Actualization.* Nashville, TN: Counselor Recording and Tests, 1971.

Fitts, W.F., and W.T. Hammer. *The Self-Concept and Delinquency.* Nashville, TN: Counselor Recording and Tests, 1969.

Galbraith, Jay. *Designing Complex Organizations.* Reading, MA: Addison-Wesley, 1973.

Gonik, J. "Tie Salesmen's Bonuses to Their Forecasts." *Harvard Business Review* (May–June 1978): 116–23.

Gordon, M.J., B.N. Horwitz, and P.T. Myers. "Accounting Measurements and Normal Growth of the Firm." In *Research in Accounting Measurement,* ed. R.K. Jaedicke, Y. Ijiri, and O. Nieslen. Sarasota, FL: American Accounting Association, 1966.

Hambrick, D.C., and C.C. Snow. "A Contextual Model of Strategic Decision Making in Organizations." In *Academy of Management Proceedings,* ed. R.L. Taylor, J.J. O'Connell, R.A. Zawacki, and D.D. Warrick (1977): 109–12.

Hershey, J., H. Kunreuther, and P. Shoemaker. "Bias in Assessment Procedures for Utility Functions." *Management Science* (August 1982): 936–54.

Hopwood, A.G. "An Empirical Study of the Role of Accounting Data in Performance Evaluation." *Journal of Accounting Research* (supplement, 1972): 156–82.

Ijiri, Y., J. Kinard, and F. Putney. "An Integrated Evaluation System for Budget Forecasting and Operating Performance with a Classified Budgeting Bibliography." *Journal of Accounting Research* (Spring 1968): 1–28.

Itami, H. "Evaluation Measures and Goal Congruence under Uncertainty." *Journal of Accounting Research* (Spring 1975): 163–80.

Jennergren, P. "On the Design of Incentives in Business Firms—A Survey of Some Research." *Management Science* (February 1980): 180–201.

Kamin, J.Y., and J. Ronen. 'The Smoothing of Income Numbers: Some Empirical Evidence on Systematic Differences among Management-Controlled and Owner-Controlled Firms." *Accounting, Organizations and Society* (October 1978): 141–57.

Kerr, S., and W. Slocum, Jr. "Controlling the Performances of People in Organizations." In *Handbook of Organizational Design*, vol. 2, ed. W. Starbuck and P. Nystrom. New York: Oxford University Press, 1981, 116–34.

Kim, D.C. "Risk Preferences in Participative Budgeting." *The Accounting Review* (April 1992): 303–19.

Lecky, P. *Self-Consistency*. New York: Island Press, 1945.

Leibenstein, Harvey. "Allocative Efficiency vs. 'X-Efficiency'." *American Economic Review* (June 1966): 392–415.

———. "X-Efficiency: From Concept to Theory." *Challenge* (September–October 1979): 13–22.

Levinthal, D., and J.G. March. "A Model of Adaptive Organizational Search." *Journal of Economic Behavior and Organization* (May 1981): 307–33.

Lewin, Arie Y. "Organizational Slack: A Test of the General Theory." *Journal of Management Studies* (forthcoming).

Lewin, Arie Y., and Carl Wolf. "The Theory of Organizational Slack: A Critical Review." *Proceedings: Twentieth International Meeting of TIMS* (1976): 648–54.

Litschert, R.J., and T.W. Bonham. "A Conceptual Model of Strategy Formation." *Academy of Management Review* 3, no. 2 (1978): 211–19.

Locke, E., and D. Schweiger. "Participation in Decision Making: One More Look." In *Research in Organizational Behavior*, ed. B. Staw. Greenwich, CT: JAI Press, 1979, 265–339.

Loeb, M., and W. Magat. "Soviet Success Indicators and the Evaluation of Divisional Performance." *Journal of Accounting Research* (Spring 1978): 103–21.

Lowe, A.E., and R.W. Shaw. "An Analysis of Managerial Biasing: Evidence from a Company's Budgeting Process." *Journal of Management Studies* (October 1968): 304–15.

March, James G. "Decisions in Organizations and Theories of Choice." In *Perspectives on Organizational Design and Behavior*, ed. Andrew H. Van de Ven and William F. Joyce. New York: Wiley, 1981, 215–35.

———. "Interview by Stanford Business School Alumni Association," *Stanford CSB* 47, no. 3 (1978–1979): 16–19.

March, James G., and H.A. Simon. *Organizations*. New York: Wiley, 1958.

Merchant, Kenneth A. "The Design of the Corporate Budgeting System: Influences on Managerial Behavior and Performance." *The Accounting Review* (October 1981): 813–29.

Mezias, Stephen J. "Some Analytics of Organizational Slack." Working paper. Graduate School of Business, Stanford University, November 1985.

Miller, J. and J. Thompson. "Effort, Uncertainty, and the New Soviet Incentive System." *Southern Economic Journal* (October 1978): 432–46.

Mitroff, I.I., and J.R. Emshoff. "On Strategic Assumption-Making: A Dialectical Approach to Policy and Planning." *Academy of Management Review* 4, no. 1 (1979): 1–12.

Moch, M.K., and L.R. Pondy. "The Structure of Chaos: Organized Anarchy as a Response to Ambiguity." *Administrative Science Quarterly* 22, no. 2 (1977): 351–62.

Onsi, Mohamed. "Factor Analysis of Behavioral Variables Affecting Budgetary Slack." *The Accounting Review* (July 1973): 535–48.

Parker, L.D. "Goal Congruence: A Misguided Accounting Concept." *ABACUS* (June 1976): 3–13.

Pondy, L.R. "Organizational Conflict: Concepts and Models." *Administrative Science Quarterly* 12, no. 2 (1967): 296–320.

Radnor, R. "A Behavioral Model of Cost Reduction." *Bell Journal of Economics* (Fall 1975): 196–215.

Rogers, C.R. *Client Centered Therapy.* Boston: Houghton Mifflin, 1951.

Rosner, Martin M. "Economic Determinant of Organizational Innovation." *Administrative Science Quarterly* 12 (1968): 614–25.

Schein, V.E. "Examining an Illusion: The Role of Deceptive Behaviors in Organizations." *Human Relations* (October 1979): 287–95.

Schiff, Michael. "Accounting Tactics and the Theory of the Firm." *Journal of Accounting Research* (Spring 1966): 62–67.

Schiff, Michael, and Arie Y Lewin. *Behavioral Aspects of Accounting.* Englewood Cliffs, NJ: Prentice-Hall, 1974.

———. "The Impact of People on Budgets." *The Accounting Review* (April 1970): 259–268.

———. "Where Traditional Budgeting Fails." *Financial Executive* (May 1968): 51–62.

Simon, H.A. *Administrative Behavior.* New York: Free Press, 1957.

Singh, Jitendra V. "Performance, Slack, and Risk Taking in Organizational Decision Making." *Academy of Management Journal* (September 1986): 562–85.

———. "Performance, Slack, and Risk Taking in Strategic Decisions: Test of a Structural Equation Model." Ph.D. diss., Stanford Graduate School of Business, 1983.

Snowberger, V. "The New Soviet Incentive Model: Comment." *Bell Journal of Economics* (Autumn 1977): 591–600.

Snygg, D., and A.W. Combs. *Individual Behavior.* New York: Harper & Row, 1949.

Staw, B.M. "Rationality and Justification in Organizational Life." In *Research in Organizational Behavior*, vol. 2, ed. B.M. Staw and L.L. Cummings. Greenwich, CT: JAI Press, 1980, 154–82.

Swieringa, R.J., and R.H. Moncur. "The Relationship between Managers' Budget Oriented Behavior and Selected Attitudes, Position, Size and Performance Measures." *Journal of Accounting Research* (supplement, 1972): 19.

Thompson, J.D. *Organizations in Action.* New York: McGraw-Hill, 1967.

Thompson, W. *Correlates of the Self-Concept.* Nashville, TN: Counselor Recording and Tests, 1972.

Waller, William S. "Slack in Participative Budgeting: The Joint Effect of a Truth-Inducing Pay Scheme and Risk Preferences." *Accounting, Organizations and Society* (December 1987): 87–98.

Waller, William S., and C. Chow. "The Self-Selection and Effort of Standard-Based Employment Contracts: A Framework and Some Empirical Evidence." *The Accounting Review* (July 1985): 458–76.

Weitzman, M. "The New Soviet Incentive Model." *Bell Journal of Economics* (Spring 1976): 251–57.

Williamson, Oliver E. *The Economics of Discretionary Behavior: Managerial Objectives in a Theory of the Firm.* Englewood Cliffs, NJ: Prentice-Hall, 1964.

————. "A Model of Rational Managerial Behavior." In *A Behavioral Theory of the Firm*, ed. Richard M. Cyert and James G. March. Englewood Cliffs, NJ; Prentice-Hall, 1963, 113–28.

Winter, Sidney G. "Satisficing, Selection, and the Innovating Remnant." *Quarterly Journal of Economics* 85 (1971): 237–57.

Woot, P.D., H. Heyvaert, and F. Martou. "Strategic Management: An Empirical Study of 168 Belgian Firms." *International Studies of Management and Organization* 7 (1977): 60–73.

Wylie, R.C. *The Self-Concept: A Critical Survey of Pertinent Research Literature.* Lincoln: University of Nebraska Press, 1961.

Young, Mark S. "Participative Budgeting: The Effects of Risk Aversion and Asymmetric Information on Budgetary Slack." *Journal of Accounting Research* (Autumn 1985): 829–42.

Index

About the Author

AHMED RIAHI-BELKAOUI is CBA Distinguished Professor of Accounting in the College of Business Administration, University of Illinois at Chicago. Author of numerous Quorum books, published and forthcoming, and coauthor of several more, he is an equally prolific contributor to the scholarly and professional journals of his field, and has served on various editorial boards that oversee them.